Desert Passages

Encounters with the American Deserts
Patricia Nelson Limerick

University of New Mexico
Albuquerque

Library of Congress Cataloging in Publication Data

Limerick, Patricia Nelson, 1951–
  Desert passages.

  Bibliography: p.
  Includes index.
  1. Deserts—United States—Public opinion—History. 2. Deserts in
literature. 3. United States—Description and travel. 4. Public opinion—
United States—History. I. Title.
E161.5.L56 1985   973'.0954   84-28032
ISBN 0-8263-0794-9
ISBN 0-8263-0808-2 (pbk.)

*To Patricia and Grant Nelson,
and to the memory of Frank Prindle.*

Contents

Preface   3

Part I: Introduction   15

    Chapter One   25
    John C. Frémont

    Chapter Two   45
    William Lewis Manly

    Chapter Three   61
    Mark Twain

    Chapter Four   77
    William Ellsworth Smythe

Part II: Introduction   91

    Chapter Five   95
    John Van Dyke

    Chapter Six   113
    George Wharton James

    Chapter Seven   127
    Joseph Wood Krutch

    Chapter Eight   149
    Edward Abbey

    Chapter Nine   165
    The Significance of Deserts in American History

Notes   177

Bibliography   197

Index   215

Deserts have been shown to resist history and develop along their own lines.

—Patrick White
Voss

Desert Passages

Preface

Deserts have made fools of the wisest people.

Alexis de Tocqueville, for instance, was not easy to trick. In *Democracy in America*, Tocqueville provided the most penetrating analysis of United States culture and politics. Penetration aside, Tocqueville fell for the Great American Desert.

Tocqueville did not visit the region, but he described it with certainty. To the west of the Mississippi River, Tocqueville said, "the land becomes more and more uneven and sterile." The further one traveled from the river, "the sparser the vegetation and the poorer becomes the soil, and everything wilts or dies." If there was ever an uninviting landscape, this was it: "the soil is punctured in a thousand places by primitive rocks sticking out here and there like the bones of a skeleton when sinews and flesh have perished."[1]

In America-according-to-Tocqueville, the earth west of the Mississippi was a dry, exposed corpse. The image was, we all know now, a disservice to the Great Plains. Tocqueville had fallen for the reports of explorers like Stephen Long, and for the perspective by which the moderately arid and treeless Plains registered as full-scale deserts. Take the habits of life in a humid climate and a preoccupation with agrarian values; apply those habits and values to the dry grasslands in the middle of the continent; and the myth of the Great American Desert was a predictable product.[2]

This was, in its time, a powerful myth, powerful enough to trick wise people like Tocqueville. It was also an easy myth to recover from. Given a chance, the region of the Plains could vindicate itself.

This was not a desert: at the worst, this was grazing land, and, at the best, this was land for dry farming. There were cyclical rains, and rivers, and springs. The judgment "desert" had been hasty—and wrong.

Farther to the west, in land that had been part of Mexico in Tocqueville's time, the judgment stood—and stands. Along the eastern side of the Cascades and Sierras, extending into Southern California, are the real deserts. Regions with less than ten inches a year rainfall, with sparse vegetation, these are not deserts of myth, but of actuality.

Deserts occur in several regions of the United States. To the north, sections of the Columbia Plateau—eastern Oregon and Washington, and part of Idaho—lie in the rain shadow of the Cascade Mountains; heavy rain on the coast, and rain and snow in the mountains drain the clouds of their moisture. Rivers originating in the Rocky Mountains flow through the plateau's arid regions, but they are often deep in canyons, not having much effect on the surrounding terrain. South of the plateau, in the physiographic province known as the Basin and Range, desert conditions are widespread. The Great Basin— most of Nevada and western Utah—is a region of confined drainage; interior basins, the site of lakes in earlier geological time, absorb the available stream flow. The Humboldt Desert and the Great Salt Lake Desert represent extremes of aridity in the basin. Beyond the Great Basin itself, arid lands extend into the Southwest, connecting up with northern Mexico's deserts. The Mohave and the Colorado deserts in California, the Sonoran Desert in Arizona, and the Chihuahuan Desert in New Mexico cover a wide arc of territory. The most isolated and, by many standards, the most dramatic deserts lie to the north in the Colorado Plateau, centered around the Four Corners area where Utah, Colorado, Arizona, and New Mexico meet. While the canyonlands in this region provide spectacular geological displays, they support only a sparse population.[3]

If you have seen one desert, you have not seen them all. There are landscapes with a monotone of sagebrush, landscapes transformed seasonally with flowering bushes and cactus, and landscapes that seem in fact to be stretches of vacancy, as in the salt flats or dry alkaline basins. The topography is probably more varied than any well-watered landscape; it includes valleys, mountains, and plains with the added variation of dramatically eroded canyons, cliffs, and mesas.

With all these variations in vegetation and topography, deserts are in other ways more alike than different. First, all these deserts have a high degree of exposed rock and soil—as if the desert revealed, in Tocqueville's phrasing, the "skeleton" of the earth. Combined with the difficulty of sustaining life on uncertain water and food, this "skeletal" impression of the naked—more precisely, the flayed—earth gave deserts their almost universal associations with death.

Second, deserts give an impression of vacancy. This impression is in part a response to the absence of a thick cover of vegetation, in part an acknowledgment of the open range for sight, and in part a reaction to the absence of human beings. In the Judeo-Christian tradition, the word *desert* did in fact carry the original meaning of a deserted place, or wilderness. As George Williams has shown, the Bible recorded a world in which *desert*, in its special meaning of arid land, was in fact synonymous with *wilderness*. As the word *desert* evolved in England, the quality of aridity took second place to the quality of vacancy. Thus English colonists in New England, not noted for its aridity, could refer to themselves as planting their settlements, as the Puritan divine Cotton Mather put it, "in a Squalid, horrid American Desert."[4]

In certain territories of the Far West, the word recovered its biblical harmony. The connection between aridity and vacancy seemed to be restored. Of course no region on the North American continent was literally empty at the time of white arrival. Even the most arid deserts had at least seasonal Indian presence.[5] Certainly deserts now are not deserted, yet even a seemingly entrenched desert city has an arbitrary look about it—placed in an inappropriate setting for tract houses, lawns, swimming pools, and golf courses. Driving through a desert even today, one perceives human presence—a passing car, an isolated town, a person on foot—as a surprise and an anomaly. The desert can still seem deserted.

Finally, all deserts share the overarching fact of problematic rainfall and uncertain water supplies. This is an environment with a great power to change the form and behavior of organisms. Desert plants and animals have obviously been shaped by the irregular distribution of water. Nineteenth-century Americans certainly found their actions limited by desert conditions. In the twentieth century, the issue remained open: How much would aridity affect or limit American behavior? To what degree would humans feel themselves under the power of nature?

These questions make desert history a prime case in the study of attitudes toward nature. I will use "nature" to mean the physical world independent of human creation—the rocks, soil, air, water, plants, and animals that humans did not make. "Nature," then, will stand for the world of life and matter pursuing its own ends, independent of human design.[6]

With this definition, the desert represents nature at its extreme. Americans entering the desert entered an independent world—rock, sunlight, life, and water circulating in an integral system. This world made few concessions to human needs—the scarcity of water made both travel and settlement risky and uninviting. The desert had not been made by humans; moreover, it firmly resisted being remade by them.

Even with this definition, the phrase *attitudes toward nature* throws a thin cloak of simplicity over a mass of complexity. It is perfectly possible for an individual or group to hold what appear to be contradictory attitudes simultaneously. The same individual can experience discomfort or inconvenience from heat, cold, or a difficult terrain, inspect a landscape for exploitable resources, and admire a view, all at the same time. Nature is on one count a reminder of the individual's own biological vulnerability; on another count, a source of commercially useful material; and on a third count, a satisfying visual phenomenon.

We have then three categories of attitudes: attitudes toward nature as a biological reality in human life—vulnerability to hunger, thirst, injury, disease, and death; attitudes toward nature as an economic resource—a container of treasures awaiting extraction or development; and attitudes toward nature as an aesthetic spectacle. These three categories provide some structure for American encounters with the deserts. In the first phase, beginning with the travels of American fur trappers in the 1820s and continuing on the overland trail, the desert was simply a threat to life, an ordeal to be endured. In the second phase, beginning by one count with the Nevada silver mines in 1859 and by the other with irrigated farming in Utah, Arizona, and elsewhere, the desert turned out to be valuable—a repository of minerals, a wasteland capable of becoming irrigated farmland. In the third phase, around the turn of the century, the desert began to qualify in some circles as beautiful and suitable for appreciation. The phases suggested here did not succeed each other in clear sequence: all three overlap and continue into the present.

This is, then, a study in the history of attitudes, but attitudes that responded to concrete, actual places and led to actions that directly affected those places. In an essay entitled "On a Certain Blindness in Human Beings," the philosopher and psychologist William James told a story that effectively illustrates the questions I have tried to pursue. Traveling in the North Carolina mountains, James passed a number of valleys "newly cleared and planted. The impression on my mind," he said, "was one of unmitigated squalor." Charred stumps, girdled trees, unkempt cabins, improvised fences, and irregular planting marked the scene. "The forest had been destroyed," James noted, "and what had 'improved' it out of existence was hideous, a sort of ulcer, without a single element of artificial grace to make up for the loss of Nature's beauty."

Then a conversation with his mountaineer-driver convinced James that he "had been losing the whole inward significance of the situation." To James, "the clearings spoke of naught but denudation." But when the mountaineers "looked on the hideous stumps, what they thought of was personal victory." "A mere ugly picture" to James was to the residents "a symbol" of "duty, struggle and success."[7]

While the actual landscape is of considerable importance in this story, the intellectual focus rests on the different appearance and meaning available to different viewers. Simply looking at the landscape, and looking at the changes humans had caused, conveyed no understanding until James awakened to "the whole inward significance of the situation," to the awareness that both his judgment and the mountaineers' made sense. In matters of landscape, one man's "ugly picture" could well be another man's "improvement."

But the mountains of North Carolina made the situation deceptively clear. By William James's time, mountain and forests had an established aesthetic value. It was no personal eccentricity that caused him to lament the ruining of the forest, the "denudation" of the land.[8]

How would he have felt in a landscape that was naturally and originally in a state of "denudation"? What range of opinion would there be for an environment that seemed initially a "wasteland"—a harsh, unattractive, vacant space? Who could regret the transformation of wasteland into mines, farms, and towns? When in history would certain visitors to the desert be able to replicate James's experience in the Carolina mountains? When would a glimpse of desert "improvements" became an occasion for regret? Whether or not they carried universal support, by the turn of the century the conventions were in place for regretting the destruction of forests. "O woodman spare that tree" made sense long before any comparable sentiment for deserts—"O farmer spare that greasewood"—had even been imagined.

Even the sentiment for preserving forests was a comparatively recent one. Roderick Nash has offered an anthropological argument to explain the hatred for wilderness revealed in American history. Early humans, he explains, left the forests of their ancestors and moved to "open, spacious environments" where vision was at a premium. When humans return to forests, fear increases with the lost "security of vision." Accordingly the American "pioneers' obsession was to clear the land and bring light into darkness." James's tree-killing mountaineers were thus, by Nash's argument, following an anthropological imperative.[9]

The corollary to Nash's proposition was this: open spaces—areas where vision was not interrupted by trees—made pioneers feel better. Reaching the Great Plains, for instance, "suddenly they could see and their spirits brightened."[10]

By this argument, the pioneers should have felt very good indeed when they reached the deserts. No trees obscured the view; horizons stretched into the distance. Contrary to the theory, the more they saw, the worse they felt. With sparse, unfamiliar vegetation, spotty water sources, and the endless exposed ground to look at, free vision was not much of a consolation.

Nash's survey of attitudes toward wilderness is otherwise thorough and insightful. This one oversight appears to be symptomatic of the fact that deserts have not figured very largely in studies of American attitudes toward nature. The omission is understandable; deserts do not fit well in generalizations designed with better-watered landscapes in mind.[11]

The difficulty of fitting deserts into easy generalizations has reinforced my preference for structuring this inquiry around eight individuals. Personally as well as professionally, I have a great faith in the synecdoche, the part that stands for the whole, the grain of sand that reveals the universe (or at least a significant part of it). The pathway to the universal, Eudora Welty has said, leads through the local and particular and, I would add, the individual.[12]

I have chosen this approach for a simple reason: I think more effectively when I can pay attention to individuals. In teaching, I prefer small seminars to large lecture classes. In meeting a new group, I learn more by talking separately to a few individuals than by listening to their collective pronouncements. In individuals and in their relationship to their groups and settings, I find my most rewarding opportunities to shed light on complicated situations.

While I believe that close study of the thought and expression of individuals reveals a great deal about their times and their settings, I also recognize the risks and limits of this approach. The local is not interchangeable with the universal; as an inquiry gains in specificity, it also can lose in typicality. I have tried to suggest the ways in which these individuals represent larger units of opinion and action. Nonetheless, I concede that there will still be much to learn about deserts and Americans, once my eight main characters have had their moment in the spotlight.

The major advantage of this approach is that one does not have to simplify complex patterns of thought and behavior. In close examinations of individuals, there is room to acknowledge subtlety, contradiction, and paradox. One could simply say, for instance, that reclamationists disliked the untransformed desert and wanted it made into farmland. But a close examination of the irrigation propagandist William Ellsworth Smythe establishes that there is considerably more to the story than that simple statement. Faith in reclamation involved a complicated set of ideas about democracy, the distribution of power, the mechanisms of change in history, and human character in general. There may be ways in which these complexities could emerge in a study of groups and not individuals. Nonetheless, when I tried to discuss the attitudes of groups, I felt as if I were orchestrating a performance in which no one wanted to sing in the chorus, and everyone wanted the solo. Individual voices were simply too strong to subordinate to a choral effect.

The individuals did submit to division into two sections: Part I, in which dislike of the unimproved desert predominates, and Part II in which appreciation supplants dislike. The explorer John C. Frémont and the overland traveler William Lewis Manly fit into the first phase of desert history, in which human physical vulnerability dominated the desert traveler's experience. The writer and former prospector Samuel Clemens, while recording the first stages of the desert's emergence into usefulness, also kept the viewpoint of the irritated traveler. The irrigation promoter William Ellsworth Smythe was wholeheartedly in the camp of utility, announcing the arrival of a new age in which the desert would become fully useful, mastered in the best interests of the nation. While the unchanged desert was the essential raw material for Smythe's vision, he saw it as a flawed landscape urgently in need of improvement.

Part II begins with the art historian and professional traveler John Van Dyke, who led the way in announcing that desert qualities others found repellent were attractive to persons of the proper sensitivity. The promoter George Wharton James was a highly representative hybrid, echoing Smythe at times and Van Dyke at others. Joseph Wood Krutch and Edward Abbey, writers and intellectuals, both represent the convictions and dilemmas of mid-twentieth-century desert appreciators.

In each of these eight chapters, there are three main characters: an individual, a desert, and the American nation. The focus on individuals raises an important question of scale. By and large, the individuals themselves were aware of their relative size in the scale of nature and nation. Most of them admitted that the desert had a way of making an individual feel small and insignificant. The balance of power was not ambiguous; in a contest between person and desert, one would not bet on the person.

In the twentieth century, the dwarfing of the individual developed a particular twist. While people could still feel reduced by the desert, they were as likely to feel dwarfed by the nation and its mass society. Appreciators declared that they enjoyed the sense of insignificance they felt in the desert and resented the insignificance they felt in mass society. The twentieth-century appreciator, in fact, felt his most acute sensations of powerlessness through his inability to stop the mass society from transforming the deserts he wanted to preserve.

When the individual "compares himself with all his fellows and measures himself against this vast entity," Alexis de Tocqueville wrote, "he is overwhelmed by a sense of his insignificance and weakness."[13] The desert, that other "vast entity," had a similar effect, afflicting the vulnerable with intense disorientation.

In an era of highways, airplanes, and air-conditioning, it takes an effort to realize how disorienting the deserts were for their first American visitors. The reasons for aridity and the best mechanisms for coping with it mystified many travelers and settlers. If one were to assemble nominations for the category of "most disoriented," a sailor named George would be a front-runner. George crossed the Nevada and Utah deserts in 1855, after persuading the French scientist and traveler Jules Remy to take him on as a servant. The party—Remy, his companion Mr. Brenchley and George—traveled from California to Salt Lake City. Soon after they left the Sierras behind and struck out into the Humboldt Desert, George began to decline.

The carcasses of draft animals, victims of the overland migration, lined their path. Heat and bad water wore on them. Snakes visited their beds. Inheriting the results of friction between Indians and emigrants, the Remy party even faced direct attack. "One felt the desert," Remy recalled, "and it was a desert indeed."[14]

George, it appeared, felt it the worst. He became utterly unreliable; left to stand watch over the animals, he slept and let them drift away. "He could not even kindle a fire," Remy wrote, "and all thought seemed to have abandoned him. He had not only lost our pipes, but even our forks, ropes, Mr. Brenchley's powder-flask, a water-gourd, etc. He would have lost himself had we not been there to look after and guide him." He drifted to sleep at any opportunity; he fell off his mule. He dreamed in the night, "screaming without waking."[15]

Placed in the rear, George lagged behind, forcing the party to wait; placed in the lead, in an effort "to rid him of his somnolency and make him of some use," he continually drifted "out of the line we had pointed out to him, and we were compelled to gallop up to him to set him right again; for either from drowsiness or great deafness, he paid no attention to our whistling." He hid during an Indian attack and afterward, "he did not seem conscious of what had taken place."[16]

What had happened to George? Remy saw only one possible explanation: "It seemed as though the desert had paralyzed him. He was incapable of thought. . . " Evidently, it was "fear which had paralyzed all his faculties during the journey." The most striking evidence came with the arrival in Salt Lake City. With "a bright and joyful countenance," George was "no longer the same man we had seen during our journey." "Crossing the desert had, as it were, annihilated" George; "the sight of a city somewhat revived him."[17]

Something peculiar happened to George, and one would like to know if Remy was right in locating the cause: "the continuous impressions he had received from the privations and dangers of a life in the desert."[18] Whatever the full and final explanation was, there is no question that the desert was capable of producing all the fear, disorientation, and despair that afflicted poor George.

Unlike George and unlike my protagonists—Frémont, Manly, Clemens, Smythe, Van Dyke, James, Drutch, and Abbey—I was from the beginning thoroughly used to life in a desert. I was born in Banning, California, near Palm Springs. Contrary to the traditions of desert history, children in Banning were not noticeably more disoriented than children in more accommodating environments. A comfortable secondary environment of buildings, automobiles, water supply systems, and even swimming pools stood between us and the primary environment of the desert. Seasonal heat and persistent desert winds were the only reminders that we did not have the place thoroughly under control. I did not associate the desert with any particular history of hardship or struggle; I am not sure I associated it with any history at all. I was aware, for instance, of the inland lake known as the Salton Sea; I had no notion that it was a twentieth-century product of human efforts to make use of the Colorado River.

I took the landscape for granted, and I had no uncertainties about water, even if I also had no idea where it came from.

It was not until I went to graduate school in the Northeast and, by a happy coincidence, ended up in Howard Lamar's western history class, that the prosaic realities of life in the desert began to seem surprising. Everyone knows that American settlement moved at a rapid pace, but this sequence was almost beyond belief. In the 1850s, deserts were fearful places pushing overland travelers to the edge of endurance; in the 1950s we lived in our desert with utter complacency. What happened?

When I left Southern California for Southern New England, none of these questions had occurred to me. I thought I was exchanging regions of sunlight and warmth for regions of chill and struggle; I was wrong. While I struggled to make my peace with the profession, members of the Yale faculty provided encouragement that I could not have done without. John Blum, David Brion Davis, C. Vann Woodward, Edmund Morgan, R. W. B. Lewis, Kai Erikson, and Howard Lamar kept me in the business.

Lewis, Erikson, and Lamar showed extraordinary patience in waiting for a dissertation that seemed, for at least four years, to be all promises and no prose. With Howard Lamar, as all his students know, the study of western history at Yale preserves many of the more attractive qualities of the historical West: notably, a spirit of freedom, adventure, and community. That spirit gets steady reinforcement from Rose Stone, whose warmth and enthusiasm were an inspiration over eight years at Yale.

If Yale was not the emotional desert I anticipated, this was even more the case with my neighborhood in New Haven. In what surely represented the further reaches of neighborly helpfulness, Bob Balay read the dissertation while it was in progress. Others played a vital role in keeping my spirits up. Katie, Deborah, Bill, and now Meg Stewart never fail as sources of encouragement.

When I left New Haven for Cambridge, I again anticipated emotional scarcity, and I was once again agreeably disappointed. I am grateful to the Harvard history department for, in the first place, taking my exotic interests seriously, and for providing me with the time and opportunity to reduce a repetitive dissertation to a form less oppressive to readers. I am especially grateful to Bernard Bailyn, for reading the dissertation, for suggesting directions for revision, and for providing an example of intellectual energy which I will never equal but can at least imitate. Donald Worster at the University of Hawaii read the dissertation with heroic concentration and many helpful ideas. Beth Hadas of the University of New Mexico Press and my friends Helena Wall and Jim O'Brien gave the revised manuscript useful readings.

The monotony of the desert made Mark Twain feel victimized and desperate; my husband Jeff Limerick has every right to echo Twain's complaint. After first, second, and third drafts, both he and I look forward to other subjects of inquiry.

As all these people have occasion to know, while I am open to debate, I am not always open to persuasion. The flaws in this book are emphatically my own.

PART ONE

Introduction

Discovery, Exploration, and Overland Travel:
The Background to John C. Frémont and William Lewis Manly

In pinpointing the discovery of the desert, the question is not so much "when" as it is "by whom." Indians took up residence in the American Southwest as long as 10,000 years ago. The Great Basin's Desert Culture was a substained project in discovering and making the most of limited resources. In certain regions, Indians supplemented hunting and gathering with irrigated farming. In what is now Arizona, the Hohokam dug major irrigation ditches as early as 300 A.D.[1]

The Spanish began their discovery of the northern borderlands with the Coronado expedition of 1540. In the settlement of New Mexico, begun in 1598, the Spanish clustered along the Rio Grande. From regular travel from central Mexico to New Mexico, from Eusebio Kino's explorations of Arizona in the late 1600s, and from the land route to California pioneered by Juan Bautista de Anza in 1772, the Spanish became familiar with desert travel. *Jornada del muerto* was their well-chosen term for the most trying passages.[2]

While the home country remained in control, the Spanish borderlands were closed to Anglo-Americans, by national policy as well as by isolation and natural obstacles. Mexican independence in 1821 opened trade with American merchants. The Santa Fe trade exposed a number of Americans to interludes of desert travel.[3] This development coincided with an expansion of the fur trade, as American trappers traveled all the way to California, and British traders from

15

the Hudson's Bay Company explored south into the Great Basin. Fur trappers thus made many of the initial Anglo-American explorations in the deserts.[4] But trappers were erratic in their record-keeping; while they might write letters or keep diaries, these documents were not likely to command national attention.

Traders and trappers may have reached the far-western deserts in advance of official explorers, but government-sponsored explorers played a key role in setting the terms in which Americans viewed arid lands. In early American exploration, the Great Plains gathered a reputation as the Great American Desert. Zebulon Pike in 1806 and Stephen Long in 1819 traveled over sections of the Plains. While neither of them crossed the Rockies, the reports resulting from both expeditions supported an idea of the Plains as desert.[5] Zebulon Pike concluded his remarks on the aridity of the region with this optimistic interpretation:

> from these immense prairies may arise one great advantage to the United States, viz.: The restriction of our population to some certain limits, and thereby a continuation of the Union. Our citizens being so prone to rambling and extending themselves on the frontier will, through necessity, be constrained to limit their extent on the west to the borders of the Missouri and Mississippi, while they leave the prairies incapable of cultivation to the wandering and uncivilized aborigines of the country.[6]

For someone like Pike, who traveled over so much of the continent, the idea of endless national expansion was an idea that had to stop somewhere. A strip of arid, treeless land could be read as nature's statement on the limits of American expansion. Unlike many of his contemporaries, Pike had a strong enough awareness of "the wandering and uncivilized aborigines" to convince him that some place had to be reserved for them. A desert—land that Americans would not want anyway—was a perfect nomination for Indian territory.

Twelve years later, the chronicler of Stephen Long's expedition to the central Rockies, Edwin James, agreed with Pike's evaluation of the Plains. The area, he said, might "prove of infinite importance to the United States inasmuch as it is calculated to serve as a barrier to prevent too great an extension of our population westward."[7] Both James and Pike seemed to take it as self-evident that only a natural barrier—and not legislative regulation—could impose limits on the mobility of the American people. From their point of view, limits would save the union from being stretched past its capacity, and aridity was nature's best way of imposing that limit.

What would happen when American expansion actually tested this limit—not in the semiarid Great Plains, but in the authentic deserts? The reports and explorations of John C. Frémont foretold the answer, reversing the environmental determinism of Pike and Long. In the 1840s, when Frémont pursued and published his travels, he made one lesson clear: the deserts were formidable obstacles, but they were not insurmountable. Aridity did not throw a roadblock across the continent. The mesage opened the way for the mass "discovery" of the desert through overland emigration.

At mid-century, overland travel provided large numbers of Americans with their first direct experience of deserts. Probably three hundred thousand Americans of all ages and classes saw the desert at firsthand on their way to the Pacific Coast.[8] Gold in California pushed a small transcontinental migration into a mass movement. Initially, Americans crossed the deserts simply to get to the treasures on the other side. In that crossing, they were dependent on animals and not on machines, and that fact set the terms of this encounter with deserts.

Travelers to California could take a number of different routes.[9] The majority chose the central trail, departing from towns along the Missouri river, following the Platte River, crossing the Rockies through South Pass, and following the Humboldt through present-day Nevada. The Humboldt finally disappeared into a sink, leaving forty miles to the next streams from the Sierra foothills. Weakened by the desert crossing, the travelers then had to cross the mountains with the prospect of winter snows providing an inexorable timetable.

No route permitted an evasion of the desert. The southern trails allowed an earlier start because of the milder winters, but they also offered a more prolonged exposure to deserts.[10] Traveling along the Gila River in present-day Arizona and then crossing the Colorado Desert in California, emigrants faced an even more demanding test of endurance than did their counterparts to the north. In return, they escaped the burden of crossing the Sierras.

Many overland travelers were fond of nature, inclined to admire the view even while under the pressure of the journey. Without any sense of contradiction, these declared nature-lovers made an exception for the desert. The sparseness of vegetation preoccupied them. "Such a thing as a tree," one individual noted with dissatisfaction, "I have not seen since we struck this Humbug River which is nothing more than a ditch. . . ." The road led past hills "with not a particle of herbage or vegetation upon them. . . . " One could travel for a full day and see "nothing whatever growing." Such landscapes embodied, in regularly used terms, "barrenness, desolation and dreariness."[11]

Other sources of distress in the desert were far more immediate. Draft animals, worn down by the preceding months of travel, collapsed under the pressure of heat, thirst, and the effort of pulling through heavy sand. Their deaths not only left their owners in a precarious position, they left the trail littered with carcasses. "Did not see anything but bones and dead animals" was a frequent comment. The effect was more than visual; traveler also commented on the "most obnoxious hideous gases . . . arising from the many dead animals around." The dust could be "suffocating," "blinding," "almost insupportable." And water, when available, was often tainted with alkali or with the decaying bodies of animals. "We have gradually become accustomed to drinking all sort and any sort," Wakeman Bryarly noted, "and now we scarcely take a second thought whether it is very good or very bad."[12]

Other hardships rested more on the relations between humans rather than the workings of nature. The desert was for many travelers the part of the trip where rumors of shortcuts proliferated. Anxious to end the journey, disturbed by rumors of depleted grass and scarce water ahead, emigrants were at their peak of susceptibility to the promise of what might be a better route. With so many varying reports, one man noted, it was "useless to attempt to make up your mind which is preferable." Choosing a desert cutoff was a decision-making at the furthest reaches of uncertainty and insufficient information.[13]

Yet another human dilemma came in relations with the natives. The Paiutes of the Humboldt region made this one of the few areas on the trail where Indian presence was an active annoyance.[14] They made few open and direct attacks, but they were frequently successful at stampeding stock, or disabling one animal at a time. The Paiute behavior made a great deal of sense: their homeland was undergoing invasion and disruption. Emigrant cattle ate much of the available grass, and Indian livelihood relied on the harvest of grass seeds. It was predictable that Indians would take their opportunities to replenish their food supply from an alternative source: the available oxen and mules. These raids, from the Anglo-American side, were beyond toleration: emigrants' lives and continued mobility depended on the maintenance of their animals. The possibilities for reciprocal understanding were slight; it is hardly surprising that desert Indians frequently received the most abusive commentary from emigrant diarists.

Indian attack was only one among the desert's many threats to life. If the waterless stretch of the Humboldt Desert had been a few miles wider, David Potter has suggested, the rate of survival on the trail would have been cut to a fraction. As it was, few emigrants failed to escape the desert without thinking of death. "Passed the journey of death," Bryarly reported at the end of his desert crossing. "It seemed as though we had passed over the scorching valley of death to life," another Forty-niner wrote. Not all of the emigrants knew the Spanish phrase for a desert crossing, but the term *jornada del muerto* conveyed the essence of their impressions. Consensus on this issue was no surprise. "Everyone, without a dissenting voice," Bryarly reported, "cursed the desert, and yet thank God they are over it with little loss."[15]

In 1849, Sarah Royce and her family started late on the overland trail. The Royces knew the route as far as the Humboldt Sink, but from that point on, Royce remembered, "all seemed uncertainty."[16] For forty waterless miles in the Humboldt Desert, the Royces would have to travel without any precise sense of direction. In the best of circumstances, this would have been an ordeal; for the Royces, this trip was almost fatal. Traveling before dawn one day, they overshot the last camp on the Humboldt. Unaware of their mistake, they continued to travel, searching for that last camp where they could prepare for the desert crossing with provisions of hay and water.

By midday, the Royce party had to face their situation. They had unknowingly launched themselves into the Humboldt Desert, without any of the necessary precautions or preparations. There was no option but retreat.

For an overland emigrant, the need to reverse directions and then travel eastward was a terrible blow to morale. The Royces returned to the Humboldt Sink, located the camp, rested, and prepared for a second try. Even with this fresh start, the Royce party was still in serious danger. Without the help of a relief party sent from California, the Royces would probably not have made it. The relief party required them to leave their wagons behind, and the Royces arrived in California virtually without possessions, but with their lives intact. In fact, for Sarah Royce, life was not only intact—it was triumphant. "We had conquered the desert," she announced.[17] The human spirit had met nature at its most intractable and bewildering, and by simply refusing to be extinguished, the human spirit had won.

The victory did not fit in the usual pattern of the American conquest of nature. The Royces, and the other overland travelers, did not tame, transform, or punish the desert. They simply endured it. On the overland trail, in the desert, humans exerted their will to live, against the overwhelming force of inanimate matter. Triumph consisted not in mastery, but in escape.

Versions of Utility
The Background to Mark Twain and William Ellsworth Smythe

After 1859, mineral discoveries seemed to begin the redemption of the desert. Even if life in arid places was still full of discomfort, valuable minerals proved that the desert offered its own version of abundance, its own way of contributing to individual profit and to national productivity. The resources were there, they were simply hidden in a kind of cosmic treasure hunt.

The trend toward irrigated farming rested on a comparable theory of the desert as a place of concealed treasure. The desert was full of agricultural possibilities, but they were, like the minerals, waiting to be found and unleashed. Beyond a shared conviction in utility, irrigation and mining had more differences and conflicts than similarities. Mining was, by the very nature of extraction, transitory and unstable; irrigation aimed at stability and continuity.

Without minerals, Americans would have had little reason to reverse directions and travel east from California into the deserts. While most participants settled down or returned home, the California Gold Rush recruited for the West a population of adventurers—prospectors marked by the "love of excitement, the willingness to gamble on the long chance, the self-confident conviction that after life in California one could survive on any mining frontier."[18] Overland travelers told of traces of valuable minerals they had glimpsed in deserts. It was, after all, logical to assume that minerals were to be found on both sides of the Sierras. California's restless prospectors were ready to test the theory.

In 1859, the discovery of silver in the Comstock Lode set off a series of booms and rushes through what would soon become Nevada. The resulting settlements had peculiar life cycles. "Some were born, developed and abandoned within the decade," Rodman Paul noted. "Without much exaggeration, one could say of the Great Basin that it was a region in which mining made a very large number of false starts for every one real success."[19]

Aridity was part of the problem. The desert mining frontier involved "environmental and geological conditions of an unfamiliar and peculiarly demanding sort, far more difficult to cope with than anything encountered on the western side of the Sierra Nevada."[20] Shortages of water, the dearth of trees for lumber or fuel, difficult terrain for transportation of people and supplies, and chemically complicated ores added new problems to an already risky business. Fantasies of fortunes and wild speculation added a human element of uncertainty.

With the precedent set by Nevada, some form of mining eventually reached most of the arid lands. Mining was crucial in the Anglo-American project of taking possession of the deserts. It is hard to disagree with Ray Allen Billington's summation: "Instead of seeking fertile, well-watered fields, miners were attracted to mountain and desert lands that might normally have waited generations for occupants."[21] Similarly, W. Eugene Hollon has said, "the discovery of precious metals speeded the process" of desert settlement "by at least two generations."[22] Without a doubt, mining providing Americans with the crucial reason to value the desert in spite of its drawbacks.

All over the mining West, Paul has pointed out, "the distinguishing characteristic" of miners' efforts was "the uncertainty of the outcome."[23] The ephemerality of the resulting settlements was a classic characteristic of the arid West, as mining added another suggestion of mortality in the form of ghost towns. In desert mining, the betrayal of apparent promise could come from the unpredictable limits of natural resources, or from the equally unpredictable behavior of humans making exaggerated claims for the purpose of speculation. While mining had rewards for some, for many others the themes of desert experience on the overland trail—disorientation and frustration with an intractable environment—continued to hold true.

As transitory as desert mining towns might have been, they created a regional demand for food. The expense and trouble of importing food put a premium on local production. Even desert regions had river valleys where water could be used in small irrigation projects.

The origins of western irrigation were, of course, pre-Columbian.[24] Southwestern tribes engaged in irrigated farming as early as 300 B.C. The Spanish in the Southwest set their own precedents, and the Mormons, arriving in Utah in 1847, pioneered in Anglo-American irrigation.[25] All over the arid West, small farmers recognized that if rain was inadequate, ditches and canals could still produce crops.[26] Enterprising individuals undertook the organization of private irrigation companies in the 1860s and 1870s. But individuals and private companies frequently discovered the unpleasant fact that irrigation development was initially expensive. Dams, reservoirs, gates, and ditches required a large capital outlay long before farms could be brought to productive status. In the spring season, as mountain snows melted, many desert rivers carried an abundance of water. The problem, for irrigators, was to construct the substantial facilities necessary to store the spring floods for later use in the dry summer season.

The drought years of the late 1880s and early 1890s played a crucial role in organizing public interest in irrigation. Other areas besides deserts were involved in this problem. For years American settlement leapfrogged over the Great Plains, jumping ahead to the Pacific

Coast. In the 1870s, American farmers moved into the subhumid Plains, profiting from a period of uncharacteristically abundant rainfall. This move was accompanied by a proliferation of cheerful theories by which "rain follows the plow." When rain failed to follow the plow and the cycle of rainfall moved toward drought, western settlers faced the limits of self-reliance and individual enterprise.[27]

One result was a national irrigation movement, and a growing sense that the project went beyond local resources and required federal involvement.[28] The first National Irrigation Congress met in Salt Lake in 1891 and launched a variety of plans to enlist government help. By this time, converted reclamationists like William Ellsworth Smythe recognized the need for enlisting popular support. What the movement needed, Smythe said, was an active "propaganda," and he and others set about to supply it.

In 1894 Congress acknowledged the cause of irrigation with the Carey Act, a measure to allow the states to use the revenue from the sale of federal lands to support irrigation projects. The Carey Act had very limited success, and irrigationists pressed for more active federal participation. Francis Newlands, representative and later senator from Nevada, was instrumental in the design of proposals for federal irrigation. Newlands led the campaign in Congress, and when Teddy Roosevelt succeeded William McKinley, the reclamation bill at last received strong executive support. In 1902, Congress passed the Newlands Reclamation Act, providing for federal initiative and control of irrigation projects.[29]

While the Newlands Act was an outstanding accomplishment of the Progressive Era, it did not create the western utopia that enthusiasts seemed to be anticipating. In its first decades the Reclamation Service could claim only a measure of success. The dams and reservoirs provided "for only 1,200,000 out of a total of more than 18,000,000 acres of irrigated land in the seventeen western states." W. Eugene Hollon has explained what went wrong: "Because they were inexperienced in constructing large dams, the Reclamation Service had underestimated construction costs, allowed settlers into projects too soon, and in some cases tried to reclaim land that proved incapable of growing crops."[30]

In the original plan of the Newlands Act, reclamation was to be financed by a revolving fund, replenished by settlers' payments when their farms became productive. For a variety of reasons, repayment was often not forthcoming. In 1914, Congress passed a Reclamation Extension Act, extending the period of repayment from ten to twenty years. This act threw the financial efficiency of the Reclamation Service into disrepair and did not fully satisfy the discontented settlers. The agricultural economy declined immediately after World War I, and, in Donald Swain's words, "farmers on federal projects called for relief from the heavy payments, while the Reclamation Service pressed for maximum collections."[31]

The repayment problem brought federal reclamation to the edge of fianncial crisis. In 1924, a Fact Finders' Committee investigated the whole project and recommended a series of reforms. Their most significant recommendation changed the whole character of federal reclamation. Settler repayment simply could not support the projects, the committee reported. What they advocated instead was multiple-purpose river use, particularly the combined purposes of irrigation and generation of hydroelectric power. In 1928, Congress authorized the construction of Boulder Dam on the Colorado River, and desert reclamation was launched on a new scale, with hydroelectric power and urban water use placed on an equal plane with irrigated agriculture.[32]

Instead of a simple process of transforming deserts into farms, the manipulation of water in arid lands turned out to be an enormously complicated matter, with a variety of special interests competing for control.[33] But to many of its first proponents, reclamation was a matter of simple, realistic optimism. "The desert only looks like a wasteland," both miners and irrigators seemed to be saying. "Those who came before us thought it was useless, but we are ourselves not so easily fooled."

CHAPTER ONE
John C. Frémont

The whole idea of such a desert, and such a people, is a novelty in our country. . . .[1]

I

The explorer John C. Frémont was courageous, ambitious, and well connected at exactly the right moment in American history.[2] In the expansionistic 1840s, he was a topographical engineer with the United States Army, acting as an advance scout for national settlement and travel, writing widely distributed reports. Responding to the nation's growing appetite for authoritative descriptions of the Far West, Frémont and his reports played a crucial part in establishing the popular images of the region. In the 1840s, the nation grew enormously, bridging the gap between the borders of the old Louisiana Territory and the Pacific Coast. Large areas of the acquired land presented the nation with a new and difficult challenge: the desert. The writings of John C. Frémont had a major influence in setting the terms in which Americans made sense of this anomalous new landscape.

At once impulsive and lucky, Frémont was perfectly suited for the era of Manifest Destiny. His early life history provided the classic elements of a success story: discouraging odds at the beginning, a rise to fame through fortunate connections, risks undertaken with considerable reward. Evidently illegitimate, Frémont was born in 1813 "into a nomadic family of unstable finances." He received a fair education, until he was finally dismissed from the College of Charleston for "incorrigible negligence."[3] He had, it seems, fallen in love.

Academic misadventure did not damage his future; he took up teaching and eventually taught mathematics for the navy. He began, also, to meet people of influence and power. In 1838 and 1839, those connections enabled Frémont to accompany the skilled French explorer J. N. Nicollet on expeditions into the Minnesota country. From Nicollet, Frémont learned many of the techniques and concerns of scientific exploration. In 1841, he married Jessie Benton, daughter of the influential senator Thomas Hart Benton. The marriage carried other benefits; the new Mrs. Frémont would contribute much of the literary flair that would characterize her husband's reports.

With the combined qualifications of a powerful father-in-law and experience in exploration, Frémont in 1842 secured control of his own government expedition. He surveyed the Oregon Trail as far as Fort Laramie and continued past the fort, despite warnings of Indian hostility, for a brief entry into the Wind River Mountains, returning to St. Louis in the fall of 1842.

In the next year, Frémont led a much more extensive expedition, traveling to the Columbia River in the Oregon country and then south to California, returning east in 1844. His major encounters with deserts took place in this second expedition, first, as he pursued an odd, inland route from Oregon to California, through the northern deserts, and second as he traveled east from California through present-day southern Nevada and Utah.

In the 1843–44 trip, Frémont spent little more than two months in deserts. Much of that time, he was clearly preoccupied—less interested in looking at the desert than he was in looking for a way out of it. Despite the brevity of his contact with the deserts, Frémont carried away strong impressions. Through his reports, his personal experiences of frustration, disorientation, and hardship in the desert had a powerful influence on the nation's images and expectations. "It is almost impossible," Donald Jackson and Mary Lee Spence have written, "to overstate the enthusiasm with which the nation greeted the printed reports of [Frémont's] first two western expeditions."[4] In career or in character, he was hardly a "typical" American. Nonetheless, his standards for assessing value and worth in nature were solidly representative. One could well think of John C. Frémont as a real estate appraiser on a continental scale, traveling ahead of settlement and, to the best of his ability, sending back good news. With the desert the news had to be mixed: it was not an attractive or valuable place, but it was not, on the other hand, a fatal obstacle to continental expansion.

By 1844, Frémont's adventurous career had only begun. In 1845, he returned to California, arriving in time to play a role in the odd events of the Bear Flag Rebellion and the Mexican War. In a dispute with Brig. Gen. Stephen Watts Kearny, Frémont was court-martialed, returned to Washington, and convicted. In 1848–49, he led a private expedition into the San Juan Mountains in present-day New Mexico and Colorado. This expedition was a disaster, with Frémont's party left divided and stranded in the mountains, reduced to severe and— for some—fatal hunger.

With one court-martial and an exploring fiasco behind him, Frémont still went on to a brief term as a senator from California. In 1856, he was the presidential nominee of the newly formed Republican party. He served briefly and controversially in the Civil War in command of the Western Department, headquartered in St. Louis. After the war, he made an illusory fortune in railroad stock. When the stock collapsed, Frémont was left nearly penniless.

Except for a brief term as territorial governor in Arizona, from 1878 to 1881, Frémont spent his last years in unsuccessful efforts to recover his fame and fortune. In the 1840s, he had volunteered to be the confident symbol of an expansionistic nation. Late in life, he was awarded a much-needed federal pension. He died soon after in 1890, the year Frederick Jackson Turner would designate as the end of the frontier. If Frémont was still symbolic, it was no longer by his choice.

II

In his later years, Frémont tried to make money by writing his memoirs. The times had changed; his adventures were no longer a magnet for national attention. Frémont's *Memoirs*, Volume I, met with disappointing sales. Volume II never appeared.

This was a melancholy conclusion to a career that rested on the skilled production of written material—on the writing of reports. Known as the Great Pathfinder, Frémont actually discovered very little in the way of new trails or territory. Trappers and, needless to say, Indians had made the real discoveries, in the narrow definitional sense of getting there first. More than the Great Pathfinder, Frémont was the Great Path Publicizer. His reports, as Bernard DeVoto noted, "were far more important than his travels."[5]

While Frémont's wife, Jessie, helped him a great deal, the power of his reports rested on his own talent. He knew how to travel—in a way that would produce experiences easily convertible into prose. Authoritative reporting had three requirements: certainty, simplicity, and minimal self-revelation. The writer could not bog down in questions or doubts. Frémont held off doubts with two unquestioned assumptions. He believed in the legitimacy of the motives and goals of the United States's program of expansion, and therefore of his own activities as agent of expansion. And he believed in the legitimacy of characterizing places or events in a few words.

By assuming the possibility of brief characterizations of landscapes, Frémont denied complexity or ambiguity in nature. By assuming the justice of the nation's motives and of his own, he performed a comparable operation for human nature. At the same time, he steered clear of introspection, self-doubt, and any confessions of weakness or perplexity.

Frémont's reports thus had the two vast variables of nature and human nature under control. His structure of certainty naturally invited the trust of the reading audience. It was, after all, an audience poorly qualified to doubt his word, since few readers had any firsthand experience of the areas he described. Frémont's reports gave American citizens just what they wanted: a quick way of assimilating huge territories.

In Frémont's hands, the process of exploration took days instead of years, and the process of presenting those discoveries took pages instead of volumes. If Frémont in any sense "conquered" the West for the nation, it was a visual and verbal conquest: he saw with efficiency and he reported with brevity.

Frémont's style suited national style. His point of view was a perspective in motion; a traveler himself, he gathered information for travelers. His gift was for gathering impressions while in motion, a skill much in need in an expanding nation. Frémont's double standard of value—beauty and use—also fit national needs. His was exactly the perspective needed to classify the West, to distinguish good and valuable areas from worthless ones. For Frémont and for many Americans who shared his priorities, the desert met the standards for the category of worthless: it was worthless by the standards of both beauty and use.

III

In all his travels, Frémont never showed the slightest fondness for deserts. He preferred mountains and plains—the mountains for their greater scenic interests, the plains for their animation, supplied by buffalo and Indians. For deserts, he had an arsenal of adjectival abuse: "forbidding," "inhospitable," "desolate," "bleak," "sterile," "dreary," "savage," "barren," "dismal," "repulsive," and "revolting."[6]

Unrewarding as it was for someone attempting to explore and report, the desert still could not be avoided. Deserts had a way of standing between Frémont and the valuable places, particularly California. A transcontinental traveler, he found, had to confront and cross deserts.

In 1843, Frémont was under no compulsion to travel extensively in the deserts. His official mission was over when he reached the Oregon coast. His instructions said nothing about desert side trips. Leaving Oregon, Frémont recrossed the mountains and wandered along the western edge of the Nevada desert. His intention was to give the Buenaventura River one last chance to reveal itself. Represented on a number of contemporary maps, the Buenaventura was a supposed water connection between the Great Basin and the Pacific. First conceived of by the Spanish explorers of the eighteenth century, the river was a prime instance of western wish-fulfillment geography.[7] Providing an easy passage through the deserts and the Sierras, the Buenaventura was such a good idea that it stayed alive in the realm of imagined possibility. Frémont set out to find it— again, on his own initiative and not on official orders.

On December 17, 1843, Frémont reached "a country where the scarcity of water and of grass makes travelling dangerous. . . ."[8] Simply choosing a direction became a trial of leadership: the scarcity of water and grass could make a trivial mistake into a disaster. Pursuing the mythical Buenaventura, Frémont did not know where he was going.

Ordinarily, Frémont recorded his decisions with the confident phrasing: "I determined." The desert reversed the balance of power in his sentences. "We *were forced* by desert plains," he said, "far to the south [my emphasis]." He no longer "determined" the direction; the "course of travelling" was "*forced upon us* by the structure of the country [my emphasis]."⁹

Frémont's phrasing at times attributed even more life to the desert: he was "tempted into dead ends," "deceived" by "the dry inhospitable rock." In his wanderings, he was finding the desert virtually an animate adversary, an adversary unwilling to play by any familiar rules. In one surprisingly well-watered valley, he said, "we began to feel ourselves out of all difficulty." Assessing the landscape, Frémont felt "it was reasonable to conclude that this stream would . . . conduct us into a better country." By the next morning, "our hopes were once more destroyed."¹⁰ The valley led only to another dry basin.

Frémont recorded this incident in the tone of an individual who would like to lodge a complaint. He had been deceived. The terrain had given a promise of "better country" and then defaulted on the promise. Frémont felt his expectations were reasonable; this was evidently a territory in which reason did not rule.

Under this pressure, Frémont's usually confident and determined persona had a few encounters with doubt. In his report, he kept these attacks of hesitation to the unlikely unit of "a moment." On December 29, a snowstorm added to his perplexity. "For a moment," Frémont admitted, "I looked around in doubt on the wild and inhospitable prospect."¹¹ Two days later, on New Year's Eve, the scale of doubt had expanded. He wrote, "Here we concluded the year 1843, and our new year's eve was rather a gloomy one. The result of our journey began to be very uncertain; the country was singularly unfavorable to travel. . . ."¹² An "uncertain result" could have meant anything from delay to death—that part of his statement was ambiguous. But the rest of the content was clear: the desert was "singularly unfavorable to travel," providing obstacles that Frémont found extremely difficult to decipher.

Would a guide have helped? Frémont made an effort to secure help from the Indians. "I tried unsuccessfully to prevail on some of them to guide us," he said, "but they only looked at each other and laughed."[13] From the Indian angle, the laughter was a thoroughly sensible response; from Frémont's perspective, it was another obstacle and frustration.

In mid-January, Frémont found "a broad and plainly marked trail." Immediate uncertainty was at an end: "On a large trail there is never any doubt of finding suitable places for encampment"—sites with water and grass.[14] The discovery of a reliable trail, however, did not in itself save Frémont from further hardship. He could have spent a mild winter in the Truckee Valley, living on fish and wild plants. Evidently he preferred the challenges of mountains, even in midwinter, to prolonged association with deserts. Without any advance exploration, he turned west into the snow-filled Sierras on January 19, 1844. On March 6, Frémont's exhausted party finally reached refuge in the Sacramento Valley.

IV

Leaving California, Frémont first traveled south through the Central Valley. Experienced travelers at Sutter's Fort had told him to follow the Old Spanish Trail, an established route that curved to the south through present-day southern Nevada—an area that was at the time, like California itself, still a Mexican possession. But traveling to the south in order to head east began to make Frémont impatient. Why not travel directly east and save time and distance?

On the edge of this impulsive decision, still in the eastern Sierran foothills, Frémont encountered an Indian from one of the Spanish missions. Pointing to the desert to the east, the Indian warned Frémont of the great risk he was courting. "There are the great llanos," the Mission Indian told him; "there is neither water nor grass—nothing; every animal that goes out upon them, dies!"[15]

Frémont heeded this warning and stuck to the established trail—a fact which in itself may not seem remarkable. But in his impulsive character, caution was more often the exception than the rule. Contrasting Frémont's receptivity to warnings in April 1844, on the edge of the desert, with an act of defiance two years before in Wyoming, reveals a great deal about the special conditions of desert travel.

In the earlier incident, in 1842 at Fort Laramie, local authorities warned Frémont that he risked Indian attack if he traveled farther west. His intrepid guide, Kit Carson, took that occasion to make his last will and testament. Did this ominous act inspire caution? It inspired in Frémont the will to go on. "I had determined," he told his men, "to proceed. . . ."[16] For Frémont, there were few pleasures in life comparable to the exercise of defiant free will.

Recording his defiance at Fort Laramie, Frémont offered several reasons for fearlessness in the face of Indian hostility. First, his party was "well-armed"—guns were a portable precaution that made caution itself less essential. Second, Frémont employed an interpreter— a mediator to deal with failures of understanding on the spot. Third, Frémont claimed that much of the threatened danger was just a matter of words—"rumors," he said, subject to "much exaggeration." Fourth, Frémont insisted that Indian hostility was one of the familiar and predictable hazards of western travel—in his words, "accustomed," "ordinary," "every day," and "expected."[17] Step by step, in the statement he said he had made to his men, Frémont reduced the fearfulness of the prospect until a situation of high adventure began to seem almost humdrum.

The dangers Frémont dismissed at Fort Laramie in 1842 were exactly the dangers he could not avoid in the desert in 1844. Guns were of no use against desert uncertainties; guns could not force the landscape into disclosing water sources or viable traveling routes. Given the scarcity of natives to speak to, interpreters were of hardly more use than guns. The desert's dangers were physically evident and undeniably actual; they could not be dismissed as dangers of words, "rumors," or "exaggeration." Finally desert hazards were in no sense familiar. The words Frémont used to describe Indian hostility— *accustomed, ordinary, expected*—only needed to be reversed to describe his experience in the desert.

When the Indian in April 1844 told Frémont to follow the established trail, he was manifestly a "good" Indian. He was "well-dressed" and spoke "Spanish fluently." He "belonged," after all, "to one of the Spanish missions."[18] This was an individual conspicuously assimilated to European culture; Frémont could get the benefit of aboriginal knowledge, safely certified with European respectability.

More than that, Frémont knew enough from personal experience to credit the warning. From his wanderings in northern Nevada during the preceding winter, he knew something about the disorientation and deprivation of desert travel. When the Indian suggested that it was an act of folly to enter a desert in ignorance, Frémont knew enough to believe him. He spent much of his career defying human beings, ranging from Indians to Mexican officials to his commanding officers. Nonetheless, nature in the deserts gave Frémont a brief course in submission, at least transitory training in controlling his impulsive will.

V

"Dismal to look upon," "apparently illimitable," the desert's principal offense lay in its discouraging prospect for mobility. Its border, Frémont explained, marked "the eastern limit of travel, where water and grass terminated."[19] "Travel" was Frémont's highest concern. The information in his reports was not only collected *by* traveling; the purpose of collecting that information was to offer a guide *for* traveling. In his records, "traveler" is almost interchangeable with "American"; even so-called settlers were more familiar to him in their temporary state as "emigrants." With the desert, the only information of significance was information with a direct bearing on mobility— how to get across it.

"A *road* to travel on, and the *right* course to go," Frémont admitted, "were joyful consolations." The Old Spanish Trail gave a bedrock of certainty to the trip, but it offered no exemption from hardship. The trail was "the roughest and rockiest road we had ever seen," very hard on the feet of horses and mules. There were still jornadas to be endured, "long stretches of 40 or 60 miles, without water." Even Frémont, habitual minimizer of suffering, had to admit that this was discomfort of a high order: "Travellers through countries affording water and timber can have no conception of our intolerable thirst while journeying over the hot yellow sands of this elevated country, where the heated air seems to be entirely deprived of moisture."[20]

"The continual rocks and want of water and grass"—the features of desert travel repeated themselves in a monotone.[21] The journey may have been an ordeal, but it did not seem to be, in Frémont's terms, much of a story. With nature a monotone of hardship, he had to find his story in human behavior.

On the edge of the desert, Frémont recorded an uncharacteristic moment of traveler's self-consciousness. "Our cavalcade made a strange and grotesque appearance," Frémont said, "and it was impossible to avoid reflecting upon our position and composition in this remote solitude." He went on to sketch a portrait of the party—a mixture of French, German, American, and Indian men; "four or five languages heard at once"; "American, Spanish and Indian dresses and equipment intermingled"; the whole procession "stretching a quarter of a mile." The party "looked more like we belonged to Asia," Frémont thought, "than to the United States of America."[22]

Why did Frémont begin the narrative of the desert crossing with this group portrait? In mountains or plains, he always found much to be interested in: scenery, geology, plants, wild animals. In the desert his attention went to the human drama as if the desert were a vast, ominously bare stage. He became aware, with a new intensity, of his companions. Most dramatically, he became aware of their differences: the diversity of dress, language, origin. The party was as separated in space as it was in character, spread out along "the dreary path" in what was, in fact, still Mexican territory.

Having noted the diversity of the party, Frémont did not go on to say what he made of it, or what fears and dangers it suggested. What force, if any, would unify such a diverse group of beings? The answer came in the incidents of violence that marked the journey.

On April 24, a man and a boy, Andreas Fuentes and Pablo Hernandez, came into Frémont's camp from the east. Their small party of six had been traveling with thirty horses in advance of the annual caravan to Santa Fe. They had camped at Archilette Springs to await reinforcement. Lured into a "security which proved fatal," they were attacked by Indians. Fuentes and Hernandez fled, abandoning Fuentes's wife, Hernandez's parents, and one other man to apparent disaster. Frémont took the refugees in and "promised them such aid as circumstances might put it in my power to give."[23]

It might have seemed a bit late for "aid." Archilette Springs was still two days' travel ahead; rescue of the abandoned party was not likely. But "aid," it turned out, meant revenge.

Kit Carson and Alex Godey volunteered for the mission. Trailing the stolen horses, they located a camp of Indians, "fired their rifles upon a steady aim, and rushed in." Scalping an apparently dead Indian, Carson and Godey were taken aback when he sprang "to his feet, the blood streaming from his skinned head, and uttering a hideous howl." Carson and Godey "did what humanity required, and quickly terminated the agonies of the gory savage."[24]

What did Frémont make of all this? His assessment is worth quoting at length:

> The time, place, object and numbers, considered, this expedition of Carson and Godey may be considered among the boldest and most disinterested which the annals of western adventure, so full of daring deeds, can present. Two men, in a savage desert, pursue day and night an unknown body of Indians into the defiles of an unknown mountain—attack them on sight, without counting numbers—and defeat them in an instant—and for what? To punish the robbers of the desert, and to avenge the wrongs of Mexicans whom they did not know. I repeat: it was Carson and Godey who did this—the former an *American*, born in the Boonslick country of Missouri; the latter a Frenchman, born in St. Louis—and both trained to western enterprise from early life.[25]

Frémont fitted the incident triumphantly into "western adventure," that secularized battle of good and evil, civilization and savagery. The last line, nonetheless, was puzzling. What was the point of citing so emphatically the international origins of the victims and their avengers?

One thinks of the earlier passage in which Frémont "reflected" on the diversity of his party. What force would transcend that disunity? The answer, evidently, lay in Frémont's emphasis on the French, American, and Mexican collaboration against the desert Indians—the common enemy. "We rejoiced," Frémont said, "that Carson and

Godey had been able to give so useful a lesson to these American Arabs, who lie in wait to murder and plunder the innocent traveller."[26] Of course, he did not know if the "brutal" and "loathsome" "savages" killed by his men were individually responsible for the Mexicans' deaths. His was obviously a concept of crime and punishment that dealt in groups, not individuals.

In the desert, there were two kinds of humans: "brutal savages" and "innocent travellers." The "savages," Frémont said, were characterized by "an absence of thought—and an action wholly impulsive."[27] Although Frémont never noticed it, his characterization of "savages" fit "innocent travellers" as well. In 1844, the desert surrounding the Old Spanish Trail was a very dangerous place. Anyone who traveled "innocently" into it, assuming that the desert owed him a safe passage, was showing "an absence of thought—an action wholly impulsive." Anyone who acted on the presumption that the desert owed him a safe passage was "innocent" to the point of being dangerous to himself and his companions.

Frémont and his men showed all the signs of that dangerous innocence. As they approached the eastern edge of the Great Basin, a member of the party named Tabeau lingered behind in search of a lame mule. The next day, Frémont found the spot where Tabeau had been killed and his horse taken. His death left the party gloomy and bereaved: "Men who have gone through such dangers and sufferings as we had seen, become like brothers, and feel each other's loss." Grief meant vengeance, but desert conditions once more forced Frémont to uncharacteristic caution. "We wished to avenge his death," he said, "but the condition of our horses, languishing for grass and repose, forbade an expedition into unknown mountains."[28]

Possibly revenge might have taught a lesson in discouraging further attacks. It was just as likely to bring a reciprocal response from the Indians, inspiring attacks on later travelers who had played no part in these events. Most important, the desire for revenge enabled Frémont to ignore the underlying dynamic of the conflict: an intrusion into Indian territory by armed foreigners.

Frémont was fortunate that he encountered death in terms of actual homicide, with evident Indian responsibility. His response to death was an immediate desire for revenge—for someone to blame, punish, and unite against. Blaming and punishing Indians placed no strain on his system of explanation. What, one wonders, would have happened if a member of his party had died from the effects of the desert—from thirst, or overexposure, or sheer exhaustion? Would Frémont have felt the same immediate inclination to revenge, to blame, and to punish? And what would have been his next move, on finding no human to bear the responsibility?

In such a situation, Frémont would seem to have had two options. He could blame himself for his folly in leading his men into the desert, which would mean an unparalleled self-examination and self-criticism. Or he could blame the desert, which would require an unparalleled attention to two almost theological questions: What kind of entity was the desert? Why was it what it was?

Fortunately for Frémont, the Indians, both the "good" ones and the "bad" ones, saved him from the trouble of either introspection or reflection. The Christian Indian persuaded him to travel on the Old Spanish Trail and thus reduced the risk of desert-caused death. The desert Indians killed in ways that left Frémont free to think of death in terms of crime, blame, punishment, and revenge. The question of human nature stayed clear and simple. The "good" humans transcended their differences to unite in a self-righteous urge for revenge. The "bad" humans were the ones who made this unity possible, this definition by opposites.

VI

When Frémont looked at desert Indians, he claimed he saw animals. They had, he said, "an expression of countenance resembling that in a beast of prey; and all their actions are those of wild animals." Living in an environment of scarcity, the Indians were "driven to any extremity for food and eat every insect, and every creeping thing, however loathsome and repulsive." Humans whose "sole employment is to obtain food" were, in Frémont's opinion, "the nearest approach to the mere animal creation."[29]

Desert Indians, Frémont was sure, lived to eat and ate to live. In his thinking, to concentrate the efforts of body and mind on subsistence was to live in a peculiar borderland. Such an overriding concern with consuming and digesting was a betrayal of humanity, and a surrender to animality.

What was Frémont's conception of animals? In his few brief descriptions of animal behavior, the animals were more than likely to be eating each other. When a prairie snake ate a swallow, or wolves chased a buffalo, he showed a curious need to intervene, even to punish the offender.[30]

While Frémont could recognize that animal life involved a continuously operating food chain, he still reacted to each link in that chain with more sentiment than science. Despite his treasured stance of scientific detachment, he still saw the animals in the food chain in terms of victim and villain. Swallows were victims, snakes were villains; buffalo were victims, wolves were villains.

Without intervention, the good animals lost more often than they won. Frémont was more than willing to intervene on their behalf—to kill the snake that insisted on ingesting swallows. His behavior here made it clear that ecological principles we take for granted never occurred to him. There were, Frémont said, "innumerable" swallows; the snake, by cutting short the lives of individuals, was, according to modern views of ecology, doing a service to swallows in general. A world without this particular set of predators would have been a world burdened with starving swallows.

Far-reaching ecological consequences were not Frémont's concern. He noticed that it was characteristic of animals to devote themselves to the pursuit of food, and he was quick to associate this observation negatively with desert Indian behavior.

Frémont, one might assume from this, would be far above a concern for food. His text would verge on the ethereal, as he and his men rose above animality and pursued the higher good of exploration. The most limited concern with consistency would make him nearly ascetic.

Consistency aside, Frémont lived in a very food-oriented world. In the three hundred pages of his report on the 1843–44 expedition, there are at least 110 references to food. What evidently set him off from animals and Indians, in his own mind, was that he and his party ate either fresh game or provisions.

This division rested on some subtle distinctions. When wolves chased and ate buffalo, it was a case in the oppression of the weak by the strong. When Frémont chased and ate buffalo, it was exhilaration, adventure, and fine sport.[31]

When fresh game was unavailable, provisions were Frémont's route to independence. Provisions freed him from dependence on local resources, from the need to know or understand those resources. No necessity focused his attention on the signs of food. His vision could aim at the horizon and barely pause at the ground underfoot.

How did Frémont justify exempting himself from the censure he applied to every other carnivore? How did he resolve the contradiction by which every other creature's appetite was degrading, while his was merely practical? Thanks to an unacknowledged categorization, he never had to notice his contradictions. Rock, plant, animal, Indian, and American were each separate categories. Rules that applied to one did not necessarily apply to the others.

Beyond these divisions were two overarching categories. Rock, plant, and animal went under the label "nature." "American," for all practical purposes, took the title "human." While the desert Indians represented a perplexingly intermediate category, Frémont took every opportunity to return them to the jurisdiction of "nature."

Ordinarily, Frémont found nothing perplexing in his own status. He was human, civilized, and American and therefore quite different from Indian or animal. By dramatizing human biological vulnerability, the desert raised the possibility that the difference might not be as great as he hoped.

VII

In terms of day-to-day travel, Frémont's time in the desert was not a source of satisfaction. But in terms of his career as an explorer, his tour of 1843–44 carried considerable reward. He had made, as he said, "an immense circuit" of the Great Basin—the region of internal drainage bounded by the Sierras and the Rockies. While he was not the first to travel through the basin, Frémont took the opportunity to reflect on its "leading features and general structure," thereby becoming, as William Goetzmann has noted, "in a real sense its discoverer."[32]

Reaching the edge of the basin, Frémont interrupted his narrative "to look back upon our footsteps." What the backward look revealed was a "peculiar and striking" country, differing "essentially from the Atlantic side of our continent. . . ." The mountains were "higher," and "more numerous"; in the whole circuit, Frémont was "never out of sight of snow." And in contrast to the proliferation of rivers on the Atlantic side, major rivers on the Pacific side represented a distinctive "unity and concentration of waters"; only the Columbia River connected the interior to the coast.[33]

Altogether the most distinctive feature of the Far West was the Great Basin itself. "Interior basins, with their own systems of lakes and rivers, and often sterile, are common enough in Asia," Frémont said, ". . . but in America such things are new and strange, unknown and unsuspected, and discredited when related."[34] He had found North America's great geographical anomaly. The Great Basin might not have been his preferred form of landscape, but it *was* his discovery.

While it was by no means an ideal place, the basin was not beyond hope. "It is called a *desert*," Frémont said, "and from what I saw of it, sterility may be its prominent characteristic." But it was surrounded by snow-topped mountains; "where there is so much snow, there must be streams"; and there were, therefore, places with "good soil and good grass, adapted to civilized settlements."[35] There was hope for limited agriculture in the basin; Frémont's news here soon proved an inspiration for Mormon leaders looking for a refuge in the West.

Moreover, scientists as well as settlers had reason to value the desert. "I flatter myself," Frémont said, "that what is discovered, though not enough to satisfy curiosity, is sufficient to excite it." For all its discomforts, the desert did have status as an intellectual challenge; its very novelty provoked and conceivably could reward curiosity. "[A]lthough a desert," the country "afforded much to excite the curiosity of the botanist." Why did Frémont not pursue this opportunity? "[L]imited time, and the rapidly advancing season for active operations oblige me to omit all descriptions, and hurry briefly to the conclusion of this report."[36]

The "limited time" and "advancing season" were references to Frémont's time back in the East, writing his report, and to his eagerness to cut off his sojourn in civilization and return to the trail.

Something of the actual urgency in getting across the desert and on to the more satisfying places seemed to have entered the organization of the narrative here. Frémont "hurried" to the conclusion of the report, just as he attempted to hurry to the further limit of the desert.

Nonetheless, he did acknowledge that, given the time and opportunity, the desert would provide things to study. In two or three passages, he noted the fact that would preoccupy twentieth-century desert admirers: for a land so easy to characterize as sterile and barren, the desert is oddly life-filled, stocked with its own adapted flora and fauna. "[T]hroughout this nakedness of sand and gravel were many beautiful plants and flowering shrubs," he noted. "Even where no grass could take root, the naked sand would bloom with some rich and rare flower, which found its appropriate home in the arid and barren spot."[37] A "barren spot" filled with plants? One realizes that this is a specialized version of the word: the desert was "barren" by virtue of the absence of familiar and usable plants, especially forage for domestic animals, and by virtue of the lack of a continuous ground cover.

In fact, in 1844 Frémont was seeing the desert at its most attractive season—in April, after what must have been adequate spring rains. This was the desert spring, the proliferation of blossoms that would astonish twentieth-century observers. Frémont did acknowledge the presence of "numerous" plants, "with flowers of white, yellow, red and purple." But these acknowledgments were brief and eclipsed by references to the more pressing discomforts of the road: "a burning sun," "the continual rocks, and want of water and grass."[38] For very understandable reasons, Frémont and party could not forget their hardships in a celebration of the desert spring.

In retrospect, with the risks and injuries safely behind him, Frémont was able to adopt his proper stance as a scientific explorer and find merit even in a barren and sterile land. Like every other element in the continental resources, the desert deserved study; the first priority, in fact, was to learn more. "The contents of this Great Basin," Frémont noted, were "yet to be examined." Information was, on all counts, sadly lacking; most of what he had heard proved to be "a tissue of falsehoods."[39] In the burst of mid-century optimism and expansion, all regions would submit to exploration; in matters of geography, no place—not even the most forbidding desert—could claim a right to privacy.

VIII

John C. Frémont had an almost sublime gift for remaining matter-of-fact. It was possible, he knew, to see everything in the world from one unified and stable perspective, and that reliable perspective happened to be his own. He could confidently collapse vast spaces into brief phrases, containing complexity in one or two adjectives. He could put his impressions through an almost industrial process of production, the raw material of place passed rapidly through stages of visual and verbal refinement to emerge as a report.

Much of Frémont's faith in the reliability of his own observations rested on a certainty borrowed from science. His cart of instruments—the barometer especially—certified him. The astronomical observations at the end of most of his daily entries were a constant reminder that this was not simply an adventure, but a search for knowledge.

Frémont's sense of certainty did not rest on any expressed religious faith. The extent of the spaces he traveled, the complexity of the landscape, the narrow margin of survival he lived on, the enormous role of luck in his own career—all these provocations would have led, one would think, to some theological expression. They did not. Frémont wrote with a sense of polite expression: religion was likely to provoke controversy, and it was not the terrain of scientific explorers.[40]

Polite expression, however, put no limits on his desert commentary. Frémont saw no reason to temper his dislike of the desert. There were no property owners, no investors, no territorial officials, no lovers of arid landscapes to feel any injury or insult.

For purposes of description, Frémont found that the desert was most clearly defined by what it was not. Definition by opposites was the essence of his thinking. "Savages" were the opposite of "travelers"; deserts were the opposite of "better countries," "countries with grass and water," "countries where humans could live." Indians and deserts shared common qualities: wildness, irrationality, danger, intractability, unpredictability. Deserts summed up the disturbing side of nature, as Indian character summed up the disturbing side of human nature.

Deserts, in fact, brought out the worst in human character. The Great Basin was "peopled," as Frémont said, "but miserably and sparsely." To his eye, "humanity here appeared in its lowest form, and in its most elementary state."[41] The desert was, in other words, a peculiar and primitive place that had forced the natives into remaining peculiar and primitive themselves. Humans, in Frémont's thinking, traveled on a narrow edge in resisting their animality, and prolonged residence in the desert made balancing on that edge next to impossible. Not that Frémont was himself threatened by that possibility, since he stayed in motion. Environmental determinism could hardly hit a moving target.

Frémont got through safely, with his life intact and his convictions unshaken. He escaped doubt more narrowly than he escaped death. The desert was the most unreasonable place he traveled in: its distances deceptive, its promises unreliable, its whole reason for existence uncertain. But Frémont had no changes in conviction to report from his confrontation with irrationality. Endurance was, in his opinion, all the desert had asked for and all that he gave it.

A great enthusiast for natural scenery, Frémont had found little beyond transitory wildflowers to praise in the desert. This lover of the wilderness made a major exception for the arid wilderness. The blossoming of the cactus, he said, "wonderfully ornaments this poor country."[42] Even the wildflowers could not redeem the impoverishment of the land at large.

Forty years later, writing his memoirs, Frémont had evidently chosen to forget this contradiction. Summarizing at the end of the first (and only) volume, he drew a dramatic contrast between his earlier life in nature and his later life in politics and business. In the first phase, when he met obstacles, they were "natural ones and I could calculate unerringly upon the amount of resistance and injury I should have to meet in surmounting them." The challenge of these natural entities worked perfectly for an oppositional temperament: "Their very opposition roused strength to overcome them." The struggle was "honest and simple."[43]

In his romanticizing, Frémont then took a giant step in restructuring the past. "No treachery," he insisted, "lurked behind the majesty of the mountain or lay hidden in the hot glare of the inhospitable plain." Nature in all its forms gave fair warning: "the sterile face of the desert warned the traveller off; and if he ventured there it was with full knowledge of his danger." When he entered politics and business, Frémont said, his "path of life" left the "grand and lovely features of nature, and its pure and wholesome air." He entered instead "the poisoned atmosphere and jarring circumstances of conflict among men."[44]

Frémont purchased his dramatic contrast here at the price of selective memory. National politics was not his first experience with treachery and irrationality, with the refusal of an outside entity to play by the rules of behavior he believed in. Nonetheless, in his old age, Frémont wanted to reduce his definition by opposites to its broadest terms. Nature was clear and honest in its challenges; human nature was deceptive and duplicitous.

To reach his final arrangement of good and evil, Frémont had to forget the doubts the desert had once begun to raise. He had to forget that the desert had seemed to be a place where the boundary between nature and human nature became indistinct, a place where mind and eye might be devoted to tracking water and food, and not to writing reports.

CHAPTER TWO
William Lewis Manly

I

The majority of participants in the Gold Rush accumulated more in the way of experiences than riches. The overland trail was a mine for stories—a veritable mother lode of narrative. As movements through time and space, journeys remembered and retold are automatically narratives; the narrator does not just describe places, he tells stories. If a scholar then catalogues the descriptions while editing out the stories, a vital connection has been severed.

For most overland travelers, crossing the desert was an ordeal, but it was at least limited in duration. For William Lewis Manly and his party in 1849, pursuing a "shortcut" through unexplored desert, the ordeal seemed endless. In duration and intensity, Manly's desert experience was far from "representative." But if one wants to explore a dramatic illustration of the reasons why overland emigrants dreaded the desert, the story of William Lewis Manly and his friends has a clear right to prolonged consideration.

To cross the southern Nevada deserts in the mid-nineteenth century, wise travelers followed the prolonged, southward loop of the Old Spanish Trail. To travelers unfamiliar with the terrain, substituting a straight line for that loop looked like a victory of rational thought over irrational and irregular nature. In 1844, the logic of the straight line nearly persuaded John C. Frémont to launch his party into the deserts. Warned just in time, he relented and made an uncharacteristically cautious choice for the known trail.

In 1849, the mystical power of the shortcut led a party of overland emigrants, including Lewis Manly, to take the trip Frémont turned down.[1] Like Frémont, they were warned; unlike Frémont, they could not draw on recent memories of disorientation in deserts to add substance to the warning. Frémont got his advice from a visibly "civilized" and therefore trustworthy Indian; the 1849 emigrants got their advice from Mormons—white people who, for reasons unintelligible to the emigrants, had made themselves outsiders to "civilization." Given the option of trusting the Mormons, the emigrants preferred to trust the magical promise of a shortcut.

A twenty-nine-year-old frontiersman, William Lewis Manly did not lead in choosing the shortcut, but he came to carry a disproportionate burden of responsibility. In 1849, he saved eight people from thirst and starvation in the desert. In 1894, publishing *Death Valley in '49*, he tried to save them from anonymity.

As his story revealed, Manly had spcial reasons to hate the desert, but his feelings were by no means unique. The overland journey—and most dramatically, the journey of Lewis Manly—carried one clear message: If you cared about human beings and their survival, you had good reason to hate the desert.

II

Lewis Manly went to some trouble to explain his origins. He was born in 1820 in St. Albans, Vermont, on a family farm "carved . . . out of the big forest that covered the cold rocky hills." In that setting, Manly's childhood provided no training in leisure or abundance. "Economy of the very strictest kind" governed the farm.[2] Everyone, including the children, worked.

"The whole plan," Manly remembered, "seemed to be to have every family and farm self-supporting as far as possible." Looking back to those "days of real independence,"[3] Manly may not have drawn an accurate social history of his homeland, but he did set up an interesting background for his later career. The remembered economy of his childhood was a narrow but stable balance of sufficiency, maintained with limited natural resources and unrelenting human labor.

Families were small units of loyalty and shared effort. Economic and social activity had little relation to commerce or money. The detachment from a competitive concern for money was, in fact, a measure of what Manly called "real independence."

This might seem an unlikely prelude to the career of a Gold Rush adventurer. But Manly's heritage included a counterimpulse to stability. Early in his childhood, "people began to talk about the far West." Manly's father "got the Western fever," sold his farm, and moved to Michigan.[4] Training in mobility got off to an early start.

Once in possession of their Michigan land, the family found that they were susceptible to another variety of western fever. "There came a regular epidemic," Manly remembered, "of fever and ague and bilious fever, and a large majority of the people were sick." Manly's father was "the first one attacked," and, at the peak of his illness, he "talked and acted like a crazy man." For a time, the burden of nursing and cooking fell on the young Lewis Manly, "the only one that remained well."[5]

At age twenty, Manly found himself with another burden of responsibility. The farm was too small to be divided among four sons. As the oldest, Manly found it his duty "to start out first and see what could be done to make my own living."[6]

When Manly left home, his parents gave him advice, advice he claimed to remember clearly fifty years later. Directing him to "depend upon yourself," to "weigh well every thing you do" and to "do nothing to be ashamed of," this parental advice might seem close to platitude.[7] What took the advice beyond platitude was the fidelity with which Manly would follow it in extraordinary circumstances. Moreover, Manly's dutifulness in recording it illustrates vividly a particular kind of character development.

The exchange between Manly and his parents encapsulated, in David Riesman's phrase, the installation of a "psychological gyroscope," the mechanism of "inner-direction." The social context of inner direction involved "an increased personal mobility . . . and an almost constant *expansion*: in exploration, colonization and imperialism." In the context, "behavioral conformity" was not enough: "too many novel situations are presented, situations which a code cannot encompass in advance." The problem of choice, then, "is solved by channeling choice through a rigid though individualized character." In inner-direction, Riesman said, "the drive instilled in the child is to *live up to ideals*."[8]

Manly's life could have provided Riesman with a superb case study. Personal mobility in a phase of expansion certainly set the context of his life, presenting him with situations "novel" to a point beyond any possible anticipation. His steering would hold steady, with parental instructions operating very much in the manner of an internal gyroscope—to keep him, as Reisman put it, "on course."

Not surprisingly, Manly's departure from home, as he later remembered it, was not marked with a sense of liberation. "It seemed the beginning of another chapter in my pioneer life," he wrote, "and a rather tough experience."[9]

III

For the next eight years, Manly traveled and worked on the Wisconsin frontier, relying on his fine skills as a hunter. He took his profits from trapping and bought "eighty acres of good government land."

Feeling "very proud" to be a "land owner," Manly might seem to have reached the end of his adventures. He was ready to follow in the family tradition: to carve out by "main strength and muscle" a self-sufficient farm, to give up a concern with money now that it had served its proper purpose in the purchase of land, to put an end to adventuring and enjoy the stability of manhood.

Manly did indeed follow in his family tradition, but in the tradition of restlessness and not stable farming. "Rumors of a better country to the west" reached Wisconsin, and "western fever" began to "break out." Manly came down with a "touch of the disease" himself and began to prepare for a journey to Oregon. His preparations were interrupted by news from California in the winter of 1848–49. Manly had become close friends with another Wisconsin pioneer, Asahel Bennett. He was living with Mr. Bennett and his family when "a regular gold fever" hit. "Nothing would cure us," Manly and his friend decided, "but a trip."[10]

The trip began badly. The Bennetts departed, carrying Manly's supplies. Two weeks later, Manly set off. Their imprecise plans for meeting failed, and Manly could not find any trace of his friends. Desperate, he hired himself as a driver to a less-than-likable man named Charles Dallas. Realizing that he had made himself dependent on a willful and unreliable employer, Manly faced a stark situation: "I was in for it," he said, "and no other way but to go on."[11]

Realizing he was too late to cross the Sierras before the winter snows, Manly's employer decided to fire his drivers, rather than support them through the winter at Salt Lake. The drivers came up with a drastic plan. They "put a great many 'ifs' together" and decided to exchange land transportation for a boat.[12] They would descend a westward flowing river to the Pacific Coast. Manly and his friends, in other words, were hoping for a version of the Buenaventura River, the mythical river connecting the interior to the Pacific Coast that Frémont claimed to be searching for in his northern Nevada wanderings.

In an abandoned ferryboat, seven young men thus set out on an unintentional exploration of the Green River and the Colorado River. Manly's greater wilderness skills made him their chosen leader. Cheerful and confident at first, they congratulated themselves on "taking the most sensible way to get to the Pacific" and "wondered that everybody was so blind as not to see it as we did."[13] They were, of course, on their way to the Grand Canyon.

Before the party could drift to disaster, Indians warned them of their danger. Like the Christian Indian who saved Frémont from his Mojave cutoff, the Ute Indian described the prospect ahead, making "signs of death to show us that it was a fatal place."[14] Manly left the river and led his men overland to Salt Lake City. Outside the city, he approached a collection of emigrant wagons and discovered his lost friends, the Bennetts.

At this point in his story, Manly had demonstrated a remarkable combination of folly and wisdom—folly in leaping into an enterprise with little knowledge of its conditions, wisdom in dealing responsibly

with the consequences of his folly. His progress revealed the substantial ignorance of western geography possible in overland emigrants; it also revealed the extraordinary ability of those people to
proceed confidently in the midst of ignorance.

It was to Manly's credit that his group gave up their happy vision
of a river shortcut to the Pacific and heeded the Utes' warning.
Having been saved once from the mistake of foolishly chosen route,
Manly was ready to make the same mistake again.

IV

The Bennetts and Manly were not the only travelers to find themselves forced into an unexpected Salt Lake stopover. A substantial
party of California emigrants, realizing that they were too late to
cross the Sierras, hired a Mormon guide, Jefferson Hunt, to lead
them on the Old Spanish Trail. Hunt, on his return from service in
the Mormon Batallion, had become familiar with the trail. He was
by all reports a competent and responsible leader.

The Bennetts had developed a strong friendship with the Arcane
family, and Manly was still traveling with John Rogers, a veteran of
the Green River trip. As a recent study of social relations on the
overland trail has shown, this alliance between a single man and a
family was not at all unusual. Both parties profited from the pooling
of labor, resources, and companionship.[15] Manly, Rogers, the Bennetts, and the Arcanes all joined Hunt's party.

"Before they moved," Captain Hunt told his emigrants, "they must
organize and adopt rules and laws which must be obeyed." The hazards
of the trip were such that "they must move like an army," and Hunt
himself was "to be dictator in all things" unless overruled by a majority. Considering the risks of desert travel and the need for cooperation, Captain Hunt's request for authority was not extreme. "All
possible trouble that we could imagine might come," Manly remembered, "was provided against in our written agreement, and all promised to live up to it."[16]

There were factors, however, which the plan failed to take into
account. Impatience, excessive confidence, unwillingness to trust
Mormon leadership, and a fondness for the straight line characterized

a large number of the non-Mormons in the company. Under those pressures, the group agreement to which "all promised to live up" lasted less than a month.

A passing traveler circulated a map which seemed to sketch a direct westerly route to California. Enthusiasm began to mount. Captain Hunt said he would stay on the Old Spanish Trail as long as one wagon chose the route for which he had agreed to be the guide. On November 4, 1849, the wagon train divided.

Manly does not seem to have participated very actively in choosing his fate. His statement was brief: "My friend Bennett whose fortune I shared was among the seceders. . . ."[17] When Manly chose his traveling companions, he evidently surrendered his right to further choice.

For the seceders, fragmentation continued. One group reconsidered and returned to follow Hunt. Those still on the shortcut divided further: "those without any families did not care to bind themselves to stand by and assist those who had wives and children in their party." Choosing haste, the single men left the families behind. Reflecting that Mr. Bennett "had been faithful to me and my property when he knew not where I was," Manly "decided to stand by him and his wife at all hazards."[18]

Beginning the journey, Bennett had asked Manly to "look around and kill what game" he could. In the journey on which they were embarked, there was no more trying assignment. Hunting had been Manly's strong point, but as the land grew drier, the game grew scarcer. "Though I was an experienced hunter," Manly said, "where no game lived I got as hungry as other folks."[19]

It was also Manly's responsibility to climb hills and mountains in search of some clue in choosing their route. This was as hopeless as hunting. Each hilltop view showed the country becoming more barren and more vacant, with fewer and fewer prospects for water.

Each confrontation with these hopeless views was a terrible test of loyalty. "Prospects now seemed to be so hopeless," Manly remembered, "that I heartily wished I was not in duty bound to stand by the women and small children." Without dependents, he said, "I could pick up my knapsack and gun and go off," travel fast and save himself. But saving his own life would come at too high a price: "I felt I should be morally guilty of murder." Tracing this "dark line of thought" repeatedly, Manly "always felt better when I got around to the determination, as I always did, to stand by my friends."[20]

In passages like this, Manly demonstrated the operations of his internal gyroscope, a return to the character-training he had received from his parents. His desert dilemma could not have been foreseen by anyone, but his parents' advice turned out to meet the navigational requirements of even this test. He envied the freedom to escape that the other single men had, but he knew he was bound by ties of personal loyalty—ties very similar to the ones he felt for his own family. He knew that any physical escape from those ties would still have left him bound emotionally. Escape would be treachery, and the betrayal of women and children, in the desert, would be murder. Manly's return to loyalty, after a round of temptation, had the relief of a return to balance and sanity.

Manly's thoughts did in fact return to his home. In his worst moments, looking at "the most wonderful picture of grand desolation one could ever see," confronting "the serious question of our ever living to get" to California, Manly "thought of the bounteous stock of bread and beans upon my father's table." What had once seemed a narrow balance of subsistence now seemed like abundance. The contrast was overpowering: "here was I, the oldest son, away out in the center of the Great American Desert, with an empty stomach and a dry and parched throat." As grim as the present was, the future looked worse. "Perhaps," Manly said, "I had not yet seen the worst of it. I might be forced to see men, and the women and children of the party, choke and die, powerless to help them."[21]

Read out of context, a passage like this might seem melodramatic. For anyone who thinks seriously about the situation in which Manly found himself at the end of the year 1849, each phrase carries authenticity. A skilled and self-reliant frontiersman in any well-watered environment, Manly was utterly at a loss in the desert. Failure to keep moving was a guarantee of starvation, but with utter ignorance of the route ahead, movement was equally perilous.

The project made Manly's responsibilities enormous. Not only was he to be the guide where there were no landmarks or trails, and the hunter where there was no game. He also had to be the monitor of the group's knowledge and emotions, providing encouragement and edited information, while at the same time maintaining his reputation for honesty. "I knew I must not discourage the others," he wrote. "I must keep my worst apprehensions to myself." He had to keep each individual's "heart and hope and faith" intact, at the same time that he struggled with his own feelings of helplessness.[22]

When Manly's thoughts "almost made [him] crazy," he seems to have fought for control in a secular arena, without connecting himself to a lineage of believers tried and tested in deserts. It is striking, in his text, to note the absence of religious content. Deserting his friends, he said, "would be to pile everlasting infamy on my head."[23] The word *everlasting* was his closest approach to a theological reference; Manly recorded his ordeal with few references to the word *God*. This was, in the words he chose to tell it, a secular and psychological ordeal. Revived faith came without visions or voices: it came with a return to the recognition of the indissoluble ties among humans. Believing he could "see the future," tempted to treachery, Manly had to stay within the circumference of his own mental resources.

V

Despite his best efforts, Manly could not discover a workable wagon route over the desert mountains. The group reached a collective point of despair. The idea of a Gold Rush began to seem absurd. "The home of the poorest man on earth was preferable to this place," Manly said. "Gold pieces" would have given them "no temptation to touch a single coin, for its very weight would drag us nearer death."[24] The groups had reached a bedrock—a measure by which money was only dead weight, and the only final value was in the chance of sustained life.

Desperate, Mr. Bennett offered a new proposition. Two men could travel ahead to the California settlements and return with supplies and a knowledge of the route, while the others waited at a waterhold. Not surprisingly, there were no volunteers. But Bennett nominated Manly, and Manly consented. John Rogers, Manly's companion from

the Green River trip, was the second nominee, and he also consented.

Bennett thought their round trip would require ten days. The trip
from Death Valley to the Mexican settlements in California and back
took, in fact, nearly a month. Returning with supplies and one
extremely durable mule, Manly and Rogers "had the greatest fear
that the people had given up our return and started out for themselves
and that we should follow on, only to find them dead or dying."
These doubts became nearly unbearable, and Manly and Rogers endured "desperate thoughts, that were enough to drive reason from
its throne."[25]

Reunited with the two families, Manly was certain of a workable
route out of the desert. His own battle with uncertainty was over.
He could devote himself to encouraging the others, particularly the
women, "who were so tired and discouraged that they were ready to
die." Courage was no abstract value in this situation; it could be
measured in actual steps taken across the desert. In stark fact, Manly's
project in encouragement was a battle of words against death. "Life
was in the balance," he knew.[26]

On March 17, 1850, the group climbed the last mountain and
saw coastal California below. Grazing cattle in meadow shaded by
live oaks—the contrast was almost beyond belief. "Such a scene of
abundance and rich plenty and comfort," Manly wrote of his first
glimpse, "bursting thus upon our eyes which for months had seen
only the desolation and the sadness of the desert was like getting a
glimpse of Paradise."[27] The image of California as paradise would
never find a more receptive audience than the members of the Manly
and Bennett party.

Doubt, of the desert variety, was indeed over. Day-to-day survival
was no longer problematic. Manly had recovered his physical sense
of location and direction. But the escape from Death Valley returned
him and his friends to a set of problems the desert had suspended.
Writing in 1894 about those returned doubts, Manly shifted uncharacteristically into the present tense: "How we, without a dollar
are to proceed, to get our food and things we need, are questions
we cannot answer."[28] In the desert, money had lost all consequence

as a measure of value. In California, money had regained its centrality as a motive, a measure of success, and a means of survival.

The shift was not easily or rapidly made. "We were happy, encouraged, grateful, and quite contented in the plenty which surrounded us," Manly remembered, "and still there was a sort of puzzling uncertainty as to our future, the way to which seemed very obscure."[29]

VI

While they might face their future with bewilderment, the Bennetts, the Arcanes, Manly, and Rogers would never have to confront any uncertainty in their judgment of the desert. Untroubled by any ambivalence, Manly could write of the desert with full and vigorous abuse, cataloging "the dreadful sands and shadows of Death Valley, its exhausting phantoms, its salty columns, bitter lakes, and wild, dreary sunken desolation." It was "a corner [of] the earth so dreary that it requires an exercise of the strongest faith to believe that the great Creator ever smiled upon it as a portion of his work and pronounced it 'Very good.' "[30]

In an earlier section of the book, describing his visits to Wisconsin, Manly had confessed: "I was always a great admirer of Nature and things which remained as they were created." Without the slightest sense of contradiction, Manly could be an "admirer of Nature" who hated the desert. Remembering Wisconsin, Manly thought it was "the most beautiful and perfect country I had seen."[31] Remembering the desert, Manly could hardly believe that such things had been intentionally created. The desert had been not merely the scene of human disaster; Manly was willing to go further and condemn the whole place as a disaster in the history of the earth's creation. With the desert, the Creator's plans and purposes went wildly beyond the power of human understanding. Could the architect of this "horrid Charnel house" be accused of intentional cruelty—or worse, of unintentional failure? Did God set out to make a garden—and did he produce a desert by mistake?

Like Frémont, Manly found the desert to be virtually negative space, the antithesis of both beauty and use. Land in that useless form might as well be an ocean floor. "If the waves of the sea could flow in and cover its barren nakedness," Manly concluded, "it would be indeed a blessing, for in it there is naught of good, comfort or satisfaction."[32] His prolonged and painful ordeal had made Lewis Manly one of America's most qualified desert-haters.

On Manly's scale of values, one of the desert's worst offenses was the scarcity of familiar game. Accustomed to rely on the use of his gun as a base line of survival, he complained repeatedly of his frustrations as a desert hunter. Manly was thoroughly aware of the ways in which human character could be affected by the deprivation of food. "Hunger," he said, "swallows all other feelings. A man in starving condition is a savage." Manly shared Frémont's idea that an obsessive concern with food led to a slide down the continuum, from civilized man to savage to animal. Unlike Frémont, Manly claimed no exemption for himself or his friends. He had seen his own acquaintances under this pressure, their faces "a mixture a determination and despair, the human expression almost vanishing." He recorded his own behavior on discovering an ox several days dead. "Some may say they would starve before eating such meat," he said, "but if they have experienced hunger till it brings down the life itself, they will find the impulse of self preservation something not to be controlled by mere reason."[33]

Unlike Frémont, Manly thought that a preoccupation with food was a basic element of human nature in desert places and not a concern particular to desert Indians. If anything, the Indians seemed to be behaving better than the whites on the issue of subsistence. Repeatedly Manly warned his party against stealing from Indian food caches. "I considered it bad policy to rob the Indian of any of their food," he said, "for they must be pretty smart people to live in this desolate country and find enough to keep them alive." With all the burdens of desert travel, Manly did not want to court the hostility of resourceful enemies.[34]

While he was no champion of Indian rights, Manly knew that he was traveling as an intruder in hostile territory, and he tried to take all possible precautions against conflict. He did not find in the Indians evidence of a borderline condition of animality. They were, like humans everywhere, trying to stay alive.

VII

Unlike Frémont, Manly wrote with no intention of offering geographical information to travelers. Travelers in 1894, Manly knew, would only need directions to the railroad station, not precise guidance to trails and waterholes. His desert knowledge had been transcribed into his memory by sheer painful familiarity—long hours with nothing to do but walk, and nothing to think about but the prospect ahead. From this kind of familiarity, one would not expect an expert map, but one might well hope for what Manly provided: a psychological geography, a record of emotions in response to a particular place.

Manly wrote one version of the story in 1851 and sent it to his parents. Within a year their house burned, destroying his manuscript. Manly did not write another version until, in his later years, "an accident befell me so that I could not work."[35] Reduced by an injury to a state of uncharacteristic helplessness, Manly wrote *Death Valley in '49.*

More than anyone, Manly knew that California settlement and development had exacted an inestimable price in human suffering. If Frémont's reports in the 1840s expressed the extremes of confident anticipation, Manly's reminiscences in the 1890s represented the reflections on consequences that Frémont avoided.

Manly did not, finally, know what to make of those consequences, or of the motives that provoked them. Was it solely a matter of gold? Were the sufferings and the deaths sacrifices to the goal of individual profit? Manly was in a poor position to argue with this interpretation. Gold prompted his trip, as it did that of the Bennetts. Traveling independently, Manly might never have realized the seriousness of the gamble he had undertaken. But his friend Mr. Bennett had risked the lives of his wife and children on the prospect of gold. The presence of these captives to the plans of men was what transformed the desert passage for Manly from adventure to ordeal. The presence of families brought on Manly's internal struggle to keep "reason on its throne," to follow parental guidance in situations which parents could never have forseen.

When the party arrived in California, the Arcane family left first, after only a day or two's recuperation. In parting, Arcane said to Manly and Rogers: "I can never repay you . . . for I owe you a debt that is beyond compensation."[36] Leaving the desert, Manly had indeed returned to a way of life in which the power of money was reasserted, even in the figures of speech with which rescued men expressed their gratitude.

Manly's desert passage had been a prolonged encounter with the prospect of death. He heard the voice of Providence in that encounter, but he was never able to make out the exact words of that message. The escape from Death Valley was an occasion of rebirth, as Manly recognized: "We were dead almost, and now we lived."[37] But there were no desert visions, conversions, or restorations of faith to report along with this redemption. Having narrowly retained their lives, Manly and his friends went back to making a living.

VIII

In 1862, providing the ultimate proof of the power of the fortune-hunting habit, Manly returned to Death Valley on a prospecting tour. Led by a man named Charles Alvord, the party included Manly's old associate Mr. Bennett. The first trip turned up moderately promising results, and Alvord returned for a second search, this time without Manly. Alvord's companions on that trip became discontented and deserted him in the desert. Hearing that news, Manly and Bennett decided to go to his rescue. "When I concluded that it was my duty to go once again to Death Valley," Manly remembered, ". . . it seemed to me that I was born for the unwelcome task of rescuing the unfortunate of that terrible valley." Headed back into the desert, he pursued a predictable line of reflection: "I thought how foolish I was, to go over this trail again."[38]

The first phase of the expedition proceeded happily. The rescuers discovered Alvord, who was nearly out of food and understandably grateful for his "narrow escape." Bennett and another man took the mules and left the valley to get supplies; Manly and Alvord would remain to prospect, and the two others would return with more food. Then the good luck wore thin. "We remained here the length of time that was agreed upon, for their return," Manly said, "and no one came."[39]

Roles had reversed in an extraordinary way. Running short on food, with Alvord becoming increasingly lame, Manly awaited help from his friend Bennett. Help did not come. Manly and Alvord got out of the desert on their own resources, with no clue as to what had become of their friends. "Some years afterwards, " Manly said, "we learned that the party we sent for supplies became snowed in and nearly perished, and believing that we would starve or go out of the valley before they could reach us, had failed to return." In those intervening years, Manly was left to wonder why his friend had abandoned him. "I helped, in 1849, to save Bennett and others from starvation in Death Valley," Manly put it, "and why he had left Alvord and myself to perish, seemed strange."[40]

Nature in the desert had its mysteries, but they were met and matched by the mysteries in human nature: the persistence of the prospector's urge in the face of the worst discouragement, and the vulnerability of human values to the biological pressures of hunger and thirst. The mysteries of nature and human nature did, in fact, intersect; scarcity in the desert put the constancy and changeability of human loyalty to a wrenching test.

In August 1849, far to the north of Lewis Manly's scene of operations, an overland party including a man named Alonzo Delano had been talked into taking a "cutoff" through Nevada's Black Rock Desert, the site of Frémont's wanderings in 1843. Like the Manly shortcut, this one led to increased hardship and disorientation. Walking in the desert, near the end of the cutoff, Delano met a young woman and her small child, left behind in a wagon: " 'Where is your husband?' I inquired, on going up.

" 'He has gone on with the cattle,' she replied, 'and to try to get us some water, but I think we shall die before he comes back.' "[41]

Without complete certainty as to the location of the next spring, Delano gave her his water flask. For Manly, Delano and many others, the desert put loyalty to a stark test. The allocation of scarce resources, and of personal loyalty, was no abstract question. "Life," as Manly had said, "was in the balance."

CHAPTER THREE
Mark Twain

I

Samuel Clemens went to Nevada in 1861. Eleven years later, under the pseudonym Mark Twain, Clemens published *Roughing It,* a semi-fictional memoir of his time in the arid West. In the book, he told the story of an excursion to Mono Lake, a lake that, in its inhospitable waters and harsh setting, stood for the anomaly of the desert. On an island of "ashes," in the middle of this lake, Twain found one tree. Standing alone, it contrasted "with its dead and dismal surroundings" like a "cheerful spirit in a mourning household."[1]

When Samuel Clemens began to write and compile *Roughing It,* he was in a comparable dilemma.[2] In July 1870, married, living in the Northeast, and determined to make a living by writing, Clemens signed a contract to write his western book. In August, his father-in-law died. Olivia, Clemens's wife, had a nervous collapse. In September, a visiting friend named Emma Nye developed typhoid fever. Clemens's bedroom became Nye's sickroom, and the scene of her death. In November, Clemens's son Langdon was born. The child was premature and sickly, and the mother was returned to invalidism. In February, Olivia had typhoid fever. In March, Clemens wrote to his publisher:

> You do not know what it is to be in a state of absolute
> frenzy—desperation. I had rather die twice over than
> repeat the last six months of my life. . . . Do you
> know that for seven months I have not had my natural

> rest but have been night and day sicknurse to my
> wife? . . . If I ever get out of this infernal damnable
> chaos I am whirling in at home, I will go to work and
> amply and fully and freely fulfill some of the promises
> I have been making to you—but I don't dare! Bliss—
> I don't dare! I believe that if that baby goes on crying
> three more hours this way I will butt my frantic brains
> and try to get some peace.[3]

Not surprisingly, Clemens could barely function as a writer.

In March 1871, the family began a move to a more peaceful environment. Olivia's health began to improve, and Clemens began to recover his facility in writing. *Roughing It* had gained a new interest. Clemens had decided to rewrite one character thoroughly. "It's no fool of a job, I can tell you, but the book will be greatly bettered by it," he told his brother. "The character he rewrote," Justin Kaplan explained, "was that of the narrator himself, Mark Twain."[4] In 1872, with the persona of the fool at the center, *Roughing It* appeared.

Both Frémont and Manly had shown considerable folly in their desert travel, in their choice of routes, and in their general stance of impatience and haste. Participants in folly, neither Frémont nor Manly had chosen to capitalize on those credentials. It was left to Mark Twain to inaugurate a tradition of self-declared fools in the desert.

Before he left Salt Lake and headed into the desert, Twain had himself firmly set up as the fool. His older brother had been appointed secretary to Nevada Territory, and Twain was traveling west as the "secretary to the Secretary." In Utah, the officials, with Twain in tow, went to call on the Mormon leader Brigham Young. Twain made "several attempts to 'draw him out' on federal politics," but Young resisted those efforts and continued to converse with the officials. Ignored, Twain fumed. At the end of the audience, Young finally recognized Twain: "He put his hand on my head, beamed down on me in an admiring way and said to my brother, 'Ah—your child I presume? Boy or girl?' "[5]

Why was this an ideal self-characterization for a desert traveler?

The advantage of a fool's position is that he can admit what the rest of humanity struggles to conceal. He can admit to his own sense of helplessness. When the fool feels vulnerable, powerless, deceived, or tricked, he confesses it, and even exaggerates it for the effect of the joke.

The desert had inconvenienced and threatened many American travelers. They had felt themselves to be small and helpless against its vast size and intractable character. In mid-journey, they may have decided they had been fools to enter the desert at all. When it came to recording their experiences, most Americans faced an obstacle similar to the one Frémont faced: the need to maintain the appearance of an unshaken dignity.

Samuel Clemens, speaking through Mark Twain, faced no such obstacle. Crossing the desert, Twain took the stance of a strident, outraged child. When Frémont abused the sterile, repulsive, barren, dreary desert, he offered the description as objective fact, uncolored by emotion. In Twain's abuse of the desert, his emotions were evident. These emotions were common ones for desert travelers—helplessness, bewilderment, and the fear of death.

II

Twain traveled by stagecoach. A week or two in a coach on variable roads was still a major exercise in endurance, but it did, in comparison with overland travel by wagon, look easy.[6] Brevity was only one advantage. The individual traveling by wagon had a constant burden of responsibility to preserve his own life and health and that of his family and draft animals. Constant decisions, on routes and timing, called for attention. By contrast, the stagecoach passenger, with his fare, hired a business to make the decisions and look out for the animals. The passenger was left to manage himself, to control his own discomfort and impatience.

The passenger who managed to sleep had achieved the maximum in anaesthetized and insulated travel—the best possible way to travel in a desert. "It was easy enough to cross a desert in a night while we were asleep," Twain recalled, "and it was pleasant . . . to reflect that we in actual person *had* encountered an absolute desert and could always speak knowingly of deserts in presence of the ignorant thenceforward."[7] What was the desert like? It hardly seemed to matter. The desert was a geographical celebrity, and just being near it was an achievement.

The unseen nighttime desert presented itself with amiable passivity: an occasion for reflection, a subject for letters home. It was admirably literary and, viewed from the stagecoach in darkness, safe. If it was all "very comfortable and satisfactory" to cross a desert at night, Twain claimed to have even higher hopes for the prospect of a daylight crossing, sure to be "fine—novel—romantic—dramatically adventurous." Unprotected by sleep and darkness, the high hopes crashed. Twain's "stern thirst for adventure" lasted less than an hour. "The poetry," Twain announced, "was all in the anticipation—there is none in the reality."[8]

The poetry demolished, Twain invoked the desert reality: "Imagine a vast, waveless ocean stricken dead and turned to ashes; . . . imagine the lifeless silence and solitude; . . . imagine a coach creeping like a bug through the midst of this shoreless level, and sending up tumbling volumes of dust."[9] In a comparable moment, Frémont had reflected on the appearance of his party. The empty desert evidently invited a pictorial overview in which the travelers could be seen from the outside. Just as Brigham Young's view from the outside had demolished Twain's dignity, this external point of view left the human dwarfed beyond vision, passengers in a coach itself on the scale of a bug.

Monotony—eventless, boring, desperate, "aching monotony"—led Twain to the familiar act of defining deserts by vacancy: "there is not the faintest breath of air stirring; there is not a merciful shred of cloud; . . . there is not a living creature visible in any direction . . . ; there is not a sound." By a repetition of negatives, Twain joined others in making it clear that the desert was most notable for its absences and opposites. The central opposition was of life and death—the absence of any of the usual sights and sounds of animal presence. Silence was the principal suggestion of death, a silence more wearing and irritating to Twain than any noise could be. In the stillness, sounds from the coach's mules only accented the emptiness, "making one feel more lonesome and forsaken than before."[10]

Accompanying the silence was a series of physical affronts. Twain was happy to catalogue his discomfort: "And it was so hot! And so close! And our water canteens went dry in the middle of the day and we got so thirsty! It was so stupid and tiresome and dull!"[11] This was certainly the tone of a bored and irritated child, incredulous that the world could treat him so thoughtlessly.

Compared with the driver and the mules, the passengers were protected. Nonetheless, the desert had ways of invading the coach. "The alkali dust cut through our lips, it persecuted our eyes, it ate through the delicate membranes and made our noses bleed and *kept* them bleeding."[12] The heat, dust, and aridity all combined in an assault on the integrity of the human body. Sight, taste, and smell were thus impaired—or forced to sense only the disagreeable; hearing was already useless in desert silence. The dust finally brought on that incontrovertible evidence of human vulnerability: blood, in the un-dignified form of a nosebleed.

"Truly and seriously," Twain declared, "the romance had all faded far away and disappeared, and left the desert trip nothing but a harsh reality—a thirsty, sweltering, longing, hateful reality!"[13] The desert crossing was a battle in the war between romance and reality, a battle in which reality gained total victory, and romance made an undig-nified retreat. Romance was impossible where physical reality in-truded so aggressively on bodily comfort, and where visual reality refused to provide interest or amusement. When dust, heat, duration, and monotony combined on the side of reality, romance had a few resources to draw on for its defense.

When reality was intolerable and romance was in retreat, where did Twain turn? To the purely verbal joke. He concluded the desert passage with an admittedly lame joke: "To try to give the reader an idea how *thirsty*" the mules were "would be to 'gild refined gold or paint the lily.' " He had been, he explained, desperate to get that "graceful and attractive" phrase in somewhere; the effort had left him "distracted and ill at ease." Leaving it with the mules, he thought, would "afford at least a temporary respite from the wear and tear" of trying to introduce the quotation.[14]

With that joke, Twain was out of the stagecoach and back in the writer's study. The genuine ordeal of the desert faded out of focus, and the mock ordeal of the writer took over. Genuine relief at reaching the end of the desert became comic relief at having found a place for a homeless phrase.

Twain's leap to a joke—from alkali dust and thirst to "gilded gold" and "painted lilies"—gave all the signs of evasion, a timely retreat before the seriousness of the desert cut off the avenue of comic escape. Facing the emptiness and stillness of the desert, Twain retreated to a word-centered refuge. If the words were inappropriate and irrelevant, they would still fill the silence.

III

After the desert came the Goshoots. The war between romance and reality continued as Twain directed his anger at two targets, the desert Indians and James Fenimore Cooper.

The Goshoots, in western Utah and eastern Nevada, Twain said, were "the wretchedest type of mankind I have ever seen," "a silent, sneaking, treacherous-looking race," a group of "prideless beggars."[15] In the nastiness of his name-calling Twain carried on as if he had received a personal offense, as if the Goshoots' principal treachery lay in the damage they did to Twain's vision of human nature.

Like Frémont, Twain found the prime offense of desert Indians to be their appetite. They were "hungry, always hungry, and yet never refusing anything that a hog would eat, though often eating what a hog would decline; hunters, but having no higher ambition than to kill and eat jackass rabbits, crickets, and grasshoppers."[16]

Twain briefly acknowledged the constraints of the Goshoots' environment, "one of the most rocky, wintry, repulsive wastes that our country or any other can exhibit."[17] But the harshness of their homeland earned them none of Twain's tolerance or sympathy. He was evidently thrown into a fury by the vision of humans living on a narrow margin of subsistence, reduced to a state bordering on animality.

As usual, Twain's anger moved on to an attack on romance and the deceptiveness of the written word. Before meeting any Indians, he insisted, he had been "a disciple of Cooper and a worshiper—of the Red Man." The "disgust" and even "nausea" provoked by the Goshoots set Twain to "examining authorities, to see if perchance I had been over-estimating the Red Man when viewing him through the mellow moonshine of romance." The resulting "revelations" were "disenchanting." "The paint and tinsel fell away" from the Indian, "and left him treacherous, filthy and repulsive."[18]

Once more, Twain claimed, he was the innocent, victimized by romance. Cooper and his novels had created illusions of primitive nobility and charm. The desert Indians, with their active appetites, had destroyed those illusions. Lost in the exchange of illusions were the actual Indians, and not only the Goshoots. "Whenever one finds an Indian tribe," Twain asserted, "he has only found Goshoots more or less modified by circumstances and by surroundings—but Goshoots, after all."[19]

Racism aside, Twain seemed to have forgotten his stance as a fool. Damning the Goshoots or damning Cooper, Twain proclaimed his opinions with a self-righteous certainty comparable to Frémont's. The overall tone was utterly lacking in the usual self-mockery, the self-characterization so well handled in the interview with Brigham Young.

Both the desert and the Goshoots unnerved and angered Twain. If the desert made him feel small, weak and foolish, the Goshoots restored him to a precarious platform of superiority.

IV

If the desert was an ordeal, the capital city of Nevada Territory registered a little short of a refuge. "Visibly our new home was a desert," Twain noted, "not a tree in sight" and "no vegetation but the endless sagebrush and greasewood." Living in a chaotic boardinghouse, watching his brother adapt to the irrationalities of territorial government, Twain was also introduced to the "Washoe Zephyr," the desert's way of guaranteeing that the town would remember its setting. The zephyr made regular afternoon appearances: "rolling billows of dust" carrying the freight of attempted settlement, "hats, chickens and parasols sail in the remote heavens; blankets, tin signs, sagebrush and shingles a shade lower" and nearest the ground, "a scurrying storm of emigrating roofs and vacant lots."[20]

With the zephyr's daily opportunities for mobility, Twain still had his own internal defense against the monotony of settling down. His own restlessness would keep him in motion. Hearing stories of Lake Tahoe, Twain and his friend Johnny set off for the mountains, vaguely in pursuit of a fortune in timber.

At Tahoe, Twain found the antithesis to the desert: an environment that supported life as forcefully as the desert opposed it. "Three months of camp life on Lake Tahoe," Twain insisted, "would restore an Egyptian mummy to his pristine vigor, and give him an appetite like an alligator."[21] Hunger among Goshoots was a mark of depravity; hunger among Tahoe campers was a measure of health and vigor. Similarly, solitude in the desert was deprivation while solitude at Tahoe was liberation.

Nature, at Tahoe, acknowledged and satisfied all of Twain's requirements. This was nature at its best: "always fascinating, bewitching, entrancing," and evidently feminine.[22] Recognizing how well Tahoe treated Twain, it comes as a surprise to realize how Twain treated Tahoe.

In the midst of preparation for supper one night, Twain let his fire get out of control. Escaping to their boat, Twain and Johnny watched the shore become a "tossing, blinding tempest of flame." Watching the fire and its reflection in the lake, Twain was thrilled: "Both pictures were sublime, both were beautiful."[23] Twain had translated the failure to control his campfire into a success at providing himself with a spectacle. He neither mentioned nor recognized his other success: a change in the relation of human to nature.

Previously the sufferer and endurer of deserts, Twain at Tahoe took a hand in desertification. He did as much as one human could do to transform a life-filled forest into a place of "solitude, silence and desolation," his words for the desert. He left the next morning without regret. The fire had fascinated him; the ashes only bored him.

V

In Twain's world, caution was an anomaly; neither the individual nor the group in Nevada had any internal braking system. "I would have been more or less than human," Twain remarked, "if I had not gone mad like the rest."[24] Madness here had the particular meaning of silver fever, and Twain had the perfect character for the condition. He was naturally susceptible to the lure of miracles and sudden fortunes. He would rush into risks without pausing for the calculation of costs; he would take on deserts without forethought. Few voluntary activities involved greater privation than desert prospecting, but Twain found no mystery in the willingness to suffer for the sake of uncertain future wealth.

Equally logical and prosaic to Twain was the chaos of mining speculation. The owner of thousands of feet in inflated mining stock, he was deeply in debt to the grocer. His monetary abundance was abstract; his hunger was concrete. Subsistence came by begging from the grocer, a form of behavior Twain did not connect to the begging behavior of the despised Goshoots.

On a journey to inspect a distant property, Twain and two companions found themselves trapped in an isolated inn on the flooded Carson River. With the river gone wild, the inn was "on an island of mid-ocean." In all directions, "there was no desert visible, but only a level waste of shining water." The desert, so frequently compared by Twain and others to a dead ocean, had taken the comparison literally. Twain was undergoing the desert equivalent of shipwreck but not, however, on a deserted island. The inn had a full "swearing, drinking, and card-playing" crowd.[25]

A week of monotonous, quarrelsome, unwelcome company left Twain's party desperate to escape. After a precarious crossing of the river, they found themselves lost in a desert snowstorm. One member of the party assumed leadership and led them in circles. A fresh start took them to an apparent trail. The snow-covered sagebrushes made smooth mounds and seemed to define a road. Here, the party discovered themselves tricked by the behavior of desert plant life: the almost uniform spacing resulting from competition for water. "In any direction that you proceeded," Twain said, "you would find yourself moving down a distinctly defined avenue, with a row of these snow mounds on either side of it." Such a setting provided the ultimate in relativism: brief exploration convinced each individual that "*he* had found the true road, and that the others had found only false ones."[26]

An attempt to build a campfire failed, but their efforts succeeded in frightening the horses into bolting. The party admitted "the conviction that this was our last night with the living." Facing mortality together, Twain and his companions wept together. They forgave each other. They gave up their vices, wishing that they had the prospect of a longer life in order to be an example to the young. "We were all sincere," Twain said, "and all deeply moved and earnest, for we were in the presence of death and without hope." Embracing each other, they awaited the "drowsiness that precedes death by freezing." At last, "a delicious dreaminess wrought its web about my yielding senses. . . . Oblivion came. The battle of life was done."[27]

In the dawn, Twain returned to consciousness. The snowstorm was over, and the party was at last able to see its position. They were camped fifteen steps from the stage station. "The whole situation was so painfully ridiculous and humiliating," Twain said, that "joy in our hearts at our deliverance was poisoned." Restored to life, they were "angry with each other, angry at ourselves, angry at everything in general."[28]

With life came the longing for the relinquished vices. Within an hour, the reformed sinners had discovered each other behind the barn—smoking, drinking, and playing cards. They shook hands and returned to life without reform.

Several others were not so lucky. The night of the storm, two sheepherders were lost and "never heard of afterward." Back at the Carson River in the snowstorm, Twain had watched a Swede singing a monotonous song cross the river and set off walking, disappearing "in the white oblivion. He was never heard of again."[29] Twain's phrasing of the fate of the Swede and the sheepherders was perfectly suited to his sense of the desert and death. They were "never heard of again"—they disappeared into silence. That silence was at once attractive and fearful. In Twain's imagined death, it was a "delicious dreaminess," he was "conquered" and "yielding," taken for once beyond chattiness, word play, and the sound of his own voice. After the silence came the "poisoned" sense of return: to life, to vice, to speech. The desert was no longer a place of accepted silence and transformation, a final place of rest. It was once more space to be crossed and endured.

The remarkable quality of this whole story was the absolute thoroughness of its mockery. Sincerity, brotherhood, conversion, death, and rebirth were all heartily undermined. The story reads like a parody of Lewis Manly's experience and the experience of many other desert travelers in the peak periods of overland crossings. The adventure, in Twain's case, served to discredit the authenticity of everything: desert, death, and victim. Twain had, he claimed, been "in the presence of death," and the encounter seemed to have left him with a sense of injury. He had been betrayed, for once, into a serious silence. Death and the desert had succeeded in fooling the fool.

VI

Frustrated in prospecting, Twain turned to a holiday at Mono Lake. The vacation was not to be a duplicate of the earlier trip to Tahoe. The two lakes and their settings were another instance in definition by opposites. If Tahoe was nature at its best, Mono was nature's version of a bad joke. Mono Lake lay "in a lifeless, treeless, hideous desert."[30] Desert qualities extended into the water. Heavily charged with alkali, the lake was as much a failure of natural hospitality as its surroundings.

A few animals had been able to make their peace with an alkali environment. The waters of Mono Lake contained no fish, only "a feathery sort of worm" which supported both flies and ducks, as well as furnishing food for local Indians. Observations of this worm allowed Twain an occasion for biological and theological reflection. "Providence leaves nothing to go by chance," he asserted. "All things have their uses and their part and proper place in Nature's economy: the ducks eat the flies—the flies eat the worms—the Indians eat all three—the wild cats eat the Indians—the white folks eat the wild cats—and thus all things are lovely."[31]

Even in a lake, the starkness of the desert made the operations of the food chain impossible to ignore, providing equal opportunities for insight, disgust, or absurdity. Twain attempted a combination of all three: insight into the actual interdependence of desert animals; disgust at the inclusion of humans in this unrefined chain of consumption; and absurdity, with the attribution of all this to Providence. "All things" were particularly "lovely" since the white folks were the only ones exempted from nurturing others.

With all its oddity, Mono Lake was a challenge to the curiosity of white folks. Twain and his friend Higbie embarked on "a voyage of discovery" to an island in the lake. The island proved to be a "hill of ashes—nothing but gray ashes and pumice stone," without a supply of fresh water.[32]

While Twain and Higbie searched for water, a storm took over the lake, and their unmoored boat drifted off. They seemed to be "prisoners on a desolate island," and Twain was in yet another desert situation of helpless captivity, once more in the presence of death. This time, Providence aided them: the boat drifted close to shore, and Higbie made a successful leap for it. The twelve-mile return through high seas was an ordeal, but one in which Twain did not appear to have been troubled by monotony. The danger of capsizing added an edge to every moment. Immersed in the alkali water, they would have been "eaten up so quickly that we could not even be present at our own inquest."[33]

The white folks, it turned out, were not invulnerable to the chain of consumption Twain had sketched in his reflection on Providence and biology. White people could also be "eaten up"—not by an individual predator perhaps, but by the elements themselves—dissolved and digested by the waters of Mono Lake.

VII

Setting to work on *Roughing It* in 1870, Samuel Clemens was immersed in mortality—the death of his father-in-law and a visiting friend, the ill health of his wife and newborn son. It is hardly surprising that his concern with death was at the center of most of the jokes in *Roughing It*. Death was only one aspect of the uncertainty that troubled Clemens. He was equally concerned with the variability of human fortunes, the complexities of human nature, and the difficulties of self-expression. With his effort to make a living as a writer, it was natural that those issues would revolve around the problem of words—the relation of literature to life, romance to reality.

In *Roughing It*, Clemens made his peace with uncertainty by embracing it, building it into the very structure of his narrative. His endless punning and his inclination to undercut serious descriptions of discomfort with a purely verbal joke were one way of reducing doubt. But Clemens's principal means of mastering uncertainty by incorporating it into his structure was to write through the invented character Mark Twain.

With Mark Twain as narrator, everything was doubtable. There was never a clear line to be drawn between what Clemens experienced and what he invented. It was not, after all, Clemens's story. *Roughing It* was Mark Twain's narrative, and there were no narrow limits of accuracy and honesty to be placed on him.

Somewhere behind the created public fool Mark Twain was a man deeply troubled by a dark side to both nature and human nature. The prospect of final darkness was a fact with which the creator of Twain could not make his peace. His feelings about death ranged from anger to attraction. They did not come near tranquility.

For Samuel Clemens, the desert resonated with suggestions of death. Its heat and sand made no concessions to the support of human life. Its scarce supplies of food and water put an extreme limit on both mobility and settlement, the principal manifestations of the American version of life. More than anything, desert monotony suggested to Clemens a version of death-in-life, a helpless entrapment in sameness. Clemens rescued himself from the monotony of desert reality by emphasizing and accelerating his activity as a writer, containing desert-inspired fears with barricades of words.

Using his words to distance himself, Clemens made a mockery of the actual suffering undergone by Americans in desert crossings. For the overland travelers of the 1840s and 1850s, the desert meant an exhausting struggle against death. For the stage passenger of 1861, the desert was a comparatively brief interlude of dust and annoyance. For the reminiscent writer of 1871, the desert was material for jokes. It could be presented as a foolish act of nature—the product of nature in a clown's mood, making a joke of landscape.

Nature as jokemaker showed its hand most clearly in the so-called rivers. The Humboldt, for instance, was a bad pun on the word *river*, appearing unspeakably paltry to the eye of a former Mississippi riverboat pilot. Certainly part of Clemens's anger with the desert involved the deprivation of the transportational experience he enjoyed the most. There were no rivers for leisurely raft trips or for steamboat adventuring. What was one to do with the Humboldt? Clemens offered his cynical suggestion: "One of the pleasantest and most invigorating exercises one can contrive is to run and jump across the Humboldt River till he is overheated, and then drink it dry."[34]

Desert rivers, such as they were, disappeared into sinks, never completing the river's proper function of reaching the sea. If the Humboldt was a bad pun on "river," than a "sink" was a worse play on "lake." Similarly, Mono Lake made a mockery of proper lake behavior.

Nature as a joke maker had gone the furthest by the very act of hiding minerals in the desert. Placing valued resources in irrational and difficult locations, nature seemed to have planned a silly, dangerous treasure hunt, with gold and silver as the lure that Twain and his fellow fools could not resist.

Included in desert mockery was human behavior under stress: the experience of rescue and conversion. Lost in the snowstorm, Twain and his fellows had reformed their lives and converted to brotherly solidarity in the presence of death, only to suffer from offended dignity in the morning. While it met all the standards of conventional sentiment, conversion in the face of desert mortality proved to be only a more extreme kind of folly, in which the fool was himself deceived by his momentary appearance of sincerity.

A writer of extraordinary, if also uneven, talent, and a writer not bound by any narrow allegiance to accuracy, Samuel Clemens was hardly a typical or representative perceiver of the desert. Nonetheless, transmuting his western experiences into a popular book led him to perform a significant intellectual act. Prospecting and adventuring provided the raw material; nearly a decade of storytelling and of selective forgetting refined the raw material; and the intention to write a commercially successful book formed the last stage of the process. In writing *Roughing It*, Clemens was in possession of the essential factors of desert experiences—dust, thirst, discomfort, vulnerability, doubt, disorientation, monotony, and, particularly, suggestions of death. From a distance of three thousand miles and several years, rearranging and recombining experiences and images of the desert became something of a sport—imagination at play with the elements of a gritty reality. The relationship of *Roughing It* to more prosaic desert experience was one of mockery and exaggeration, but it was a direct relationship nonetheless. The process of literary exploitation was not unlike the process of mineral exploitation; as much as Clemens refined and manipulated his resources, the raw material still came from the desert itself.

A degree of distance was, in fact, crucial to the workings of perception. In one part of their journey, the stagecoach companions had taken the precaution of bringing along bread, ham, and hard-boiled eggs. "It was comfort," while the supplies held out, "to sit and contemplate the majestic panorama of mountains and valleys spread out below us and eat ham and hard-boiled eggs." "Nothing," Clemens concluded, "helps scenery like ham and eggs."[35]

Clemens had made the admission that Frémont could never make directly: visual appreciation required a bedrock of comfortable nutrition. Without ham and eggs, or their equivalent, geographical space was territory to be traveled across and endured. It only became "scenery" to be "contemplated" when one's "spiritual nature" could move beyond a preoccupation with food and survival. Nature appreciation rested on a foundation of prosperity and security—a foundation difficult to achieve in the mid-nineteenth-century desert.

Roughing It did not add much to the store of factual knowledge about American deserts, but it supported the judgment emerging from the overland experience. The desert, travelers agreed, was an anomaly in the American landscape. "Prov'dence," Clemens quoted a western storyteller, "don't fire no blank ca'tridges, boys."[36] The question that baffled Frémont, Manly, Clemens, and many others was this: What had Providence been aiming at in the creation of the desert?

CHAPTER FOUR
William Ellsworth Smythe

I

Like Lewis Manly, William Ellsworth Smythe thought it would be a "blessing" if water were unleashed on the desert. Unlike Manly, Smythe tried to make it happen.

If the waters of the sea invaded the desert, Manly felt, it could only be an improvement. Nineteenth-century travelers might be disturbed and even infuriated by the sense of helplessness with which the desert afflicted them, but that same helplessness put limits on their plans for revenge or retribution. When they said they had "conquered" the desert, they meant they had survived it.

At the turn of the century, prospects for human control over aridity began to improve. The mastery of water resources, it began to seem, might lead to the mastery and even eradication of the desert. Manly's dream of a flooded desert might come true, but with a significant variation. With the unleashing of the waters, the desert would be transformed not to ocean, but to farmland. And the farms, according to some of the planners, would recreate the community of Manly's remembered childhood.

Reminiscing about his home in Vermont, Manly had written: "The whole plan seemed to be to have every family and farm as self-supporting as far as possible." The days of self-sufficiency "were the days of real independence."[1] In his own youthful career as a gold-hunter and an adventurer, he did not show a great deal of loyalty to this agrarian "plan." A few years before his death, he might have

77

been reassured to discover that the plan and the values of "real independence" attached to it had attracted at least one devoted advocate—the irrigation crusader William Ellsworth Smythe.

Smythe's loyalty to the family farm was only equaled by his antipathy to the unimproved desert. *The Conquest of Arid America,* first published in 1900 and revised in 1905, presented both positions with force. Smythe was also a committed and even emblematic Progressive, as his book *Constructive Democracy* (1905) made clear. He was extremely religious, a believer in the existence of a "universal Purpose" and in his own qualifications to act as the Purpose's spokesman in matters relating to western North America.

Smythe was by no means a native westerner himself. He was born in 1861 in Worcester, Massachusetts. He worked for several Massachusetts newspapers, including the Boston *Herald.* At age twenty-seven, he accepted an invitation from a Nebraska town-site developer to edit the Kearney *Expositor.* In the next year, he transferred to a job as an editorial writer at the Omaha *Bee.*[2]

In 1890, Smythe underwent a personal conversion and a corresponding career change. "Drought struck Nebraska," and Smythe watched men "shooting their horses and abandoning their farms." At the same time, "fine streams" flowed through these devastated areas. "There were the soil, the sunshine, and the waters," Smythe said, "but the people did not understand the secret of prosperity, even with such broad hints before their eyes."[3]

The secret was irrigation. Smythe went on to write a fateful series of articles for the Omaha paper. "How many lives those articles influenced," he admitted, "I do not know; but they changed my life completely."[4]

"I had taken the cross of a new crusade," Smythe proclaimed.[5] He was quite serious. The desert had invaded Nebraska, and Smythe moved to defend the farms. He launched a campaign that would move from defense to offense, taking on desert areas where farming had never achieved a first foothold.

Over the next decade, Smythe went on to play an active role in the National Irrigation Congress, and in the movement's publication *Irrigation Age. The Conquest of Arid America* was his key work. In 1905, the same year he issued a revised edition of *The Conquest,* he also published *Constructive Democracy: The Economics of a Square Deal*. With this book, Smythe tied the cause of irrigation to the Progressive movement, playing on all the familiar themes of efficiency, independence, and progress.[6] Irrigated farms became a way of providing places for an uneasy middle class, a group under pressure from both the corporate rich and the ambitious poor.

II

What had gone wrong with the middle class? In part, the problem stemmed from the growth of the corporations. While Smythe lamented the dominance of a plutocracy and the loss of opportunity, he celebrated the efficiency of consolidation. Pernicious as it could be, the corporation was one of the devices "employed by a mysterious Providence in carrying on the work of social progress."[7] With deserts or corporations, Providence was perfectly capable of using nasty means for beneficial ends. When business was rationalized into federally chartered corporations, with strictly regulated profits, then, Smythe felt, the corporation would have reached its ordained goal.

In the meantime, Smythe's concern was with the innocent victim of Providence's financial plans, the man who was "so palpably wounded in the economic strife that his wounds cannot be hidden," the surplus man.[8]

The surplus man, in a definition Smythe repeated with evident satisfaction and emphasis, was "*one who, under the conditions that surround him, is unable to satisfy his reasonable wants, according to his accustomed standard of living.*"[9] The line setting off the surplus man from his fellows was not, Smythe insisted, a division between an upper and a lower class; the line was instead perpendicular, running vertically through all classes. The division ran between those profitably employed by the new economic order and those who were losing both status and income in the transition. Only the factor of loss counted. By this standard, a rich but declining banker deserved—and got—more of Smythe's concern than a poor but rising worker.

In drawing this distinction, Smythe put on a remarkable display of the limits of Progressive humanitarianism. Underpaid immigrants were not surplus men; there was always room at the bottom. A primitive standard of living, Smythe said, permitted immigrants to find their small wages abundant. "Poor" people were hardly to be pitied; scarcity and privation were ultimately a matter of point of view.[10]

On the other hand, an individual with an advanced standard of living was made authentically miserable by even slight losses. The banker who lost his bank to consolidation was, as Smythe presented him, beyond consolation. Once adapted to abundance, the banker could not bear retreat. If providence granted an individual a degree of upward mobility, there had better be no reneging on the bargain.

In his concern for the surplus man, Smythe gave a classic demonstration of the anxieties the white middle class faced at the turn of the century. The problems of status so preoccupied him that he could dismiss the problem of poor laborers without a moment of troubled consciousness. "Everything is to be viewed from relative standpoints," he reminded the reader and then went on to make his own nonrelative claim: "It is the man whose situation is growing worse who is to be regarded as the real economic problem."[11]

There were, Smythe felt, advantages to poverty: "The man who is frankly poor has no social state to maintain. He may economize in every possible way, without injury to his prospects in life."[12] By contrast, the middle-class man "must maintain certain appearances, or suffer an immediate loss of income and social standing." The man in decline was a man who would be shunned. "The world is merciless to the unsuccessful."[13]

For a middle-class man bearing "marks of failure," the cities and developed regions of the United States offered no refuge. Human nature, unleashed in competition, had created a situation of riches for some, an unrecognized and insignificant privation for the poor, and a slow decline into scarcity for the surplus men. In the social and economic transitions of the early twentieth century, the man in the middle was helpless, a victim of forces beyond his control. The surplus man, Smythe was careful to insist, had reached his situation because of the "conditions that surround him, and for no fault of his own."[14]

Smythe's plan was to offer the displaced middle class an alternative environment in which they could recover control of their lives. The desert had seemed to be the place where nature overpowered Americans. Now Smythe had selected it as the place where victims overpowered by their society could regain control.

III

It was Smythe's faith that the arid regions of the American West would be both the location and cause of the nation's redemption. Irrigated farming would offer Americans a fresh start in the direction of self-sufficiency, independence, *and* community. The "conquest of arid America" would also involve the conquest of certain pernicious elements in human nature. The recalcitrance of nature in deserts would provide the necessity for planning and cooperation among settlers, putting an end to willful self-interest. In the irrigation age, speculation—or the subordination of all other human values to monetary profit—would go the way of other relics of barbarism. America would at last have a stable, sensible civilization.

"Agriculture," Smythe offered as an axiom, "is the basis of civilization."[15] He was a champion of the agrarian tradition, a firm holder of the faith that a society received its stability from a basic stratum of land-owning small farmers. The transformations of his day only emphasized the vital role of farming. Subsistence provided by the family's own labor would be a bulwark against the tyranny of the surrounding social forces. The farm, in Smythe's hands, was a fortress for human dignity, holding off the threat of dependence.

Conventional farming, however, was itself an exercise in dependence and contingency. Relying on rainfall was a "crude, uncalculating, unscientific" and even "childlike dependence on the mood of the clouds."[16] In the regions west of the hundredth meridian, with a rainfall below twenty inches per year, scarce and unpredictable rain would force the farmer to give up his dependence on weather. Irrigated farms represented a resolution on the part of Americans to take control of the last remaining natural variable. With the mastery of water, Smythe believed he had found a way to combine both tradition and innovation, to use the newest scientific methods in the restoration of old values.

In restoring the agrarian past, Smythe acknowledged that rural

America had never been paradise. "The bane of rural life," he explained, "is its loneliness." Young people left the farm to "seek satisfaction" for their frustrated "social instincts." "The starvation of the soul," Smythe insisted, "is almost as real as the starvation of the body."[17]

Desert farming was his antidote to both varieties of hunger. Irrigation would require intensive culture, and the farms would be much smaller than the traditional 160 acres. "A very small farm unit" would then make it "possible for those who till the soil to live in the town." The western settlements would be "a long series of beautiful villages" and observers would be hard put "to say where the town ends and the country begins."[18] Farm virtues and city refinements would mingle, and the original landscape—the unimproved desert—would disappear.

The project of desert irrigation, Smythe declared, was an undertaking in which Americans were "conforming their methods to the laws of the universe."[19] Science was the means by which physical conditions could be assessed, and the laws of the universe determined. And the result was an answer to the question that had baffled nineteenth-century Americans: What was the purpose of the desert?

Smythe developed his explanation of the desert with a strong sense of plot. The initial main characters were God and Man.[20] The desert was not a character; it was something closer to a playing field or stage. God created the desert, along with the rest of the earth, but the desert He left unfinished, barren, arid, and uninhabitable. This was not an oversight or a failure on God's part. When His other creation, Man, was ready for maturity, the desert would be his test and his opportunity. His assignment would be to finish what God only began. In this enterprise, Man would become a partner in creation, empowered to create fertile land from that most unpromising of raw materials: desert.

Before the partnership could be formed, the second main character fragmented. Man became men. Men, in their plural state, sought their own individual fortunes, and the result was disaster: irresponsibility, speculation, and improvidence. The crucial element in the test of the desert was that it would give men a second chance at unity. Undertaking the collective irrigation projects necessary in deserts, men would take a step toward the primary status of Man. This was crucial for Smythe's optimism: men, individually, could and did behave badly; but Man, collectively, was an entity in whom Smythe had full faith. By some intricate moral chemistry, the re-unification of human nature enhanced virtue and cancelled the vice that had been so evident in the behavior of divided individuals.

Along with God, Man, and desert, a fourth element entered in the plot—the American nation, or Uncle Sam, the final defense against doubt. "When Uncle Sam puts his hand to a task, we know it will be done," Smythe declared. "When he waves his hand toward the desert and says, '*Let there be water!*' we know that the stream will obey his command."[21] Smythe, in other words, was a full believer in the romance of the federal government. Nearly a pretender to the throne in an American version of Genesis, Uncle Sam stood for efficiency and resoluteness and thoroughly masked the realities of divided authority and interest politics.

Having secured the support of both God and Uncle Sam, Smythe had taken his desert narrative as far as he could. The plot had to remain a cliff-hanger. He knew what should happen next, but how was he to enforce his vision of the future? How did he know he was right?

IV

Like many reformers, Smythe was engaged in an effort to outlaw uncertainty. He offered Americans a fresh start at "industrial inde-pendence"—"the guarantee of subsistence upon one's own labors," or "the ability to earn a living under conditions which admit of the smallest possible element of doubt with the least dependence upon others."[22]

Promoting the cause of certainty, Smythe found himself obligated to take on that most uncertain of human enterprises, prophecy. Nearly every passage in *The Conquest* demonstrated his claim to exemption from the limitations imposed on human vision, or ex-emption bordering on a claim to omniscience. Others might have "less imagaination"; the "average woman," for instance, "cannot see the fields and towns which are to be, through the clouds of dust that come swirling from the treeless land."[23] Peering into the future might strain the ordinary human eye, but dust and mirages did not restrict the vision of a prophet.

In irrigation, Smythe claimed to have found "a philosophy, a religion, and a programme of practical statesmanship."[24] He meant it. He did not have to "prove" his program any more than he had to "prove" the Bible. The mandate for irrigation was revealed religion: "God wrote it on the face of the earth in His own indelible characters."[25]

The divine message could be read both by history and by science. American history, according to Smythe, was the record of "continental conquest" alternating with actual war. Veterans of the Revolutionary War went on to conquer the trans-Appalachian frontier, and veterans of the Civil War took on the trans-Mississippi West. In the interludes between the interhuman battles, "it remained to wage war on the forest, the plain, the desert and the mountain."[26]

From Smythe's point of view, the human war against nature was unambiguously heroic. It was an effort to make the continent habitable, to improve it, to put it to the uses for which it was intended. Beyond any doubts, the earth and its resources were intended for human domination. Despite any token resistance it might offer, the highest destiny of any land was to be farmland.

The war to transform wilderness into submissive farmland succeeded until, in the late nineteenth century, the troops hit the one hundredth meridian. "Upon this strange boundary of prosperity," marked with "indelible lines," the army of settlers "trembled and hesitated for several years, then fell back baffled and disappointed." The army had crossed the line beyond which rainfall dropped below the level needed to sustain most crops. They had "encountered an obstacle beyond the power of the individual settler to overcome."[27]

To this point, the conquering army had proceeded with a rare informality of organization. Each individual had been his own strategist and commander. The individual, Smythe was delighted to announce, was no longer a viable unit for the campaign. In the well-watered East, "the individual acted alone and exclusively for his own benefit." In the arid West, "the association and organization of men were the price of life and prosperity." The "alternative" to cooperation "was starvation."[28]

In addition to its powers of cooperation, the army of homebuilders had a new element in its arsenal: the methods of applied science. Smythe used the word *science* with reverence. To identify a practice as "scientific" was to place it in an almost sacred realm of certainty. The forces of scientific industry may have been to a large degree the forces responsible for the creation of the surplus man, but the irony did not trouble Smythe. Neither were science and religion at odds. Science was in fact a way of gaining access to the divine will, deciphering physical conditions to find the mandate hidden within them.

Smythe maintained his certainty with science, history, and divine authority. If he recognized any tenuous connections or unsupported assumptions in his arguments, he seldom admitted them directly. He was, by his own admission, writing to persuade. What his movement needed, he had decided, "was an organized propaganda, alive, tireless, sleepless."[29] Providing that propaganda, he kept his doubts to himself, or wrestled them to the ground in grand, dramatic, and obviously staged gladiatorial exchanges.

To examine his ideas closely is, in fact, to take unfair advantage of him. His style of expression was always more oratorical than literary, reflecting years of extensive speechmaking. His sentences were arranged to strike the ear and the emotions, not the intellect.

"Can there be any reasonable doubt," Smythe concluded a typical chapter, "that if the policy of material conquest over new areas can find another field on which to operate, . . . it will confer another century of prosperity?"[30] His question had an obvious answer: in human affairs, there can always be reasonable doubt. But it was just as obvious that the question did not ask for an answer. Doubt was raised and dismissed in the same gesture.

In essence, Smythe was planning to shape the future by proclamation. Declaring an end to land speculation, he insisted that the "fury" of gambling for profits had subsided into "the calm current of these saner times."[31] Were the times in fact saner, the current calmer? Smythe's own sense of urgency would have suggested otherwise.

V

Smythe did not write with a sense of leisure. In fact, he charged into the future as resolutely and impatiently as John C. Frémont charged into deserts. For both, caution was folly.

Explaining this urgency, Smythe made an admission that called his whole program into question. The western country, he said, "is growing enormously; . . . new towns and agricultural districts are springing up where silence and desolation have reigned for ages; the region is measurably free from domination by great capitalists." All this seemed cheerful and optimistic, and then Smythe made his admission: "Doubtless the time will come when the same economic forces which closed most of the commercial avenues to small capital in the East will produce the same result in the West, but it has not come yet." When would it come? "There is probably another generation of prosperity for enterprising men who follow the tide of settlement to the Western valleys and mountains."[32] Elsewhere, Smythe expanded his vision to vast time scales—new eras in civilization, new relations with the Creator. Echoing under the expressions of cosmic confidence was his admission here: "probably another generation of prosperity," and inevitable population growth and economic expansion would put an end to this most recent round of fresh starts and new beginnings.

After this admission, Smythe's optimism seemed a little tinny, insistent to the point of stridency. Nonetheless, he persisted in asserting that desert farming was a fully fresh start. In his conquest the western man "is born again. He turns over a new page in his life history." Both individuals and institutions were to be reborn, and the condition of rebirth meant a liberation from error. Given a fresh beginning, the westerner did "not intend to repeat the old mistakes."[33]

How was he to avoid them? Smythe's own words suggested that he would not. The western man, he said, "realizes that his relation to the natural resources of the region is like that enjoyed by the men of a century ago in the place whence he came. *They* planted hamlets which grew into cities, and thereby enriched their descendants; *he* will do the same. His heart swells as he thinks of his own and his children's future."[34] His heart, it would seem, might just as well sink. The western man had felt impelled to leave the cities founded by his forefathers, and he had moved west in order to create his own. He would raise children as he had been raised, and in a generation or two, he would have duplicated the situation that he himself had fled. The "wilderness" would now be peopled, the hamlets would be cities, and his descendants would be troubled by the same ancestral restlessness. Intentionally or not, the "old mistakes" would have been replicated.

Smythe's scenario for the future came fully equipped with paradox and unintended consequence. With rare exceptions, Smythe ignored those complications and confined himself to declarations of inevitability. The direction he pointed out for America was the direction that had to be taken "because we then move with the great trend of events which no man or party or nation is directing, and which none can prevent or divert." Irrigationists were "merely conforming our institutions to meet the inexorable demands of the cosmic process."[35]

What role could individual choice play in an "inexorable" and "cosmic" trend? Even the option to hesitate was gone. "The unseen forces which have driven us thus far will drive us farther,—and there is nowhere to go, except to the goal."[36] Taking on the role of prophet, Smythe had to present his hopes as predetermined facts. The effect of this strategy was to negate the role of individual will, an unpleasant effect for an advocate attempting to persuade men to voluntary action.

Smythe's dilemma was only one in a long tradition of Protestant perplexity, in which free will and determinism were in unstable co-existence. Unlike others in this tradition, Smythe did not reflect on its paradoxes. He recognized that his cause would require strenuous exertion on the part of individuals. He took it as his mission to persuade the individuals to volunteer for that exertion. He explained, as one of the principal methods of persuasion, that the cause had the backing of the deity. Beyond those limits, Smythe did not go in for philosophy.

VI

And what of the desert? The desert seemed oddly irrelevant. It appeared in Smythe's world as an enemy, and not a very interesting enemy at that. Smythe's colonizers would "drive the desert back inch by inch."[37] It was as if the land itself had been held in captivity by the desert; liberated from the tyranny of aridity, the land would take its proper role as farmland, and the desert would cease to be.

"Homeseekers," Smythe declared, would "grapple with desert, translate its gray barrenness into green fields and gardens."[38] Conquered enemies might conventionally undergo enslavement or exploitation; it was unusual to find one facing the prospect of "translation." Smythe's odd word choice emphasized that this was a conquest in which the enemy was to be turned into something else entirely. The phrasing also emphasized the seductiveness of Smythe's world of words. In a written or spoken sentence, "gray barrenness" easily became "green fields and gardens," sliding along a rhetorical continuum well greased by familiarity. The reader could follow along with Smythe, never having to notice that this particular "translation," so effortless in writing, might present enormous difficulties in actuality. Moreover, the desert's "gray barrenness" was an abstraction, without any particular physical reality. The "translation" thus seemed to take an abstraction and make *something* of it—"green fields and gardens." Who could regret the change?

The victorious homeseekers would also "banish" the desert's "silence with the laughter of children."[39] Like Twain, Smythe was evidently fond of the human voice and the sounds of life; the desert's speechlessness was deeply unnerving. Replacing the silence with "the laughter of children," Smythe would prove that a waste place had been transformed to a scene of normal family life.

"*For every surplus man there is a surplus place, where he may use his peculiar talents and experience, and where he may satisfy his reasonable wants according to his accustomed standard of living.*"[40] In Smythe's basic plan, the desert was in fact irrelevant and uninteresting, valuable only for its vacancy, its status as unused surplus. But on a less prosaic level, the desert had a cosmic significance—in his own phrase, as a "Promised Land."[41] By 1905, the concept of a Promised Land might have seemed a lost cause to some. For Smythe, the cause was not lost but in need of redefinition and decoding. Until humans were ready for their role as translators, the gardens of the Promised Land would masquerade as desert.

VII

Predictably, for a man who had "taken up the cross of a new crusade," Smythe had his tests and trials.

His own efforts to put theory into practice were of limited success. In the second decade of the twentieth century, he directed the founding of several colonies in arid areas of California.[42] Independent groups of Little Landers ("a little land and a living") founded farm communities in three locations: San Ysidro, south of San Diego; Los Terrenitos, outside Los Angeles near present-day Tujunga; and Hayward Heath in Northern California. Each colony foundered in fairly short order. Soil, in all three sites, was generally poor. A few colonists in the San Ysidro settlement received better soil and produced better crops. They were reluctant to share their profits with less fortunately situated members. The Hayward colony had unworkable hillside soil, and the Los Angeles area group found themselves attempting to farm in a virtual rockpile.

After several years' effort, all three groups gave up and tried to sell out. Only the Los Terrenitos group found that occasion to be a happy one. Interest in suburban sites for Los Angeles residents was on the increase, and the Little Landers finally found a way to make a living on their undertaking: by subdividing and selling out to developers.

Smythe dreamed of small independent farms; he got suburbs and agribusiness. He imagined federal dams for democratic irrigation; the economically successful dams produced hydroelectric power and water for cities. He declared an end to the improvidence and inefficiency of land speculation; gambling in land values remained a fundamental western enterprise. He rested his theories on the assumption of unlimited water resources; depleted underground water tables and over-allotted rivers eventually mocked that assumption. The "conquest of arid America" remained incomplete.

By 1921, Smythe was evidently finding his optimism to be a precarious perch. His last book, *City Homes on Country Lanes*, sketched a version of the old faith. The plan now included the entire United States in a network of garden cities, with each family relying on its one-acre garden.

The first line of the book sat alone and unparagraphed: "I am an optimist." The old life on the land had failed and was "doomed to pass away." After the transition, Smythe said, "the land is to be the healing and the saving of the people." The next line sat grimly alone, unparagraphed: "There is no other refuge."[43] If this was optimism, it was optimism in a stark and almost desperate setting.

With William Ellsworth Smythe and irrigation, man and cause were blended past division. The anxiety and urgency evident in his books were, however indirectly, self-revelation. Uneasy with the course of events, moved to intervene, the author could not be sure of the intervention's success. Manly at least knew he had rescued the Bennetts; Smythe could not be sure he had rescued the nation.

When he finished the first edition of *The Conquest*, Smythe explained in the second edition, he and his wife had been living on a remote ranch in the desert country of northeastern California, twelve miles from the nearest house (" 'and no one living there,' as my wife caustically remarked"). Six years later, Smythe insisted, author and cause had prospered coincidentally. Smythe had moved to San Diego and to national prominence. The irrigation movement of 1899, he said, had been "domiciled in distant deserts." The irrigation movement of 1905 was "planted in the heart of populous towns."[44]

To be "domiciled in distant deserts" was to be in exile and in isolation, a proposition equally true for authors, their wives, and especially their causes. With an urgency reminiscent of Lewis Manly and nineteenth-century emigrants, Smythe searched for a route out of the desert and back to civilization.

PART TWO

Introduction

From Vulnerability to Complacency:
The Twentieth-Century Background to John Van Dyke, George Wharton James, Joseph Wood Krutch, and Edward Abbey

Traveling on the overland trail, prospecting for minerals, or creating irrigation projects, Americans had to acknowledge their initial vulnerability to the desert. Early in the twentieth century, complacency began to replace the awareness of vulnerability; it became possible to live in desert towns and cities with a comfortable faith that water would be there when needed. With this shift away from uncertainty, the deserts could be properly nationalized; they could offer the replication of modern urban society, in a sunnier, snow-free climate.[1]

How did this happen? Transportation was the key to the change, as access to the desert became at once easier and a matter of choice. After 1869, one could see the northern Nevada desert through the window of a Central Pacific railroad car. During the 1880s, transcontinental lines extended through Arizona and Southern California as well. With the proliferation of automobiles and roads in the early twentieth century, desert travel and urban living had become a matter of comparative comfort. In the familiar cycle, growing towns and cities required roads, and with more roads, towns and cities and their demands grew even larger.[2]

With the ordeal of travel eased, and with the installation of the technology and equipment of a hydraulic society dependent on the large-scale manipulation of water, more and more Americans found themselves in a position to think of the desert as interesting and even beautiful. Scientists and naturalists investigated the intricacies of biological adaptation to the desert. As this information made its way into popular understanding, plants and animals that had formerly seemed ugly became elegant models of appropriate design. In the mid-nineteenth century, the desert had seemed alien and alarming in contrast to familiar landscapes; in the twentieth century, with a margin of safety established, the desert by its very novelty qualified as a site worth seeing. The more that Americans felt themselves insulated and protected from the desert, the more they felt safe to appreciate the desert for, as many of them put it, its "reality."[3]

Not surprisingly, the appreciation of deserts lagged behind the appreciation of mountains, meadows, and seacoasts. The mountain-lover John Muir was known to thousands, the desert-lover John Van Dyke was known to a select few. Popularizing a favorable image of the desert was no easy task, given the balance of negative judgment in the past.

The ideas of four men—George Wharton James, John Van Dyke, Joseph Wood Krutch, and Edward Abbey—provide a record of the course of appreciation in the twentieth century. The last three represent an almost unbroken chain of intellectual continuity; George Wharton James forms the exception, who was nonetheless most representative of popular opinion. Unlike Van Dyke, Krutch, and Abbey, James worked both sides of the street; with masterful inconsistency, he was both appreciator and irrigator.

Writing over eight decades, Van Dyke, Krutch, and Abbey shared a remarkable degree of agreement, revealing something one might call the desert appreciators' consensus. They liked the desert for its tranquility, authenticy, and solitude. They found the adaptiveness of desert plants and animals intriguing and inspiring. They liked the wide spacing between individual organisms; in times when the nation seemed crowded, they treasured what might become the lost luxury of vacant space. Men with a strong sense of themselves as outsiders, they were gratified by the idea of belonging to the desert, fitting into an environment that did not compromise individuality. They were proud to be individuals of distinctive and advanced taste, able to find interest and beauty where others could only see useless matter.

Life in the desert, they felt, stood in direct contrast to life in modern mass society, and this was to their minds very good news.

The terms of power, the appreciators felt, had reversed: from a situation in which humans needed to be protected from the desert, the situation had become one in which deserts needed to be protected from humans. Their effort to defend deserts had its pitfalls. In claiming that the desert was in fact fragile and vulnerable, they were in the position of defense attorneys attempting to arouse sympathy for a rough and unconcerned defendant, visibly a tough customer. They met another obstacle in their own tendency to fatalism; defending deserts against commercial exploitation often struck them as a lost cause, with only the long-range consolations of a restored balance in far-off geological time. They could not comfortably cross over into the larger dimensions of pantheism; unhappy with both reductive science and inflated mysticism, they wandered with some bewilderment in the middle.

Certainly the most confusing element of their thought concerned their attitude toward human beings. As they condemned the ecological crimes of mankind, it did seem at times that desert-loving and misanthropy went hand in hand. Yet as individuals with fairly low opinions of human nature, they seemed to be oddly proud of themselves—proud of both their sensitivity and good sense. Generalizations that applied to the failures and flaws of the species evidently did not apply to the authors themselves.

And yet the need both to sell books and to recruit supporters for preservation drove the appreciators back into relation with other less certifiably redeemed people. With many of the characteristics of elitists, they nonetheless had to attempt the popularization of their point of view. To resist the forces of commercial development, they had to issue repeated invitations to other Americans to visit deserts, and to care about them. In what might have been the most uncomfortable irony, they were forced to appeal to individual choice and to attempt to change individual minds when, in their own terms of an overpowering mass society, such an effort was both futile and silly.

In the writings of the appreciators, the desert became an attractive place, well on its way to becoming desirable real estate. The resulting towns and cities developed an ever-increasing need for water and power. The progression from Van Dyke to Krutch to Abbey took place against this backdrop of growth and development in dams. The rising sense of urgency in the desert-lovers correlated to this development; if Van Dyke made his observations at the beginning of the federal reclamation era, Abbey drew his conclusions from the consequences—the transformation of the desert's river systems into a network of ditches and reservoirs. A society needed technological sophistication in order to transform the desert; a society needed aesthetic sophistication in order to appreciate the desert untransformed. The desert-lovers could only hope that the second kind of sophistication stayed ahead of the first. On that matter of close timing, they rested their faith.

CHAPTER FIVE
John Van Dyke

I

In the conquest of arid America, William Ellsworth Smythe assumed that the desert was his enemy and humans were his allies. Who could possibly choose the hostile and desolate desert over the forces of progress and improvement?

John Van Dyke did. An art historian from New Jersey, he was an exact opposite to Smythe. "The deserts should never be reclaimed," he said. If the proponents of progress had their way, Van Dyke claimed the long-range victory. "Nothing human is of long duration," he said, with satisfaction.[1]

If Smythe felt he understood and could speak for the Creator, Van Dyke felt he had similar connections to the Creation. Nature, he said, "intended" that lands of plenty and lands of scarcity "should remain as she made" them. With or without reclamation movements, "when man is gone," nature would restore order. "The sand and heat will come back to the desert."[2] Van Dyke's prophecies of triumphant deserts and vanquished humans were for him a source of reassurance rather than doom. Where Smythe was at times ill at ease with the demands of his optimism, Van Dyke seemed to have made a complacent peace with his pessimism. The peace relied on two attitudes: a distrust of human nature, bordering on misanthropy, and an admiration for nature, bordering on pantheism. He demonstrated both attitudes in *The Desert: Further Studies in Natural Appearances*, first published in 1901.

When John Van Dyke first visited the desert, he was already in middle age.[3] He was born in New Brunswick, New Jersey, in 1856. His family moved to Minnesota in 1868, and Van Dyke spent much of his boyhood outdoors. He left Minnesota to earn a law degree from Columbia University. In 1878, he became librarian of the Sage Library of New Brunswick Theological Seminary, an affiliate of Rutgers. His position allowed him leisure and travel time to pursue his interests in art. In 1889, he became a professor in the history of art at Rutgers.

Van Dyke was always an energetic traveler and a fluent writer. Beginning in 1883, he wrote a number of art history handbooks. In 1893, he published *Art for Art's Sake,* an introduction to a philosophy of art appreciation. In 1898, he published *Nature for Its Own Sake,* applying to nature much of the philosophy he had formerly applied to art.

In late 1897, at age forty-one, Van Dyke underwent a decline in health and left New Jersey for California. His brother, Theodore, had become an enthusiastic Californian and the author of books that described the state and celebrated hunting and the outdoor life. After visiting Theodore, John resolved on a desert tour. In the early summer of 1898, equipped with a desert pony, a fox terrier, and fifty pounds of supplies, Van Dyke traveled through the San Gorgonio Pass and into the Colorado Desert. In the next three years, he made a series of journeys through the Colorado, Mojave, and Sonoran deserts. "I kept no record of my movements," he said, "I was not travelling by map."[4]

In May 1901, Van Dyke completed the manuscript of *The Desert.* "It will sell," he told his editor at Scribner's, "but not up in the hundreds of thousands. It is not so bad as that. My audience is only a few thousand, thank God."[5] John Van Dyke was a man of unpopular opinion—and proud of it.

In 1893, in *Art for Art's Sake,* Van Dyke gave the painter the sole responsibility for mediating between human awareness and natural beauty. Humanity, in which Van Dyke was willing for once to place himself, shared a blindness to the omnipresent attractions in nature. Artists were the only seers. Transforming nature into pictures, artists could share their sight with the less fortunate.[6]

Van Dyke never lost his respect for art, but he did revise his opinion on the possibility of a direct approach to nature. He, for one, was by no means dependent on the mediation of painters. For several years he had kept his eyes fixed on canvases that drew on the resources of nature and transformed them. Gradually his eye moved from the translations and transcriptions to the original. His response to unmediated nature, he discovered, was just as intense as his response to art. The same values of form and color were there to be discovered and savored. The major difference between art appreciation and nature appreciation was simply this: with nature, Van Dyke confronted an unsigned creation. He admired the work, without knowing much about the artist.

In 1898, When Van Dyke published *Nature for Its Own Sake,* his preferences were clearly formed. Nature at its best was nature with the least evidence of the existence of humans. The failure of the desert to present itself as a habitable and hospitable environment would be the basis of its charm. The desert was as close as Van Dyke could get to "nature for its own sake."

II

John Van Dyke was not burdened with excessive fondness for the human species. "After the making of Eden came a serpent," he said, "and after the gorgeous furnishing of the world, a human being." Why had Providence ordained the existence of evil? "Why the existence of the destroyers? What monstrous folly," Van Dyke asked, "ever led Nature to create her one great enemy—man!"[7]

Nature's other creatures had the sense to fear humanity, "the great annihilator," whose "civilization meant their destruction." The progress of civilization left a trail of injury: "grasses and wild flowers perish"; "mountains are blasted"; "plains are broken by the plow and the soil is gradually washed into the rivers." Finally "the artificial desert—the desert made by the tramp of human feet—begins to show itself."[8] Like Smythe, Van Dyke recognized humanity's claim to a role in creation. Smythe claimed for mankind the power to make green places out of deserts. Van Dyke found mankind expert in making deserts out of green places.

In this wholesale condemnation of humanity for crimes committed against nature, where did the author and his readers stand? In condemning humanity, could Van Dyke occupy both the prosecutor's chair and the defendant's? What part did a self-declared "lover" of nature play in the collective entity "man"?

Van Dyke never addressed these questions directly, but his general stance would indicate that he was claiming an exemption from the crimes of mankind. In a combined preface and dedication, Van Dyke addressed an unnamed "you." The pronoun *he* stood for man, "the great annihilator." *I* and *you* were thus set off from that guilty and destructive *he*. Those lucky enough to earn Van Dyke's second person pronoun gained a seat with him in the spectators' gallery overlooking the arena of human errors and crimes, a gallery where observation replaced complicity.

III

Characteristically, Van Dyke in looking at a landscape saw a moment in time as well as a location in space. When he rode toward a range of desert mountains, he saw "the surviving remnant . . . of some noble range that long centuries ago was beaten by wind and rain into desert sand."[9] Placed in a nonhuman time scale, the desert was in motion, its mountains declining into hills, and then into plains.

Van Dyke's vision was not only unusually flexible in its time scale, it was also openly uncertain and prey to deception. "Who of the desert has not spent his day riding at a mountain and never reaching its base?" Van Dyke asked. "The vision is so cleared that the truth itself is deceptive."[10]

Frémont, Manly, Twain, and many others had felt angered and betrayed by the tricks that deserts could play on human vision. Van Dyke, however, took the desert's deceptiveness as an invitation to a contest with a worthy rival. He pitted his considerable resources of perception against the desert's trickery of light, air, and color. Victory in this contest might always go to the desert, but that did not reduce Van Dyke's enthusiasm for the sport.

Beginning to climb his mountain range, Van Dyke found sugges-

tions of a trail. Discovering the print of a deer hoof, he was about
to conclude that the trail was a recent animal path. But the hoof
print turned out to be "sunk in stone instead of earth—petrified in
rock."[11] Desert time made one of its sudden extensions, taking the
apparent evidence of a deer's recent presence and extending the
evidence back into centuries.

Arrival at the top of the mountain was also an arrival at another
variety of time and duration. "Gradually," Van Dyke reported, "I
make out a long parapet of loose stone"—"the ruins of a once fortified
camp." The site included an apparent burial ground, and Van Dyke
was launched into reflections on the scale of man in nature. "The
traces of human activity are slight," he said. "Nature has been wearing
them away and reclaiming her own on the mountain top."[12]

Had the Indians chosen this site for the view? Van Dyke thought
not. "A sensitive feeling for sound, or form, or color, an impres-
sionable nervous organization, do not belong to the man with the
hoe, much less to a man with a bow." Here was the familiar theme
of Americans in deserts: a concern with food and subsistence distracted from the higher human faculties. But Van Dyke reversed the
idea that the preoccupation with food was in some way unhealthy.
"It is to be feared," he said, that the higher sensitivities "are indicative
of some physical degeneration," or "some abnormal development of
the emotional nature." Aesthetic sensitivities "travel side by side
with civilization and are the premonitory symptoms of racial decay."[13]
Civilization, Van Dyke had already claimed, brought the destruction
of natural beauty. Civilization was also the agent of sophistication,
making it possible to appreciate beauty. One could only hope that
the acquisition of taste kept a narrow margin ahead of the destruction
of nature.

Confronting the desert, what did the aesthetically advanced person
find to appreciate? The "simplicity" of open spaces and clear lines
was in itself attractive. The horizontal line was "restful." "Things
that lie flat are at peace, and the mind grows peaceful with them."[14]
For earlier desert travelers, "things that lie flat"—and things that
were at the same time silent—were suggestive of death, a special
variety of "peace."

Van Dyke himself never evaded the desert's suggestions of death.

On the contrary, he savored them. The negation of humanity was, after all, what he liked best about the desert. "The weird solitude, the great silence, the grim desolation, are the very things with which every desert wanderer falls in love."[15] Aesthetic sensitivity might be "an abnormal development of the emotional nature" at the expense of physical vigor. Enfeebled or not, Van Dyke could face "desolation" without flinching. He not only faced it, Van Dyke wanted it clear, he loved it.

IV

The desert, Van Dyke said, was no simple "sea of sand." It had instead all the variations of feature "common to all countries": plains, valleys, hills, and mountains. How then did "the desert differ from any other land?" By a single variable: "water—the lack of it." Nature worked by a strategy of deprivation, withholding the key element for the veiling of the earth's surface with "pretty"or "picturesque" vegetation.[16]

The desert was like a city under siege: with nature running an unbreakable blockade on water, the inhabitants fought among themselves for the reduced resources. "At every step there is the suggestion of the fierce, the defiant, the defensive," Van Dyke said. "Everything within its borders seems fighting to maintain itself against destroying forces." In this "war of elements and a struggle for existence," sun, winds, drifting sands, and sudden cloudbursts were forever disrupting the earth's surface.[17] However peaceful Van Dyke might have found the desert in an overview of its horizontality, there was no peace in the details.

The desert war was all the more intense for its silence. "There is not a sound to be heard; and not a thing moves save the wind and the sand." The fact of war had to be reconstructed from the evidence of the battlefield. "You look up at the worn peaks and jagged barrancas, . . . you look about at the wind-tossed, half-starved bushes; and for all the silence, you know that there is a struggle for life, a war for place, going on day by day."[18] Again, accurate perception required an extension of time scale: what looked like an established landscape had to be seen as a particular moment in time.

While William Ellsworth Smythe had been equally preoccupied with the idea of war, his was a war of conquest initiated and conducted by humans against a passive enemy. In Van Dyke's war, humans were utterly irrelevant, late arrivals in a war which preceded them and which would certainly outlast them.

In a steady "war for place," few plants won. "All told there is hardly enough covering to hide the anatomy of the earth." The desert was "bare and bony," with rocks protruding at sharp angles, with the "backbone and ribs" exposed.[19] Sparse ground cover had alarmed earlier desert travelers, provoking their impressions of barrenness and death. Characteristically, Van Dyke was more intrigued than alarmed, and also more willing to extend the metaphor. The "naked" desert was not simply earth unclothed; it was earth without flesh, dissected and displayed.

The agents of dissection were still at work. Winds, sand, and sudden floods carried on a constant sculpting of the surface. Not even mountains were exempt from the life and death cycles of plants and animals. Tracing the stages of mountain erosion, Van Dyke made an abrupt and contradictory shift back to human time scale, and back to a flagrant intrusion of human emotion into the desert landscape. The desert mountains, he said, "remind you of a clenched hand with the knuckles turned skyward." They were "barren rock and nothing more; but what could better epitomize power!"[20]

If the epitome of power was subject to steady erosion and dissolution, then power was evidently more a matter of appearance than fact. In deserts, no member or element of creation had any claim to the protection, much less the affection of the creator. No matter how "set and determined" mountains might look, the balance of power was against them. The extent of their "quiescent force" was a gesture: a clenched fist directed at the sky.

V

If the destiny of the mountains was an arrival at the horizontal, it was possible to visit the future. The Salton Basin was the lowest part of the Colorado Desert, and a place where the horizontal was unchallenged. The desert had once been an inland sea. Shoremarks were still visible; dunes, beaches, bays, and lagoons still clearly marked. The sea's history carried the familiar lesson of change and impermanence. The accumulation of silt at the Colorado Delta trapped the sea just as erosion reduced the mountain, and "finally the desert came in."[21]

This "bottom of the bowl" was a study in vacancy—the "most forsaken" place, "as flat as a table." For Van Dyke, the vacancy had the key advantage of isolating color. Light changes in the course of a day found a perfect reflecting surface. "Form" was "almost blurred out in favor of color and air." "A landscape all color," this was nature catering to the interests of contemporary art theory: "The great struggle of the modern landscapist is to get on with the least possible form and to suggest everything by tones of color, shades of light, drifts of air." Those were, after all, "the most sensuous qualities in nature and in art."[22]

This was Van Dyke's aesthetic elitism at its peak, confident that his taste for subtlety represented a universal standard of value, and evidently finding it unnecessary to mention any of the other "sensuous qualities" of the Salton Basin: heat, dry winds, uncertain water supplies, possible sand storms, poorly marked trails. Van Dyke did not ask for exemption or protection from those risks; facing up to the hardships undoubtedly added an edge to the aesthetic rewards. But he could hardly expect many Americans to share his feelings on either count: either in the willingness to accept discomfort, or the prizing of subtle light, air, and color effects.

In fact, Van Dyke did not expect to be part of anything larger than a tiny minority of desert appreciators. The power, in this transitory moment of human history, lay elsewhere. The Salton Basin was "more beauty destined to destruction." "It might be thought," Van Dyke said, that "its very worthlessness would be its safeguard against civilization, that none would want it, and everyone from necessity would let it alone." But "the industry or the avarice (as you please) of man" would not respect even this severe limit. "A great company" had undertaken "to turn the Colorado River into the sands, to reclaim this desert basin, and make it blossom as the rose."[23]

What was the point? "It is said that a million acres of desert will thus be made arable, fitted for homesteads, ready for the settler who never remains settled."[24] Enterprises on behalf of chronically restless settlers were an exercise in impermanence, a proposition that Van Dyke as an outsider to a dominant value system could confront complacently. One can imagine Smythe's shudder.

Irrigation, Van Dyke was sure, would receive a full measure of public approval. "A most laudable enterprise, people will say," he wrote. "Economically those areas will produce large supplies of food." That would be thought "commendable, too, even if those for whom it is produced waste a good half of what they already possess."[25]

What was obvious to John Van Dyke had never been obvious to the rest of the world. "The aesthetic sense—the power to enjoy through the eye, the ear, and the imagination—is just as important a factor in the scheme of human happiness as the corporeal sense of eating and drinking," he asserted; "but there had never been a time when the world would admit it." Here Van Dyke distributed democratically the condemnation that earlier desert travelers had directed at Indians. "The world" was now accused of a preoccupation with food to the exclusion of the higher faculties. The " 'practical men' who seem forever on the throne" were Van Dyke's equivalent to Twain's Goshoots living on the lower borders of human potential.[26]

Convinced that "the main affair of life is to get the dollar," the "practical men" had "stripped the land of its robes of beauty" and substituted "weeds, wire fences, oil-derricks, board shanties and board towns."[27] The benefits of the mines, lumber mills, farms, and oil wells went elsewhere, and the West was left with the detritus.

On this subject, Van Dyke had a way of writing himself into a rage. His stridency and melodramatic phrasing were in part a measure of his sense of impotence. Even if the deserts were "the breathing spaces of the West and should be preserved forever," Van Dyke could do nothing about it.[28] In his own historical time, Van Dyke's cause might be a lost one, but he had his consolations.

"Nature," he said, "will not always be driven from her purpose." The desert reclamation project that Van Dyke placed his faith in was nature's return to control. "Sooner or later, Nature will surely come to her own again," he said. "Men and their deeds are obliterated, the race itself fades; but Nature goes calmly on with her own projects. . . . When man is gone, the sand and heat will come back to the desert."[29] It was a conclusion to send chills through Smythe and his "army" of reclamationists. In Van Dyke's vision, Smythe's phrase, "the conquest of arid America," took an unsettling turn, as the desert moved into the position of conqueror.

VI

Van Dyke took mountains, rivers, Indian settlements, inland seas, and reclamation projects and followed them from their peak of vitality to their dissolution into silence. At last, he hit a subject with some suggestions of permanence. Light was an element of undeniable reality, and an element that was endlessly replenished.

Light and color offered the most comfortable border territory between Van Dyke's two lives: as an art historian at Rutgers, and as a traveler in the southwestern deserts. He moved comfortably from description to explanation, certain of his understanding of the mechanisms used to trick vision, and equally certain that understanding the mechanism did not make the trick any less effective.

Desert atmosphere carried dust particles, all of which absorbed and reflected light. Desert air became colored air. The colored atmosphere, the variation in sunlight over a day, the reflections from clouds, the colors in plants, rocks, and soil added up to a vast range of effects. A day with the desert's extraordinary air gave an art historian material for a year's reflections and study. Meanwhile, "the average unobservant traveller looks right through it and thinks it not different from any other air."[30]

The "unobservant traveller" was well advised to stay on his train and avoid staking his life on his uncertain vision. The "deception of distances" was "not infrequently accompanied by fatal consequences." Regularly, "some mining or exploring party is lost." Survivors, if any, would always report: "The distance seemed so short." Van Dyke put is simply: "But there are no short distances in the desert. Every valley-plain is an immense wilderness of space."[31]

Van Dyke was intrigued by the ways in which mind and eye cooperated, or failed to cooperate, in judging distances, mirages, and color effects. The confusion, he suggested, came less from physical causes and more from a failure of mental flexibility. "We are not willing to admit different reports of an appearance," he said. "The Anglo-Saxon in us insists that there can be only one truth, and everything else must be in error." The eyes reported the "truth of appearances," and a narrow mind rejected the report. "The preconceived impression of the mind refuses to make room for the actual impression of the eyes," he said, "and in consequence we are misled and deluded."[32]

Victims of the misunderstanding between inflexible minds and honest eyes, humans could at least appreciate the deceptions to which they were prey. This was a concession Van Dyke was happy to make. The mirage's "loveliness," he said, "is not the less when its uncertain, fleeting character is revealed."[33] This was, of course, an aesthetic acceptance of uncertainty that more vulnerable desert travelers had been unable to make. Neither Frémont nor Manly had been in a position to find the deceptions of the desert vision "lovely." Van Dyke traveled in the desert with a pony, a minimum of supplies, and no dependents. In his remarks on desert vision, he made no reference to hardship. Even his usual themes of death and dissolution disappeared.

Light and color had for him an unconditional vitality. The sights of the desert even had a value independent of the presence of a seer. When nature reclaimed the desert from the irrigators, Van Dyke closed his Salton Basin reflections, the mirage would again be "serene in its solitude, though no human eye sees nor human tongue speaks its loveliness."[34] As a denial of human significance, this can stretch one's willingness to believe in Van Dyke's sincerity. After several repetitions of the same theme, one begins to suspect that he meant it.

VII

In desert plants and animals, Van Dyke found another variety of permanence. "The individual dies," Van Dyke admitted. "Yes; but not the species." Grasping that proposition brought him "closer to an understanding of Nature's method. It is the species that she designs to last, . . . and the individual is of no great importance, merely a sustaining factor, one among millions."[35]

And what were humans to think of this arrangement? "If we have eyes only for" nature's "creative beauties we think her all goodness; if we see only her power of destruction, we incline to think she is all evil." It was a mistake to see any individual intent in this, since the plan was "carried out without any feeling." Humans in their own biological lives demonstrated the paradoxical plan of nature. "With the same indifferent spirit that she planted in us an eye to see or an ear to hear, she afterwards plants a microbe to breed and a cancer to eat." A sense of paradox was the only way to make sense of nature. "She in herself is both growth and decay. The virile and healthy things of the earth are hers; and so, too, are disease, dissolution, and death." An attempted moral judgment was only a route to befuddlement: "She is neither good nor evil; she is only a great law of change that passeth understanding."[36]

Even in the midst of change, nature was intent on the maintenance of the species, and this required the maintenance of balances of power. Nature had to deal with her creatures like a superpower in a Cold War: "How wonderfully she arms both offence and defence! What ground she chooses for the conflict! What stern conditions she lays down!" Even in the harsh desert setting, nature insisted "that something shall fight heat and drouth even here." Such "stern conditions" called for extra armaments: defenses against evaporation, systems of water storage to withstand sieges of drought, root systems virtually animate in their search for water, thorns to hold off water-hungry animals. "Put heat, drouth, and animal attack against the desert shrubs," Van Dyke said, "and they fight back like the higher forms of organic life."[37]

Were these tough desert plants "beautiful"? "If you mean something that has a distinct character, something appropriate to its setting, something admirably fitted to a designed end, . . . then the desert will show forth much that people nowadays are beginning to think beautiful." Nature was once again keeping up with trends in art theory. In deserts, form had the good taste to follow function.[38]

The function, of course, was to stay alive, to emphasize the creative aspect of nature in an environment that dramatized the destructive. Animals showed the same determination and development of "character" in a struggle with scarcity. "The life of the desert lives only by virtue of adapting itself to the conditions of the desert," he said. "Nature does not bend the elements to favor the plants and animals; she makes the plants and animals do the bending." Forced adaptation did not develop compliance and submission. "The strife is desperate," Van Dyke said, "the supply of food and moisture is small, the animal is very hungry and thirsty. . . . Everything pursues or is pursued."[39]

Van Dyke was illustrating the familiar point that desert travel called attention to the stark operations of the food chain, the ways in which organisms served as each other's nutrition. But his version was a particularly athletic one, in which the struggle for existence became a sort of multispecies Olympic event. Predators and avoiders of predators, the teams may have been well matched, but each confrontation of individuals was a microcosm of the larger conflict, and each capture or escape readjusted the score.

The vigor and violence of the animals had to earn Van Dyke's admiration. "Perhaps you shudder at the thought of a panther dragging down a deer," he said; still the panther was using its resources with "character"—a perfect harmony of design and function. If any of these desert animals failed to impress their viewers, "the fault" was "not in the subject. It is not vulgar or ugly. The trouble" as usual, was that humans lacked "the proper angle of vision."[40]

Admiration for character could not move freely in the constricted human mind. "If we could but rid ourselves of the false ideas, which, taken *en masse*, are called education," Van Dyke claimed, "we should know that there is nothing ugly under the sun, save that which comes from human distortion." Dividing plants and animals into categories of good and bad, beautiful and ugly, was "to accuse Nature herself of preference—something which she never knew."[41] In the recovery from "education," the desert pushed receptive observers—even professors—beyond their original preferences, into a recognition of an alternative standard of value, measured by "character." Recognizing the value of the species over the individual, humans took a step closer to nature's point of view. Whether that step was altogether in the interests of human mental health was a question Van Dyke chose not to raise.

Whatever effect it had on the species, the desert had been therapeutic for one human being. Riding through the foothills on his way out, Van Dyke seemed to have picked up the spirit of desert plants and animals: the will to live. "The joy of mere animal existence, the feeling that it is good to be alive and face to face with Nature's self, drives everything else into the background." "Life becomes simplified from necessity," Van Dyke said. "It begins all over again."[42]

The nature enthusiasts of the nineteenth century, Van Dyke said, "never would have tolerated the desert for a moment." The "Nature-lover of the present" had "a little wider horizon than his predecessor. Not that his positive knowledge is so much greater, but rather where he lacks in knowledge he declines to condemn." Without a way of tolerating ignorance and uncertainty, humans were trapped into condemnation. The desert began to make sense only when humans gave up their impossible demands for omniscience. "Nature never intended," he said, "that we should fully understand."[43]

VIII

At the summit of the coastal mountains, Van Dyke looked down at "the habitable portion of Southern California, spread out like a relief map." Grainfields and orchards formed an attractive pattern; "yet large as they are, these are only spots." In the uncultivated areas, the "sands of the valley have the glitter of the desert. You know intuitively that all this country was planned by Nature to be a desert."[44]

Man had had "phenomenal" success in storing mountain water and reclaiming the valleys, creating "farms, houses, towns, cities." Success aside, "the cultivated conditions are maintained only at the price of eternal vigilance." When driven, nature could be "almost human in the way she rebels and recurs to former conditions." Even with irrigation, discouraged farmers could be persuaded by two or three years of drought to abandon their farms, and "once abandoned, but a few years elapse before the desert has them for its own."[45] Looking down on Southern California, Van Dyke could only see the precariousness of maintaining life on borrowed water, an element of life in arid America that most of its residents preferred to ignore.

Behaving again like a Cold War superpower, nature was determined on a balance of power. "Out on the Mojave she fights barrenness at every turn; here in Southern California she fights fertility." In the battle against fertility, the desert had been the target of every elemental force: oceans, earthquakes, volcanoes, winds, sands, and sunlight had all been "turned against it."[46] It had until this time endured, but Van Dyke would make no claim for permanence—for the desert or for the earth itself.

Nature "cares nothing for the individual man or bird or beast; can it be thought that she cares any more for the individual world?" Old life contributed matter to a new life; old worlds might offer raw material for new ones. A planet winding down might be a planet turning to desert. "Is then this great expanse of sand and rock the beginning of the end? Is that the way our globe shall perish?"[47]

The question is difficult, of course. And yet it suggested, in its almost playful arrangement of image and idea, a second, equally difficult question. Was John Van Dyke serious?

IX

For an individual eager to recognize the unknown and the uncertain in human experience, John Van Dyke had an odd habit of writing dogmatically. Each time he expressed his conviction in human insignificance, his prose escalated to a level of self-congratulatory craft that seemed to carry its own message. He described, for instance, the effect of desert silence on the individual.

> Was there ever such a stillness as that which rests upon the desert at night! Was there ever such a hush as that which steals from star to star across the firmament! You perhaps think to break the spell by raising your voice in a cry; but you will not do so again. The sound goes but a little way and then seems to come back to your ear with a suggestion of insanity about it.
>
> A cry in the night! Overhead the planets in their courses make no sound, the earth is still, the very animals are mute. Why then the cry of the human? How it jars the harmonies! How it breaks in a discord upon the unities of earth and air and sky! Century after century that cry has gone, up, mobbing high

> heaven; and always insanity in the cry, insanity in the
> crier. What folly to protest where none shall hear![48]

Protestations of insignificance aside, judging by the effortful grandeur
of the prose, one insignificant and ephemeral human, at least, was
taking himself quite seriously.

It seems clear that Van Dyke thought his style was artistic and
effective. For a later reader with different tastes, Van Dyke's ornate
effects make it close to impossible to judge his sincerity. There were,
after all, other reasons to suspect the authenticity of the sentiment.

The writer who could go into a fury over the commercial and
industrial exploitation of nature was the close friend of Andrew
Carnegie, and the family's choice to edit the industrialist's posthu-
mous autobiography. The author who expressed a reliable contempt
for "civilization" relied heavily on the use of universities, libraries,
art galleries, and travel facilities. The champion of misanthropy seemed
to have a very high opinion of his own human resources. Van Dyke,
evidently, had resolved his doubt about the human race by reversing
nature's priorities: he gave up on the species and reserved his respect
for a few individuals.

Van Dyke's consistent feminization of nature was also perplexing.
This entity had little in common with conventional social definitions
of femininity. The harshness of the desert did after all put a considerable strain on the image of a kind and nurturing Mother Nature.
In Van Dyke's portrait, nature was violent, utterly beyond either
giving or receiving affection, and equally devoted to overseeing the
death and the life of "her" creatures.

Perhaps Van Dyke was most revealing in his division of nature's
creative and destructive aspects. "The virile and healthy things of
the earth are hers; and so, too, are disease, dissolution, and death."[49]
Van Dyke had gone to the desert to seek relief from illness, apparently
a lung condition. Like many American male intellectuals at the turn
of the century, he was preoccupied with issues of strength and weakness, health and illness, virility and impotence. He evidently had
reasons to suspect himself of a leaning toward the negative side of
those opposites. But his own temperament, and the conventions of
turn-of-the-century nature writing, would hardly let him address those
issues directly. The result was a peculiar, unresolved handling of erotic

issues: a female source of creation who made sure to supply her children with the weapons needed for their own and each other's destruction, who oversaw their health and virility as well as their "disease and dissolution."

Van Dyke's attraction to death was a significant contrast to the behavior of William Ellsworth Smythe. Smythe had been fond of organic metaphors, attributing biological life histories to movements, institutions, and political units. But Smythe used only the first half of the organic metaphor: western states were in their "infancy," great causes were "born," institutions "sprouted" and "blossomed." No entity—biological or institutional—ever got past a ripe middle age. Smythe used the metaphors of life but rigidly censored their natural connection to metaphors of death.

Van Dyke practiced no such censorship. He clearly loved figures of speech derived from mortality. Prospects of human annihilation were his consolation and inspiration. While there were predators and challenges from the elements in all environments, the desert gave Van Dyke his most exhilarating glimpses of life always operating on the edge of mortality.

Viewed in a nonhuman time scale, a dimension Van Dyke was always delighted to enter, the desert came to life, reversing its usual image of inert vacancy. Geologically and biologically, it was far from dead space. The "character of the country," a phrase Frémont and others had used casually and with no special emphasis, was Van Dyke's discovery. For all its diversity, this collection of rocks, soil, scarce water, and plants and animals coalesced into an entity, with its own processes, rules, rewards, and penalties.

There was no reason to be disturbed by this entity, Van Dyke insisted. "As for fear," he reminisced in 1922, "there was nothing to be afraid of except my own decisions about water. The fear of man was wholly eliminated."[50]

On the overland trail in the nineteenth century, the formula seemed to be clear: If you liked human beings, you hated the desert. Quite true, Van Dyke seemed to be saying, and if you had your reservations about human beings, you would love the desert.

CHAPTER SIX
George Wharton James

I

In 1889, the Methodist minister George Wharton James found himself in need of a new career.[1]

Born in 1858 in England, James married Emma Smith in 1880 and in the next year emigrated to America. His first ministerial job was in the mining camps of Nevada. His wife joined him, but she remained attached to England and resentful of her exile in sagebrush deserts. After a brief return to England, in 1888 the family settled in Long Beach, California, where James was the pastor of the town's thriving Methodist church.

In 1889, Emma James sued for divorce. The case claimed the attention of Southern California newspapers, as she accused her husband of remarkable feats of adultery and deception. James responded in kind. In 1890, he left Southern California—divorced, defrocked, and emotionally devastated.

He took refuge, finally, in the desert. In Arizona and New Mexico, he found a tranquility he badly needed. After his debacle in human relations, the appeal of the desert lay precisely in its desertedness.

After his recovery, James resurfaced with a new profession. His "ministry" now involved the recruiting and guiding of tourists. His flock was drawn from the American middle class—men and women with a surplus of leisure and savings available for investment in recreation. Over the years, James wrote more than forty books and innumerable articles addressed to that audience. In 1906, he pub-

113

lished *The Wonders of the Colorado Desert,* his most comprehensive statement on the desert.

He kept his ministerial skills in good working order with frequent lecture tours. He was a striking and handsome man, with features well able to support imposing expressions and commanding gestures. His voice was strong and resonant, and one can well imagine that phrases that appear inert in print struck live audiences with force.

In 1895, James remarried and settled in Pasadena. He had made an extraordinary return to respectability after his earlier disgrace. While he spoke frequently of the physically and psychologically healing properties of the deserts, he did not record a straightforward account of the disruption of his own life. He had the tightest boundaries drawn around authentic self-disclosure. Whatever wounds he might be concealing, James held to a public tone of hearty self-confidence.

Holding to one tone, James, of course, risked monotone. Whether he discussed indigenous desert vegetation or irrigated crops, he kept his features in the same set expression: a pleasant smile of appreciation. Like any expression held continuously, this one started to wear. Such a uniformity of response to everything—deserts and date farms, fields of cactus and fields of cotton—began to call all response into question. If the appreciator saw everything with this bland and verbose enthusiasm, was there any evidence that he was seeing at all?

When James hit on something he particularly admired, his only way to convey this was to turn up the volume, to take the familiar note of appreciation and italicize it. Reading this sort of passage—for instance, James on a dramatic sunrise—is not a very moving experience for the elemental reason that there is no movement involved. James's feelings did not move or change; they only got louder.

Worked up to his most persuasive, James resorted to his favorite device—the list. Did he ever feel "solitary" in the desert? "No!" Many entities kept him company: a "majestic mountain," springs, burros, coyotes, lizards, "an occasional rattlesnake to watch, to follow and to kill," a stream, palm trees. The list begun, James raised his question:

—can one be solitary with such companions as these, especially when, in addition, he has such stars and skies as the city dweller never sees; such a horizon as only the desert dweller knows; such sunrises and evening glows as only angels can understand the glory of; such silences; such voices out of the far away; such weirdness; such mystery; such storms; such calms? Ah no! there is no solitude in such presences for is not one with himself, with his ideals, with his dreams, with his ambitions, with the great ones of the past, and the great ones of the future, with the achievements and life of the ages, and better than all, with the source and origin of it all, with God?[2]

Could one be solitary with such presences? Obviously not; the desert seemed to be positively crowded, congested with nonstop spectacles, emotions, past and future heroes, all human achievement, *and* the deity. The desert might still look deserted to the uninformed, but wherever James was or had been, an imagined audience and crowded prose traveled with him.

At times, in this literary bombardment, James sounded like a disciple of John Van Dyke; at other times, a disciple of W. E. Smythe. He recorded his fondness for untouched desert, and his enthusiasm for commercial development, without any apparent sense of contradiction.[3]

His contradictions did not handicap his career. In fact, they probably enhanced it. Some individuals at the turn of the century may have declared themselves to be strictly preservationists or strictly utilitarian businessmen. More frequently, individuals combined a sentimental fondness for nature with a practical interest in commercial development and reclamation. In George Wharton James's mind, these contradictory components of popular enthusiasm were held suspended in a general tone of free-floating appreciation.

Having mastered contradiction, James played a leading role in popularizing the American Southwest. His books typified the literature of description and promotion. Reading them carefully and thoughtfully is an exercise in irritation, but they were not meant to be read with care or thought. He wrote big books. Their size was in part the result of a willingness to quote other writers—in bulk. In certain sections, James seemed to have brought the act of producing a book closer to clipping and pasting than writing. His own words threw an extraordinarily loose net of words at objects and experiences. One reads a James book with the disheartening certainty that this man never revised, never reduced two words to one, never looked back at all.

James's prose was evidently not an irritation to publishers.[4] Little, Brown and Company in Boston and Dodd, Mead and Company in New York were both pleased to publish his books. The Page Company in Boston cheerfully backed James in a series of description books on southwestern states. *Craftsman Magazine* and *Out West* enjoyed James's services as an editor and regular contributor. The operators of resorts, railroads, and land companies found abundant reason to value James's literary services. Promoters, if they could not raise the funds to buy his services, could use his writing style as a model of what sold.

With George Wharton James, a writing style that could work compliantly with the monetary motive was finally applied to the desert. Describing the Southwest was the way James made his own living, but he intended his descriptions to produce livelihoods for many others. For thirty years, James did his best to get the arid Southwest on record as a frontier of economic opportunity.

The region had to be made attractive for tourism and for settlement. Encouraging tourism meant a stress on the exotic attractions of the unchanged desert. Encouraging settlement meant a stress on the attractions of the desert remodeled and tamed through irrigation and town-building. The two purposes required two postures. In his passive stance, James would admire and describe natural settings. In his active stance, he would admire and promote commercial development. In neither description nor promotion would James have any recognizable individuality. Although he would make frequent use of the pronoun *I*, his observations and feelings would remain safely generalized. On the evidence of his books alone, it would be no surprise to learn that the entity known as "George Wharton James" was actually a committee of promotional writers.

II

George Wharton James and his God were on the best of terms. They had the same blandly amiable personalities; they inspected the world with the same free-floating approval; they left trails of unnoticed contradictions behind them. Religion did not raise James to a transcendant overview of earthly concerns. Instead, he took possession of religion and tailored it to his size and needs. When necessary, the Creator of the desert joined James as an enthusiastic backer of irrigation and progress. The church may have revoked James's right to occupy a Methodist pulpit, but no one had rescinded his right to preach.[5]

In the world according to James, heaven and earth no longer had mysteries; they had "surprises." As desert "surprises" or "wonders," James included all manner of natural objects and qualities, everything from the clarity of the atmosphere, the brightness of the stars, the coolness of the night, the sudden appearance of rain, to the odor of sage. A "surprise," evidently, occurred when a natural event or object undercut or reversed expectation in a safe and insignificant way.[6]

The desert had been "surprising" Americans since the 1820s, undercutting and reversing their expectations in unsettling and even life-threatening ways. The stagecoaches and railroads had changed the conditions of the American encounter with the desert to the point where "surprises" could be enjoyed. The key change was the diminishing of individual physical vulnerability. With survival removed from contingency, Americans like James showed a new tolerance—and even appetite—for measured doses of uncertainty.

James knew what "surprises" were good for. They kept "one's emotions and sensations of body, mind and soul, alert and awake, sensitive and receptive." Left to its own resources, the mind always risked becoming "accustomed" or "blasé." "Surprises" jogged the mind back to life, and this worked both for individuals and for groups. "We are a mentally alert nation in some lines," James said, "yet in others we are asleep and inert." The nation itself was in need of the tonic of the desert's "surprises." In fact, James claimed, the desert had been "waiting for us to know and understand when we first took possession of it." And yet the nation had "neglected it," "flouted it," "steadily refused to cultivate its acquaintance." Why?[7]

Nation and desert had not been introduced. And here in 1906 was George Wharton James, ready to make the introductions and to recite the opening pleasantries—ready, in fact, to give the desert a voice and let it issue its own invitations. "The desert," James announced, "is the friend of man. To you, my dear reader, it calls and says, 'Come to me, know me, lean on my heart, and you shall gain new power, strength, courage and wisdom.' "[8]

This was the greatest "surprise" of all. Frémont, Manly, Twain, Smythe, and many Americans who shared their experiences and opinions had thought of the desert as an enemy or an oppressor, hardly as a friend. Even John Van Dyke, as an appreciator, had acknowledged and valued the desert's impersonality and intractability. But George Wharton James was not to be cowed. In his campaign to appreciate everything, he would take the formerly "hostile" and "inhospitable" desert and dress it up as a friend. With a mannered act of ventriloquism, he took over the silent desert and gave it the inviting words he wanted it to say.

If the desert could be imagined as friendly, it was a great gain for human self-confidence. It was also a good way of evading questions of power. The desert, James said, had been waiting to be understood since "we first took possession of it." It was not in the usual course of things for the relationship of property to evolve into the relationship of friendship. In human slavery, many masters were fond of remarking on the bonds of affection and friendship that united them to their possessions. Encouraging Americans to take possession of the desert, James evidently found a similar consolation in the metaphor of friendship.

In fact, *The Wonders of the Colorado Desert* was very much concerned with a power struggle, with a contest between Americans and the desert to see who could take possession of whom. The pivot of the struggle was the desert's water supply.

James's description of desert rivers indicated the terms of the battle. River behavior was "capricious, uncertain, wilful, and destructive." Rivers went from "flooding," "washing out roads, carrying away bridges and railway tracks, destroying irrigating aqueducts and ditches, and ruining growing crops" to suddenly "ceasing entirely." James's judgment was absolute: like "the sterile country through which they pass, they must be tamed and made subject to the will of man before they will yield anything of beauty to the landscape, nourishment to the soil, or comfort to mankind."[9] Like Twain, James found desert rivers to be betrayals of the concept *river*—lawless, ill-behaved, and certainly not "friendly." They were the battlegrounds for the struggles between the wild desert and the will of man.

When the struggle was over, and the Colorado River was "tamed and subject to the will of man," there would be "room for hundreds of thousands" of homeseekers. "Thousands of acres of fertile land" only awaited "the magic touch of the vivifying fluid to produce abundantly." The vision brought as much gratification to James as it had to William Ellsworth Smythe. The struggle demonstrated the "indomitable energy," the "dauntless courage," and the "persistent effort" which men "were capable of making in order to carry out their inflexible will."[10]

For all his celebration of human heroism, James wrote at the time of an awkward event in the power stuggle.[11] In 1901, the California Development Company, under the direction of Engineer Charles Rockwood, had attempted to divert Colorado River water to the Imperial Valley agricultural project. In 1905, the Colorado left its main channel and entered at full force the cut in the bank made for the Imperial Valley development. Rushing into the desert, the river began to form the inland lake known as the Salton Sea. While Rockwood and staff had found it easy to make the initial cut in the bank, the sequence seemed impossible to reverse. As James wrote his book, celebrating "the inflexible will of man," the river continued to flow into the Salton Basin, flooding farms and towns.

The Salton Sea was thus a constant and disturbing presence in James's book. "Can this really be a body of water," James asked, "or is it only a fiction of a disordered brain?" It was, alas, a fact of disordered human plans. "It was with a singular feeling," James said, "that I saw the slowly oncoming waters drive back the tokens of an advancing civilization."[12]

Telegraph poles and railroad tracks were gradually undergoing immersion. The metaphor of immersion was one to which James often referred in a positive way: the immersion of the body in a soothing hot spring, the immersion of the self in the solitude of the desert. But this was all too literal—a reversal of power in which the desert seemed to have gained control of the crucial weapon of water in order to use it against civilization.

The process had an unsettling, prehistoric dimension. James knew of the earlier geologic time when the Colorado Basin had been an inland sea. The ancient channel connecting the river to the sea was, he said, very near the channel Rockwood had cut and the Colorado had appropriated. The unhappy Rockwood, therefore, was "merely doing what Nature had done centuries before." The point of view might have delighted John Van Dyke, but it neither reassured nor consoled James. "Unfortunately," he noted, "the conditions now are not so simple."[13]

The conditions were, in fact, so complex that James himself was prey to doubt. Looking at the Salton Sea, he said, "we cannot help the queries which force themselves upon us as we think how it has slowly crept up, inch by inch, during the past months: 'Will this new sea take the place of the old? If so, what will become of the works of man in this valley?' " At the time James sent in his manuscript, there were simply no answers. "Desperate efforts" to "control the unexpected flood" were under way, but their success was without guarantee.[14]

James could not resign the question to uncertainty. He preferred the prophetic voice. "I believe the Colorado will be returned to its old channel," he declared. "Man with his power and wisdom has set himself the great task. He will accomplish it." "Development" might have suffered a "decided arresting," but the river would soon "be diverted into channels of usefulness and fertility." Then, "instead of a great inland sea, we shall live to gaze upon a vast territory of cultivated lands occupied by a busy, healthy, happy, and prosperous people."[15]

If words could control rivers, George Wharton James had done everything possible to talk the Colorado back into its channel. The river did not appear to notice.

III

William Lewis Manly and his fellows did not find the desert beneficial to their health. On the contrary, it threatened to kill them.

In a few brief decades, the desert had turned healthy. "A wiser selection of a location for a health-seeker," James said, "one could scarcely find." Choosing the desert, the invalid could gain a measure of power over illness and the experience of impotence and vulnerability it represented. To move to the desert to live in "the sweetest, purest, balmiest, and most healing atmosphere of earth," was "to rationally compel health."[16]

"To see a man of mental power and activity" brought by disease "to a state of physical emaciation and exhaustion, mental inertness and spiritual quiescence, is to be filled," James said, "with despair." To see "this poor, decrepit creature" brought to the desert, "subject to the direct vivification of sun, wind, and dry air, and then to watch his sure recovery to health, strength, courage, power, and usefulness"—this was "to see the dying brought back to life."[17] Weakness and powerlessness were the intolerable effect of disease, and the choice of the desert was, James claimed, the vital step in resisting the drift to helplessness and death.

Elsewhere, James admitted the limits of the desert's therapeutic powers. Sketching a plan for a sanitarium, he noted he would admit only "those who are in the *earlier stages* of pulmonary and bronchial affections" (his emphasis).[18] Individuals with more severe ailments might test the desert's healing power at their own risk.

For all his enthusiasm for the desert as a "manufactory of health," James also followed the usual association of the desert with death. He enjoyed sketching the hazards of desert travel. "Many a poor wretch has been lost to the world forever in the treacherous secrecy of those sand-hills," James said. "Unthinkingly he has gone to his death,—been overpowered by the heat and thirst, and unable to find his way out, has fallen, to be covered almost immediately by the drifting sand and thus suffocated while unconscious."[19]

Repeatedly, James offered little sketches of the typical decline, through disorientation, to death. In incident after incident, individuals who were "too bold, too confident," faced heat, blowing sand, thirst, exhaustion, and finally death.[20] An ignorant confidence was the mechanism by which fools sacrificed themselves to the desert.

The victims in these imagined deaths were often prospectors. When James took the desert prospector and afflicted him with illness, the resulting passage carried a clear sense that the author found such a death both titillating and unnerving. If the prospector should fall ill, "who is there out in that forsaken place to care for him?" Earlier declarations on the health-restoring power of the desert were no longer operative. Alone, the invalid grows "weaker day by day," "too weak to gather wood, to go for water, to light a fire." Rattlesnakes nestle near him; "lizards run over his face"; rats approach; and finally "a great, black, bald-headed bird with hideous beak and great bleary eyes swoops down upon him, and dreams and dreamer are at an end."[21] James, in other words, milked desert death for every shudder, tracing the individual's growing weakness and the desert's growing power. Death was immersion—being surrounded and overcome by desert forces and presences.

Why on earth would prospectors run this risk? The answer, James thought, was clear: "There is no desert, however terrible in its natural conditions, that man will not dare if thereby he may gain gold." Delicately sensitive to "surprises" as James was, he found this willingness to face danger "not surprising." The prospector was "a dreamer," "an idealist." He could "see in these inhospitable, barren plains or these dreary, sandy deserts or these rough and rugged slopes pockets of the precious metals." He could see even further—to visions of "his wife in silks, satins, and diamonds," "a brownstone front, with lackeys innumerable," and the prospector himself the master of "this lordly mansion, giving orders with consciousness of power and right."[22] Visions of future abundance kept the prospector willing to submit to scarcity, with the fond faith that his privation was temporary.

Hardship was bearable because the prospector had deciphered the desert. "A place which is obviously so cursed that nothing will grow on it must have been created by the Lord of all things for some purpose," the prospector reasoned, "and the only purpose it could possibly have was to carry mineral hidden somewhere below its forbidding surface."[23]

In the prospector, James had found a very appropriate American hero for the desert. He was an "idealist" and a "visionary" whose ideals and visions fitted amiably into the materialistic ambitions of the American middle class. Capable of enduring great privation and hardship, his heroism had a straightforward and secular motive. Like so many other good Americans, he simply wanted to be rich.

IV

"The desert," James said, was "God's color showroom." It was "His divine exhibition salon to which He freely invites all men . . . to see beauty in all its nakedness." The display would be comprehended "only by those souls that love the real more than the false, the simple more than the complex, the nakedness of Nature more than the prudery of Man."[24]

Repeatedly, James indicated that life in the desert was more "real" than life elsewhere. Desert-lovers, he said, had chosen "the larger, fuller, realer life."[25] While he might long for the authenticity he attributed to the desert, James wished for it the way the prospector wished for riches. The prospector lived a life of scarcity while hoping for abundance; James seemed to have lived a life of artificiality while hoping for authenticity. For all his admiration of the desert as a type of the "real," he was himself caught up in windy rhetoric and formulaic declarations of conviction.

It was sometimes James's habit to pose contrasts between the "real" desert and "artificial" civilization, typified in the city. In cities, "everything is conventional, fictitious, unnatural." "I have felt more solitary and alone, more utterly desolate and forsaken," James said, "when walking through the streets of London and Paris, New York and Chicago, than I have ever felt in my years of desert experiences."[26] Cities were the model of what was wrong with civilization, and what was right with the desert.

And yet James was happy to applaud the expansion of towns into the Colorado Desert, and to lament the drowning of civilization by the rampaging Colorado River. Similarly, when he traced the agonies of lost prospectors, their deaths hinged on the failure "to get back to civilization." Civilization, far from being the poisonous and confining cities James abused so regularly, would have been the individual's refuge. James was happy to engage in a ritualized mockery of life in the city, while, he acknowledged, he lived in Pasadena and spent weekends in the desert.

Tranquility in the midst of self-contradiction was, in many ways, James's stock in trade; one route to that tranquility was his reliance on the list or inventory as a major structuring device. In his chapters on desert plants and animals, James simply catalogued, with a few lines of description per item.[27] The effect of listing the desert's contents was to separate and compartmentalize every subject. The possibility of connection—even the basic exchanges of the food chain— went without recognition. The result was a desert without relations, without effects or consequences.

For all his inconsistency, James was a crucial figure in the transformation of attitudes: from the vulnerability of the overland travelers to the complacency of twentieth-century desert residents. That transition required a considerable readjustment of the mechanisms of popular thought. James, as a successful popularizer and publicist, was one of the preeminent mechanics, realigning the relationship between Americans and deserts.

When the Colorado River broke loose and began to form the Salton Sea, George Wharton James kept to his faith in the human mastery of the desert's resources. In the midst of one of the worst setbacks in the "conquest" of arid America, James still found a refuge in complacency. In the long run, he made it clear, setbacks like the Salton Sea break were only temporary interruptions in a guaranteed victory; they were virtually nature's equivalent to the futile last rebellions of the western Indians. They made good stories, but they did not shift the balance of power.

How then did James help to make the transition from vulnerability to complacency? First, he reduced the significance of personal biological vulnerability and transformed contact with the desert into a generalized, primarily visual sensation. This was made possible in part by the creation of a phantom narrator. When James recounted "his" desert travels, he explained that two assistants had helped him. "Sometimes one and sometimes another wrote the description; sometimes one went alone, sometimes all of us together; but to secure uniformity in the narratives I have written all the accounts in the first person and as if we had all been together."[28] The narratives condensed to a series of views; the desert trips might have been made by conveyor belt for all the sense of motion or exertion they carried. James performed the act of literary self-amputation explicitly in these narratives, but the pattern ran through the whole book. Nearly every sentence could have been composed by committee. The intense, often painful sense of personal involvement that characterized the overland narratives had disappeared entirely. The dust, heat, and thirst that had assailed the earlier travelers could hardly find a target to hit.

Second, James transformed the fearful qualities of aridity into quaint details, reducing the desert's unpredictability and hardship to the status of "surprises," measured doses of uncertainty and novelty.

Third, he stepped away from the question of the desert's origin and purpose. Instead of a part of the Creator's work that might force a change in American behavior, and even in the understanding of the Creator's purposes, the desert became just another valuable gift to the nation from a good-natured and indulgent God.

Fourth, James happily ignored human diversity, and especially conflicting claims to the use of water. In the significant alignment of power, there were two characters: "man" and "the desert." The conflicts visible in James's own times—the conflicts between public and private irrigation projects, between municipal users and agricultural users—simply did not penetrate to the text. Overland travelers recognized that aridity meant hard choices in loyalty and in the allocation of scarce resources; James preferred not to notice.

Fifth, James made it clear that contradictions in attitude did not need to be disposed of by discarding one proposition in the interest of consistent loyalty to the other. Contradictions cease to trouble their holders, not necessarily when they are resolved, but when they are captured in formulae. For all his proclamations as an appreciator of the "uncontaminated" desert, James could put aside that sentiment at the mere thought of a progressive human enterprise like reclamation. Any mention of irrigated farming carried its contrasting description of the formerly "useless," "valueless," or "sterile" desert. Even when farming was not at issue, James was likely to describe the desert as "gaunt, harsh and desolate," or "forbidding, barren and terrible."[29] He swung randomly between characterizing the desert as beautiful, gentle, and healthful, and as hostile, deadly, and harsh. In all his vacillations, one thing was clear: this was a form of appreciation which posed no obstacle to "progress."

For a writer who dealt so wholeheartedly in contradiction and confusion, James has been very charitably judged by posterity. One literary historian has admired James's "masterful prose" and "virile character." His "defiant, hard-won optimism," another claimed, "gave conviction to James's prose."[30] After an inspection of James's writing, one responds to the claim with a bewildered question: "But conviction in what?"

There is one way of understanding the generosity with which James has been judged. The combination of attitudes he represents—an appreciation for nature and an appreciation for American enterprise—was by no means unique to him. Like James, his admirers in the mid-twentieth century were equally disinclined to perceive contradiction or strain in loyalty extended both to nature and to the growth of the American economy.

"Some years ago," James wrote of his transformed career, "I used to preach sermons regularly, taking my text from God's other book, His world—Nature."[31] Preach, James certainly did, evidently on the assumption that both texts had clear and undisputed meanings.

In James's mind, the desert did have a clear meaning. It just happened to be split in two: the angry, resistant desert still in need of taming, and the friendly, receptive desert in need of understanding. If anyone was going to figure out the relation between these two deserts, it was not going to be George Wharton James.

CHAPTER SEVEN
Joseph Wood Krutch

I

In 1929, Joseph Wood Krutch did not like deserts. In a book called *The Modern Temper,* Krutch went on record with a vision of humanity misplaced in a meaningless universe. When he wanted an analogy for despair and alienation, he turned to nature. The human world, he declared, was becoming "more and more a desert."[1]

With his horror of the impersonality and inhumanity of nature, Krutch did not seem to be a candidate to lead the cause of desert appreciation. With or without deserts, Krutch's prospects for recovery from pessimism were not promising. "Most of my subsequent intellectual history," he himself said, "has been an attempt to climb out of the pit into which I had led myself."[2]

For many nineteenth-century Americans, traveling into the desert meant traveling into doubt and despair. Joseph Wood Krutch reversed the sequence. Solidly committed to pessimism long before he saw a desert, Krutch found that the desert provided him with a route of escape from the "pit" of "skepticism" and "alienation."

Joseph Wood Krutch took intellectual dilemmas seriously. Born in 1893 in Lexington, Kentucky, Krutch wrote drama criticism for the *Nation* and taught dramatic literature at Columbia, where he had received his Ph.D. He was thirty-six years old when his gloomy book, *The Modern Temper,* was published. During the next year, he went on a lecture tour to discuss his book. Arriving in Detroit, he was met by the president of a women's club. "She approached me," Krutch remembered, "only after every other descending passenger had left the platform. 'Are *you* Mr. Krutch?' 'I am.' Her face fell. 'But you do not look as, as—*depressed* as I expected.' "[3]

The lady did not know that Krutch had already taken a step to recovery. Writing *The Modern Temper*, Krutch had purchased a microscope. Why? "If," he said to himself, "this book is a failure, I will devote myself to microscopy."[4] The ironies of this choice were enormous. His book was in many ways a lament for the damage that the revelations of science had done to human dignity. In the stress of writing, Krutch consoled himself with the acquisition of one of science's archetypal instruments.

Along with the microscope, Krutch also took on Henry David Thoreau. Returning from his lecture tour, he kept himself occupied by reading *Walden*. Then, at his wife's suggestion, Krutch moved from New York City to rural Connecticut, where he began to enjoy direct opportunities to observe nature.

Krutch published a biography of Thoreau in 1948. Soon after completing that book, he was reading a "nature essay." "It suddenly occurred to me," he remembered, "to wonder if I could do something of the sort."[5] *The Twelve Seasons*, observations of Krutch's rural Connecticut home, appeared in 1949.

By that time, Krutch was spending two or three days a week at Columbia and retreating to Connecticut. Increasingly, Connecticut was an unsatisfactory refuge. Allergies and respiratory problems beset Krutch in both city and countryside. In 1950, he had a sabbatical year and a chance for temporary relocation. In a long tradition of sufferers from respiratory problems, he chose Arizona, where he had vacationed briefly before World War II.

Krutch and his wife spent the year 1950–51 in Tucson, while he wrote *The Desert Year* (1952). After a final year in the East, he left Columbia and moved to Tucson, preparing to make his living solely by writing. Over the next years, desert areas provided him with material for several books: *The Voice of the Desert* (1954), *Grand Canyon* (1957), and *Forgotten Peninsula* (1961). His continued reflections on the condition of humanity resulted in several more books on the themes of *The Modern Temper*, all of them framed by a complicated combination of hope and melancholy, faith and doubt.

II

The Modern Temper was Krutch's obituary for faith and for meaning in contemporary Western civilization. Humans had once thought themselves to be significant—rightful occupants of a universe that valued and recognized their existence. In a "primitive" or "barbaric" state, faith in their own significance gave humans an animal vitality. As they pursued the mastery of nature and the refinement of civilization, their growing knowledge of the universe revealed a world which was alarmingly independent of human needs and values. Nature's goals had little to do with human hopes. Animate nature simply pursued nutrition and reproduction; individual organisms died, but the general processes of nature did not register grief or loss. Humans were simply another variety of animal and their lives and deaths were equally irrelevant to the life of the planet.

As the project of civilization succeeded, knowledge of the processes of the universe reduced the opportunity for irrational faith. Eventually every civilization ended in the same dilemma: devitalized by science, sophistication, relativism, and skepticism. No individual or group could will a return to the animal vitality and ignorant confidence of the primitive stages. The human project, Krutch declared, was "a lost cause."[6]

Nature, for Krutch in 1929, was fertility personified—"a desire merely to live and to propagate in innumerable forms."[7] This was reproductive energy operating without any limits of good sense or good taste. The counterpart of fertility was mortality: such a profligate production of life required an equally profligate use of death to make room for the next, equally temporary arrivals.

This line of thought led Krutch to declarations that would seem to have disqualified him for all time as a potential nature-lover. "Nature, in her blind thirst for life," he said, "has filled every possible cranny of the rotting earth with some sort of fantastic creature, and among them man is but one."[8]

With human dignity under siege, nature even invaded man's terrain, controlling and trivializing his behavior through his sexuality. The placing of human consciousness in animal bodies was perhaps nature's cruelest stroke. At earlier stages, humans might believe in the illusion of love. With the loss of illusions, the noble passion of "love" turned out to be merely a "biological urge." With aspirations for a higher life, humans were driven to self-betrayal by their relentlessly biological bodies.[9]

"Primitive" or "barbarian" people, with their vitality intact, were still deeply concerned with the processes of making a living. When "food, clothes and warmth are considered merely as instruments," civilization was in trouble. Krutch, in other words, saw material abundance as a precondition of modern despair. "Despair of the sort which has been described," he admitted, "is a luxury in the sense that it is possible only to those who have much that many people do without, and philosophical pessimism, dry as it may leave the soul, is more easily endured than hunger or cold."[10]

At the end of the prosperous 1920s, Krutch was not anticipating the onset of an economic depression. Material abundance he treated as given; the remaining problems for Western civilization were intellectual, emotional, or spiritual. He stayed close to that assumption for years afterwards. One suspects that economic issues simply bored him. Never facing privation himself, he was not noticeably interested in the dilemma of the financially disadvantaged. The provision of food and shelter was a settled issue in his mind; that aspect of human biological character did not interest him. To the same degree, political issues connected to production and distribution were of no particular interest. Political issues could only appear small and local in the scale of an alien universe and the lost soul of man.

On that scale, even if humans were finally powerless, Krutch awarded them one final achievement. "We know at least that we have discovered the trick which has been played upon us," Krutch said. "Whatever else we may be, we are no longer dupes."[11] In an absurd universe, defeated on all fronts, humans would at least refuse to be fooled.

Krutch had appointed himself the spokesman for a people defeated but refusing submission. "Ours is a lost cause and there is no place for us in the natural universe," he said, "but we are not, for all that, sorry to be human. We should rather die as men than live as animals."[12] The "lost cause" required that its supporters reject both illusion and survival.

The "phantom of certitude," Krutch said, was permanently out of reach for Western man.[13] This was the bedrock paradox of Krutch's thinking: in a voice of authority and certainty, he asserted the impossibility of faith and certitude. The declarations of science, Krutch felt, had to be absolutely credited. If science revealed a universe that was not run for human benefit, the revelation had to be accepted, even if the acceptance meant debilitation and death.

What was the difference between religious faith and scientific certainty? Faith catered to the human sense of dignity and significance and was thus an illusion. Scientific certainty mocked both dignity and human signficance and was thus reality. To a degree, the principle here was comparable to judging the effectiveness of a medicine by the nastiness of its taste: whatever went down easily was suspect.

From points of view other than Krutch's, the message of science was not an utterly hopeless one. Man "has exchanged the universe which his desires created, the universe made for man, for the universe of nature of which he is only a part. Like the child growing into manhood, he passes from a world which is fitted to him to a universe for which he must fit himself."[14] From the point of view of late-twentieth-century environmentalism, this was hardly an unreasonable request. But to Krutch in 1929, power, strength, and dignity lay in the condition of humanity-as-child; and impotence and damaged dignity were the rewards of adulthood.

The only, limited refuge was in art. What marked the worlds created by art, in contrast to the world of nature, were the qualities of wholeness, harmony, or consistency, organized by one creative intelligence. Art, alas, could not be used as a guide to living. The whole and complete world created by the human imagination was the antithesis of the actual world.[15]

Ironically, *The Modern Temper* was itself a work of "art" constructed by human imagination. For all Krutch's proclamations that "certitude" was a "phantom," he was quite certain that his portrait of the nature of the universe and the position of modern man was an accurate one. His book created a whole and consistent world, and the fact that the world so created was a trap and a mechanism for paralyzing human will did not reduce its wholeness.

The Modern Temper, Krutch thought, captured reality. But his own statements undermined that claim. "The contact of the human mind with reality," he said in a moment of radical skepticism, "is so slight that two thousands of years of epistemology have not been able to decide what the nexus is, and it is easier to argue that our consciousness exists in utter isolation than to prove that it is actually aware of the external phenomena by which it is surrounded."[16] Doubting the possibility of genuine perception of matter, Krutch was nonetheless certain he had figured life out.

III

When Krutch went to the desert, he went with the understanding that strategies and mechanisms of perception could never be taken for granted. Something seen in nature, he said, "never means much until it has become part of some general configuration, until it has become not a 'view' or a 'sight' but an integrated world of which one is a part; until one is what the biologist calls part of a biota."[17]

Was Krutch declaring his intention to live off the land, to make the desert his source of physical as well as spiritual sustenance? Had he left Columbia and the *Nation* in order to take up a hunting and gathering life as "part of the desert biota"? This was, needless to say, not what Krutch meant. He intended to live near Tucson, relying on the mass production and distribution systems of his culture. He was not, in any sense of Twain's phrase, interested in "roughing it."

In Krutch's mind, a human could become "a part" of "an integrated world" by an act of consciousness alone. While plants and animals earned their membership in "a biota" by physical adaptations, transplanted New York intellectuals could be considered to "fit in" simply by resolving to pay attention.

The very idea of "an integrated world" was itself a measure of the transformation of Krutch's ideas. In *The Modern Temper*, he had claimed that "integrated worlds" were possible only in art, when the intelligence of the author or artist created a world defined in opposition to the chaos of nature. Now Krutch had shifted ground: the "integrated world" was now the world of nature where creatures—

plants, animals, and humans—reflected their environment in the unified diversity of their adaptive choices.

Entry into this world did not require the sacrifice of individuality. The Sonoran Desert was a special world, appropriate only for certain individuals. If he did not come to know this desert, Krutch said, he would "feel all my life that I have missed something intended for me."[18] Words like *intended* suggested a possible religious dimension, but Krutch approached this very tentatively. Certainly the desert's charm was "physical," but there was also, he was sure, "a spiritual element. Nature's way here, her process and her moods, correspond to some mood which I find in myself." Even this modest statement earned a qualification. "If that sounds too mystical for some tastes," Krutch offered, "we can, perhaps, compromise on a different formulation. Something in myself can be projected upon the visible forms which nature assumes here."[19] If this was a form of theism, the desert pantheist had to work with a new and more subtle deity, a deity always forced to prove itself in the face of psychological reductiveness.

A stay in the desert, Krutch hoped, would allow him to discover "what it is that this land, together with the plants and animals who find its strangenesses normal, has been trying to say to me," and "what kinship with me they all so insistently claim." How was it that the author of *The Modern Temper*, preoccupied with the status of man as exile in the physical universe, could now feel a sense of "kinship" with nature? What did the desert creatures and Joseph Wood Krutch have in common? "Patience," "endurance," and "austerity," Krutch said, characterized the desert.[20] The same qualities had survival value for desert creatures and for veterans of twentieth-century alienation and despair, even with significant variations in the degree and kind of hardship they faced.

As a recently arrived observer, Krutch admitted having had "a certain romantic notion" that the desert was "for all its beauty, a hard and difficult land,—not I mean, that I expected any hardship, but merely that I should be living where nature and her children found it strenuous and difficult to live."[21] Krutch claimed his usual exemption from hardship; his ambition to be "a part of an integrated world" was, again, predicated on an assumption of emotional or intellectual solidarity, not to be confused with physical or nutritional adaptation.

Yet Krutch, in this case, intended to offer the exemption from hardship to other creatures. "For the desert birds and the desert animals," he said, "this is not an unfavorable environment." This was simply their home; "only to those who come from somewhere else is there anything abnormal about the conditions which prevail."[22] Adapted to their environment, desert residents redefined *normal* and learned to live with the new definition.

However easily Krutch could support the redefinition of *normal*, *adaptation* was not a word he could use complacently. "Its connotations are mechanical," he said, "and it alienates us from a life process which is thereby deprived of all emotional meaning." What was at stake in that deprivation? "What the plants and animals have actually been doing," he claimed, "is analogous to what we do."[23]

This line of thought led Krutch back to the issue which had preoccupied Frémont, Manly, Clemens, and other desert travelers: the question of the human connection to other animals. Unlike the nineteenth-century people, Krutch was unable to divide animal and human into utterly impenetrable categories. "No matter how much we may try," he said, "we cannot really separate our privileges and our predicaments from theirs. To think of them in merely mechanical terms is to come ultimately to think of ourselves in the same terms."[24] The question that preoccupied earlier desert travelers had now intersected with Krutch's old battle against the reductiveness of behavioral science and the damage done to human dignity by mechanistic explanations.

In 1929, Krutch had offered an impotent combination of submission and defiance, the proclamation of a lost cause. In 1952, Krutch's argument on behalf of human dignity would be one of extension. The crucial requirements for human dignity—choice, will, intention, freedom, even consciousness—would be extended to animals. Krutch's grounds for this extension could seem, to say the least, arbitrary. "Let us not say this animal or even this plant has 'become adapted' to desert conditions," he said. "Let us say rather that they all have shown courage and ingenuity in making the best of the world as they found it."[25] Rescuing humans from the indignity of animal status required elevating the dignity of animals.

For all his commitment to the common cause of humans and animals, Krutch did recognize a difference in their adaptations to aridity. "Animals and plants manage to survive on a quantity of water which would soon bring death by thirst to those of any other climate," Krutch noted; "man, on the other hand, digs wells, channels streams, and in one way or another manages so to modify external nature rather than himself that he uses approximately the same amount of water here as anywhere else." Krutch briefly acknowledged the greater vulnerability of the human solution, citing the earlier, irrigation-based Indian cultures: "when man does fail he fails utterly, as the story of the abandoned cliff dwelling tells so plainly."[26] With this failure acknowledged and no lesson drawn for contemporary American desert settlements, Krutch left humans behind and launched into a world of enterprising organisms who refused defeat and responded to scarcity with various strategies of water conservation.

Repeatedly, Krutch made use of words and phrases attributing intention, choice, and intelligence to plants and animals. Organisms "modify themselves," "learn the great art of doing without," "invent wings," "arrive at solutions," "remember ancient habits," "work out methods," and "adapt themselves."

How was this self-adaptation more than a poetic figure of speech? How could plants and animals be said to "learn" or "invent"? What Krutch did, in instances like this, was to play a temporal trick—to offer the history and development of a species over evolutionary time in terms appropriate to individual life history. In that way, mutation and selection over time became, in Krutch's phrasing, the learning of new habits, and the behavior of a species over millennia became the accomplishments of an individual plant or animal. Thus difficult desert conditions became opportunities for enterprise and creativity, not situations in which the inanimate bullied the living.

IV

The process by which Krutch made species history into individual history also worked in reverse. In human affairs, the dilemmas of the individual—notably, the dilemmas of Joseph Wood Krutch—became the dilemmas of the species.

Krutch had had his bouts with radical doubt, and those individual sieges shook the validity of all human perception. When, in the course of a desert year, Krutch went on an outing to a local mountain peak, the cause of human perception hung in the balance.

On this trip, Krutch half-mockingly acknowledged the religious resonance of such journeys. "In the legends of the saints, and prophets, either a desert or a mountain is pretty sure to figure." The combination was certain to be powerful: "If THE ANSWER is ever to be whispered into my willing ear, this should be the moment."[27] Having mocked the conventions of religious revelation satisfactorily, Krutch was still willing to admit that he left the peak philosophically enriched.

The power of the peak rested on its distance from the world of humans: "from where I stood there was no visible evidence that the earth was inhabited." An escape from the context of human life was, it turned out, an escape from Krutch's old enemy, behavioral science. "No man in the middle of a desert or on top of a mountain," Krutch insisted, "ever fell victim to the delusion that he himself was nothing except the product of social forces, that all he needed was a proper orientation in his economic group, or that production per man hour was a true index of happiness." As revelations go, this one might have seemed a bit prosaic, but it went further. "No such man . . . ," Krutch went on, "ever thought anything except that consciousness was the grandest of all facts." "No man in such a position," Krutch concluded, "ever doubted that he himself was a primary particle, an ultimate reality."[28]

Certainly many nineteenth-century Americans in deserts had contemplated a number of things besides "the grand fact of consciousness": the location of water, grass, and fuel, for instance, or the clues leading to mineral deposits. But this was a declaration, finally, of Krutch's experience, and in line with religious experience, the personal and the private were only a step away from the universal, with no intermediate stop at the collective and historical.

Proclaiming the centrality of consciousness, Krutch was making no retreat into solipsism. The restoration of consciousness was also a restoration of the natural world. Leaving the mountain top, Krutch took a last look at the purple glow of the sunset. To scientists, he claimed, the sunset would be "merely a subjective impression pro-duced in me by the fact that the sky *really was* transmitting to my eyes" not the color purple, but only "a rhythmic disturbance in the field of electric or gravitational force."[29]

For a time, Krutch had felt forced to yield his perception to the greater reality of the scientists. Now he wanted to fight back. "If the color purple exists only in me," he argued, "then that proves not only that I exist but proves a great deal more. It proves that there is something in the universe which would not be there if I were not." The self, purple, and the beauty of the sunset "were all there together. If one has already granted the first two, it is too late to deny the third."[30]

To assert a belief in the reality of color, the actuality of beauty, and the authenticity of consciousness was by no means, for Krutch, to assert the obvious. For a time in his intellectual history, physical actuality had been nearly reasoned out of existence. At the conver-gence of consciousness, light, and beauty, Krutch could escape doubt and skepticism. He had, he said "no impulse to do what the scientist would call 'probe deeper' into the realities of which I was aware." Perhaps perception was a matter of surfaces; "then on the surface is where I, and most human beings, are most truly at home."[31]

Humanity, in *The Modern Temper,* had been radically homeless, without a resting place in an alien universe. In *The Desert Year,* Krutch could at least imagine humanity "truly at home," trusting its weight to a surface that science continually threatened to break.

V

Like science, nature operated with certain precepts from which human dignity and integrity had to be defended. Nature worked on "the statistical criterion," pursuing "the greatest good of the greatest number." While contemporary social planners might imitate nature on this count, Krutch claimed for humanity's uniqueness the opposite value: a "concern with a mere individual."[32]

At a neighbor's swimming pool, rescuing a bat from drowning,

Krutch "had seen an individual bat as only man can see him." At Carlsbad Caverns, he thought he "had seen bats as nature sees them." Three hundred thousand bats swirling out of the cavern: this was what the female character nature, devoted to untrammeled reproduction, wanted. If one bat lost value in the midst of three hundred thousand bats, the same risk operated for humans. When humans submitted to "nature's insatiable appetite for more and more of every kind of creature," to "her immoderate desire for multiplication," they ran the risks of discovering that "men should not be too common if they are to have value."[33]

In this exhortation against fertility, Krutch's distinction between "man" and "nature" came close to defining a gender difference in ways of fighting mortality. While the profligate female character flooded the world with organisms, the chaste and careful male character set about the rescue and restoration of threatened individuals. In the meantime, the attraction of the desert gained new resonance: in the sparseness and scarcity of the desert, nature was on "her" best behavior, with "her" rampant fertility tempered for once by restraint and good taste.

This was, in fact, Krutch's answer to the long-running question, "what is the desert good for?" The purpose of the desert was to demonstrate an alternative to crowding, congestion, and struggle.

In more favorable environments, with unlimited water, "the struggle for existence is visibly the struggle of plant with plant, each battling his neighbor for sunlight" and space. In deserts, "the contest is not so much of plant against plant as of plant against inanimate nature." Since "the limiting factor [was] not the neighbor but water," the country had "a kind of peace."[34] The comparison, of course, neatly sidestepped the fact that the desert plants also struggled for place and resources, but the "battle" went on at root level. A view of the tranquil, uncrowded surface made it possible for Krutch to imagine a kind of solidarity among life forms, joined in a common cause against "inanimate nature."

Krutch felt no reservations about extending the lesson of the desert to the human world. "The human race," he said, had managed to "produce for itself a sort of artificial, technological jungle in which too many people can live somehow." In such an environment, "the struggle inevitably becomes ultimately the struggle of man against man, and not the struggle of man against nature."[35] Elsewhere Krutch would advocate empathy and cooperation with nature; here, he seemed to prefer, in the manner of William Ellsworth Smythe, a common war against nature in the interest of human solidarity.

In a world in which human population "escaped" from "the limit set to its multiplication by natural conditions," the intolerable consequences were both conflict and a diminished "respect for individuals." Krutch thus valued the desert precisely for the deprivations that had disturbed many earlier desert visitors. "The land simply will not support either too many people or too many mesquite trees," he said. "Hence we both have room."[36]

This lack of crowding was not a sign of "superior wisdom" in the human, animal, or vegetable kingdoms. "It is merely because, for all of us, the limit is sooner reached."[37] This was a view of the desert that had a long, if discontinuous history. In the early nineteenth century, explorers of the arid plains, Zebulon Pike and Stephen Long, had valued aridity as a limit on American expansion. In the intervening century, Americans had come to see aridity as a temporary obstacle to be conquered. Krutch, however, returned to the earlier view of aridity as a desirable limit.

Living outside Tucson, supported by an elaborate production and distribution system, Krutch seems to have lived with the happy idea that he had arrived just in time, just as desert population reached its comfortable peak. In the next ten years, this innocent conviction would be tested by Arizona's relentless population growth. But in 1952, the lesson of aridity was as clear to Krutch as it had been to Pike and Long. Aridity set self-evident limits, and this was what the desert was "good for."

VI

The desert's lessons came in "metaphors," opportunities for intellectual adventure comparable to interpreting "an essay by Emerson or a poem by Emily Dickinson."[38] Krutch's desert metaphors may have been illuminating, but they had a way of running to the abstract.

The basic temper, Krutch said, was one of "austerity." "In contemporary society, the all but universal ambition of the individual and the all but invariable aim of every proposed social or political movement is to get, for oneself or others, more *things*." The desert directly reversed this value: "the very fauna and flora proclaim that one can have a great deal of certain things while having very little of others; that one kind of scarcity is compatible with, perhaps even a necessary condition, of another kind of plenty." An "economy of abundance" was thus "a meaningless phrase" unless one asked "abundance of what?"[39]

In his times, Krutch declared, significant resources—physical space, leisure, contemplation, intellectuality, manners—were in short supply, and material goods were left to act as substitutes.

Krutch was not, he hastened to point out, advocating economic deprivation. "I am no ascetic," he said. "I am not praising want."[40] He was simply pointing out the desert's metaphorical lesson: material scarcity was highly compatible with spiritual abundance.

Developing ·this metaphor, Krutch kept scarcity at a comfortably abstract distance, with a complacent assumption of an assured subsistence. In these terms, desert scarcity was a visual and philosophical prospect to be admired, and not a physical fact to be dreaded.

The desert grasslands—land with enough forage to support a sparse collection of cattle—provided Krutch with another, similarly abstract exercise in metaphor. Ownership of these lands, Krutch argued, did not restrict the freedom of nonowners. "The wanderer," he said, "could not raise cattle or dig mines" on the land, but "he may exploit its spiritual resources as freely as he is able." Krutch had thus been able to take possession of vast units of land, an extent of property he never expected "to own in any legal sense."[41]

Lest anyone attribute a dangerous radicalism to these ideas, Krutch insisted on a clarification: "It is not, I hasten to add, that my idea approaches any sort of communism." "The metaphor of the grasslands" turned out to be an economic proposition no desert propertyowner needed to fear. "One can own, either rightfully or fruitfully, only those things—and only so much of a thing—as one can come into intimate relationship with," Krutch declared. ". . . One can own only what one loves, and love is always some sort of reciprocal relationship."[42]

Violations of this proposition need not be corrected with punishment or with redistribution of wealth. The rich, it seems, were only to be pitied for their failure to attain genuine, spiritual ownership. In the case of the desert, authentic ownership came to those with the proper aesthetic receptivity, while the legal property owners simply held irrelevant paper titles to the land.

Krutch's easy dismissal of the actual control of property was probably his most remarkable accomplishment in the sidestepping of economic and political issues. He had, in 1952, a cheerful faith in the limited usefulness of desert property. Confined to low-density cattle-raising, landowners would have little effect on their land, Krutch thought. Exploring his "metaphor of the grasslands," Krutch was oblivious to nonmetaphorical overgrazing, not to mention the possibilities of spreading cities and subdivisions, mining, dams, and coal-fired generating plants. For serious advocates of conservation and preservation, the power of private property presented dilemmas and obstacles that could not be controlled by the substitution of a more attractive metaphor. For Krutch in 1952, ownership in "the metaphor of the grasslands" had the same distant abstractness that scarcity had in "the metaphor of the desert." The meanings of the metaphors were easy to find in proportion of how little was really at stake.

Krutch spent his year in the southern deserts, regions tractable enough to permit conventional American towns and cities to develop, tamed enough to allow American writers to treat scarcity as a metaphor. The northern canyonlands were, Krutch realized, dramatically less tractable and tamed, and correspondingly less conducive to comfortable interpretation. In the Utah canyonlands, "the earth defies man to live upon it, and for the most part he has not challenged the defiance."[43]

With the help of a hired guide and jeep, Krutch was willing to attempt a brief visit. "The fact that I never have stayed long," he admitted, ". . . may be the consequence of a certain defensive reaction." The "alien" beauty of the canyonlands was like the beauty of the stars: "it is not well to be too continuously aware of such things, and we must take refuge from them with the small and the familiar."[44] Even a declared lover of deserts, in other words, could find his affection too severely tested by this extreme landscape.

Despite occasional shrubs, the northern desert was "a country where the inanimate dominates and in which not only man but the very plants themselves seem intruders." Where "living things are no longer common enough or conspicuous enough to seem more than trivial accidents," Krutch said, man "feels something like terror."[45]

In the further reaches of desert conditions, Krutch could find himself as unnerved as any nineteenth-century desert traveler, appalled by the exposed and naked earth. A fondness for room and space was not a fondness for vacancy. As a nature-lover, Krutch was a dedicated admirer of life, and particularly of individual organisms contemplated one at a time. Inanimate nature—soil or rock—had a value as it contributed to the support of life, and as it made adequate spacing possible.

When inanimate nature dominated, the balance of power went beyond the reach of Krutch's metaphors and abstractions. The northern landscape carried the clear lesson: "that man is small, and that life is precarious."[46] The lower Sonoran Desert provided that lesson in exactly the right balance, inanimate nature and life in just the proportions Krutch valued. But the canyonlands tipped the balance, returning Krutch by a new route to his 1929 vision of a humanity lost and impotent in an alien universe.

VII

In his desert year, Krutch learned "first and foremost generally to be 'more sure of all I thought was true.' "[47] This was not, in other words, a conversion or a shaking of first premises. Later readers could notice several unquestioned assumptions that Krutch carried into the desert and back to the publishers: the insignificance of actual property ownership and resource control; the irrelevance of contemporary Indians or Chicanos in the Southwest or, for that matter, of disadvantaged people in the world at large; the confidence that a basic, comfortable subsistence for humans was a settled issue; and the consistent feminization of the wildly reproductive nature, and the corresponding masculinization of the careful and thoughtful "man." These patterns of thought were evidently unshaken by a year in the desert.

Krutch had, however, found the desert to be a proving ground, a place to test the reconciliation of scientific revelation with spiritual revelation, to trace the universal in the specific and local, and to imagine alternatives to contemporary culture. The measure of success in his enterprise was, finally, personal restoration: the discovery of a homeland.

For Joseph Wood Krutch, personal restoration was not to be achieved once, and with permanence. For all the professorial calm of his public "I," his ideas showed a constant struggle with doubt. A conviction proclaimed with confidence might come into question in the next line; doubt eroded certainty with the persistence of a river wearing at its banks. Krutch's explorations in nature were repeated excursions to build up the banks of certainty; each reflective essay was another effort to contain the never fully conquered skepticism.

His autobiography, *More Lives Than One*, gave fuller glimpses of the character behind the measured and civilized voice of his other books. Many of the same themes—the question of inclusion or separation in particular—organized his presentation of both the desert and his own life. He evidently carried a strong sense of himself as a chronic outsider and nonconformist. In an eccentric German grandmother, Krutch found one possible influence for his "nonconformist interests, opinions and habits." In general, his rejection of Freudian and other psychologies required him to take credit for the creation of his own character, or to postulate a kind of congenital personality. "Such fears, anxieties, doubts and obsessions as I suffered from (and they were not a few), as well as such intellectual curiosities as awoke in me," Krutch explained, "were nearly all, so far as I am aware, spontaneous growths."[48]

Melancholy and pessimism, in any case, were not later forced on Krutch by his intellectual conclusions. Doubt, pessimism, and a sense of exclusion were acknowledged elements in his temperament. "Self-distrustful since childhood and temperamentally inclined to fear the worst," Krutch entered on most of his life projects with the "dark estimates of my chances I habitually set up." Completing *The Modern*

Temper, Krutch faced his "usual reaction": the "utter despair into which the anticipated failure of almost any enterprise I undertook . . . precipate[d] me."[49]

In the 1920s, Krutch's work with the *Nation* gave him an unusual sense of participation in a community of writers and thinkers. In a whirl of parties and shared beliefs, Krutch and his contemporaries celebrated "various freedoms," of which "sex freedom" was "by no means the least important." It was a rare spell of optimism in Krutch's memories: "The future was bright and the present was good fun at least."[50]

Even in the company of nonconformists, Krutch remembered, "there were fundamental elements in my temperament which made it inevitable that I should ultimately rebel against some of the rebel orthodoxies." The break came with the 1930s. Many of Krutch's formerly close associates took up an enthusiasm for communism, which Krutch could not share. His sense of exclusion was as strong as his refusal to convert, and his self-image as an outsider seemed for once to have become literal fact. "Never before," he recalled, "had I found myself so nearly surrounded by colleagues whom I knew to be enemies or, at least, not certainly to be trusted."[51]

With these glimpses into Krutch's life, one begins to develop a fuller realization of the values he must have assigned to the idea of "being part of an integrated world." "Self-distrustful since early childhood" and shaken in early middle age by exclusion from his former community, Krutch evidently found the idea of inclusion both profoundly attractive and profoundly threatening.

The issue was in many ways a religious one, but Krutch had wasted no time in turning down the chance to participate in a religiously coherent cosmos. In childhood, reflecting on a Sunday School "reference to the time when the lion and the lamb would lie down together," Krutch concluded, "If the lion ever tries it he will starve to death." Years later, learning of Darwinism, he felt he encountered only "a wonderfully rich elaboration" of this childhood insight, an insight that led him to take his "stand with Science against Religion, because Science seemed to be describing the contingencies while Religion shuts its foolish eyes upon them." By his teenage years, Krutch "had said good-bye to an important part of the old world."

Giving up on the Christian faith, he briefly "feared that what I did not believe might nevertheless be true and that my lack of faith might have the most appalling consequences." Then the fears "faded," and Krutch embarked on the life without "illusion" he would capture in *The Modern Temper.*[52]

The issues that would run through his desert books were familiar virtually from Krutch's early childhood. He had rung the changes on doubt, despair, and faith, and on the conflict of science with religion long before he left his home in Knoxville, Tennessee. Many of Krutch's preoccupations did in fact center around the concept of *home*. In 1929, he lamented the apparent fact that man had no home in the physical universe, and in 1952, he celebrated the discovery of the desert as his true home. While he insisted that his actual family home was a happy one, his childhood in Knoxville gave him a complicated set of remembered values to associate with the concept of *home*.

His birth certificate, Krutch said, described him as "White, legitimate, born alive." The three facts were all significant, and the first was by no means the least meaningful. In 1893 in Knoxville, "not to be white was frankly admitted to rightfully entail some pretty severe penalties." The belief in a fundamental difference between blacks and whites was, accordingly, "one of the very first of the things which I took for granted."[53] Congenital nonconformist that he might have been, Krutch as a child accepted the conventions of life in a former slave state. His mother's father was, in fact, known as a Southern sympathizer. Krutch had some experience with "lost causes" before he discovered the defeat of humanity by nature and science.

He had, he claimed, "no nostalgia" for his childhood. Adults and children were both "unadventurous," living in a "provincial" world that lacked "stimulation" and "excitement." But there were things to be said in favor of the old Knoxville, Krutch felt. He could not "help remembering," he said, "how relatively free it was from both the public and private pressures, tensions and anxieties of today. Civilization did not seem to be threatened, and the pattern of individual lives was more firmly established. We are now accustomed to seeing our world as a concatenation of 'problems'; few living before World War I took any such view of it."[54] This was, in other words, a coherent world, in which individual lives followed secure patterns. But it was not, in his familiar phrase, "an integrated world."

The white middle-class pace of life, as Krutch remembered it, was charming and leisured, a condition made possible by "the greatest labor-saving device of all, namely servants—almost invariably black." "Neither I nor anyone else," Krutch went on, "ever thought of 'a Negro problem' or supposed that the *modus vivendi* which seemed accepted without reservation by both groups need ever be disturbed." Subordination, Krutch seemed to suggest, had its compensations in stability. "Whether or not the Negroes actually believed themselves to be natural inferiors, I do not know," he said, "but they accepted with apparent cheerfulness and often with humor the assumption that they were."[55]

When the situation changed, descendants of both races had, in Krutch's view, "lost something as well as gained something." For Negroes as well as whites, "life has now become a series of problems. They have exchanged a possibly degrading acceptance of things as they are for anxiety, anger and a corroding sense of wrong. Because of them, tomorrow may be better; today is, in some ways, worse."[56]

With this portrait of his home, Krutch's preoccupations in nature writing gain new meanings. One begins to understand, particularly, his complacent lack of concern for the economically disadvantaged. In the old days at Knoxville, by his memory, black servants lived cheerfully with their lower status; their "problems" came from increases in freedom. Krutch's view of race relations in Knoxville is not a very useful social analysis, but it does reveal a logic in his thought. Growing up in a border state, in a time when the interaction of freedom and slavery had yielded only a partial emancipation, Krutch had good reason to adopt an ambivalent stance toward the concept of *home*. Depending on the point of view, this "home" was a refuge or a trap, a comfortably unexciting society of tradition, or a hierarchical system on the edge of disruption. Looking at the desert or looking back on Knoxville, Krutch admired a stable system in which individuals kept to their proper places in a spirit of cheerful acceptance, and he was himself an observer, unlike the others, free to determine his own place.

VIII

In 1954, Krutch had become a permanent resident of Arizona. He had written a second book, *The Voice of the Desert: A Naturalist's Interpretation*. Neither the content nor the point of view were novel to readers familiar with *The Desert Year*, but there was a perceptible increase in confidence. In the title alone, Krutch was proclaiming both the status of the desert as an entity capable of speaking its own messages, and the status of the author as a naturalist, a legitimate interpreter of the desert.

Over the next decade in Arizona, Krutch did become alarmed by the uninterrupted population growth and economic development in desert areas. *The Voice of the Desert* concluded with an exhortation for a step beyond simple conservation and toward a feeling for nature that was not predicated on use.[57] But the complicated problems of regulating the development of private property, of modifying the conventions of profit-centered land use, or of limiting the demands and aspirations of American consumers were by this time beyond Krutch's reach. His public stance as a refined and cultivated gentleman of sensibility placed him a far distance from the trade centers, banks, real estate offices, and chambers of commerce that were directing the future of American settlement in the desert.

Krutch, after all, had put together something closer to a religious belief than a political or economic program. As a teenager, and later in his mid-thirties, Krutch had declared religious faith to be an impossibility. Then he found in nature the lessons, parables, and texts of a tentative new faith. Those parables had the advantage of being undeniably actual—genuine stories of participants in a reality beyond the reach of modern skepticism. But the leap into pantheism was a difficult one for an individual distrustful of leaping. As a sophisticated intellectual, Krutch would have found an emotional proclamation of rebirth embarrassing and distasteful, even if he had had such a conversion to report.

After a number of visits to the desert, Krutch remembered, his wife had "said to several of our friends: 'You wouldn't know Joe out there. He is an entirely different person,' and I thought rather unkind the usual response, 'Isn't that nice!' " New person or not, in the desert Krutch found himself capable of moments of certainty in which he knew that "life is not a dream," and "reality is pervasive and, it seems, unconquerable." The joy in those moments was "not personal but impersonal. One no longer asks, 'What's in it for me?' because one is no longer a separate selfish individual but part of the welfare and joy of the whole."[58]

Devoted to the value of the individual, yet burdened by a sense of separation and exclusion, Krutch must have found this "impersonal" joy to be a particular relief. For once, the desert's negation of the central significance of humanity was more a consolation than an affront.

CHAPTER EIGHT
Edward Abbey

I

The plateau and canyon areas of southern Utah carry desert conditions to an extreme. Not only is vegetation sparse and water in short supply, the terrain is at its most intractable, cut by deep ravines and canyons. Travel routes are labyrinthine, and human settlements are small and scattered. Even a desert-lover like Joseph Wood Krutch found the region unnerving and alien.

An extreme and intractable landscape might, however, appeal to a more extreme and intractable man. The Utah canyonlands were in fact Edward Abbey's preferred landscape. If Krutch took the role of the gentle and sensitive observer of nature, Abbey took the part of the tough guy drawn to a tough land, the rebel fighting in defense of his chosen home.

Did such a rough environment need help in defending itself? Abbey fully respected the superior powers of the desert; he found his bedrock of faith in the long-range endurance of nature. The river that cut the Grand Canyon could certainly take care of concrete dams, given a millennium or two. "The earth will survive our most ingenious folly," Abbey said repeatedly.[1] The desert would outlast humans and, eventually, make a mockery of human pretensions to power.

And yet the desert needed protection. Humans, for all their cosmic paltriness, were still capable of major crimes. With dams and roads as their instruments of destruction, Americans seized desert wilderness—and ruined it. But if each new dam was a crime, each new road an invasion, who was the victim? Dams were hardly perceptible as events in the geological sweep of time; if they caused injuries, they were injuries on a human scale of time. Abbey might imagine long-range consolations of a restored nature, but he happened to be alive in the twentieth century. The injuries of the present hit him directly; the restorations of the future were out of his reach.

Born in 1927, Abbey grew up far from deserts but still close to nature. Raised in rural Pennsylvania, he first hitchhiked through the West as a teenager. After military service, he moved to the Southwest, attending the University of New Mexico for a time. Seasonal work as a park ranger provided him with opportunities to live in isolated areas and to observe the patterns and behavior of tourism. His literary ambition evidently leaned toward the novel, but a work of nonfiction brought him his audience. In *Desert Solitaire,* published in 1968, Abbey drew together the experiences of three summers at Arches National Monument. Personal narrative provided him with a vehicle for opinions on wilderness, American society, and prospects for the future. As his following books showed—*The Journey Home* (1977), *Abbey's Road* (1979), and *Down the River* (1982)—there was not much novelty in the thought of Edward Abbey, but there was undeniable force and vigor in his defense of the desert.

The conflict between American society and the desert had been obvious from the first meetings. What the desert offered was not what American settlers wanted. Reckoning with this maladjustment, Smythe and the irrigationists set out to change the desert, clearly to their minds the party responsible for the flaw in the relationship. The relationship between society and desert did not look any healthier to Edward Abbey, but he made a different allocation of the blame. The desert was a model of apportionment and equity, with no shortage, but just the right amount of water. The desert was fine; the problem lay in American industrial society, with its irrational demands for mastery, its efforts to coerce compliance from the desert. Smythe and Abbey, in essence, sat in the same stadium and watched different phases of the same game, but Smythe's victories were Abbey's defeats. Triumphs to Smythe, dams were disasters to Abbey; the desert tamed was the desert ruined. The place that had made innocent victims of William Lewis Manly and other overland travelers was now, in Abbey's characterization, an innocent victim itself.

Like John Van Dyke and Joseph Wood Krutch, Abbey liked the desert for the very qualities that repelled others. Not surprisingly, he and his predecessors drew similar portraits of those qualities in action. With a limited amount of water, animals and plants were in a constant contest with inanimate nature. Scarcity of water enforced the proper spacing; spacing gave the organisms the "sparseness and simplicity" appropriate to individuality; and the integrity of the environment held everything in unity. Limited vegetation left much exposed soil and rock; desert landscapes, especially the carved canyonlands, were thus glimpses of "earth in the nude." Exposed rock represented the most undeniable category of matter; the desert was "the bare skeleton of Being," the most real of environments. In its undeniable actuality, it was the most powerful reminder "that *out there* is a different world, older and greater and deeper by far than ours."[2]

Like Krutch, Abbey cheerfully drew his lessons from these observations. Nature in deserts visibly voted against crowding; modern humans persisted in crowding; humans were going against natural law. Life in deserts had made its peace with scarcity; Americans pushed endlessly for more material goods; Americans were once again going against nature. Nature, in other words, was the higher authority called in to back up Abbey's own judgments, a method of certification he shared, ironically, with Smythe. The system required Abbey to make a careful choice of examples; nature in jungles might demonstrate a preference for profligacy and waste, thus lending an alarming support to American economic habits. Abbey had the sense to stick with the desert and its meanings.

But the very notion of meaning, Abbey insisted repeatedly, was an "illusion" produced by "the displaced human consciousness." He claimed that the desert had no meaning; he wrote pages exploring what that lack of meaning meant. "The finest quality of . . . this desert landscape," he said, "is the indifference manifest to our presence, our absence, our coming, our staying or our going. Whether we live or die is a matter of absolutely no concern whatsoever to the desert." Far from "saying nothing," as Abbey repeatedly claimed, the desert in his translation made a perfectly direct statement. No conventional deity, speaking out loud or inscribing actual words on stone, could have spoken more clearly.[3]

There was certainly no reason to reject Abbey's proposition that deserts had no meaning *apart* from human consciousness. What rendered the proposition moot was the fact that deserts and human consciousness were no longer detachable. For over a century, Americans had been attributing meaning to deserts and acting on those meanings. On an uninhabited planet, deserts might be meaningless; but this, to Abbey's regret, was a world with no shortage in the supply of humans. To declare deserts without meaning was simply to award a pure philosophical position the status of greater reality, while dismissing human history as transitory and insubstantial. That very dismissal was, after all, one of the meanings humans found in the desert.

II

In the 120 years that separated William Lewis Manly and Edward Abbey, the desert did not lose its association with death. Railroads, automobiles, and airplanes, maps and marked roads had made risk voluntary; no one who did not choose it faced death in deserts. Despite that change, Manly the desert-hater and Abbey the desert-lover were nearly equals in finding the desert full of intimations of mortality. Many of his narratives, especially in *Desert Solitaire*, were journeys hinging on death.

In a desert canyon called Courthouse Wash, Abbey spent a long day rounding up stray cattle. The desert, in this instance, was in its conventional role as an environment that strained endurance and stressed human biological vulnerability. In that setting, the cattle drive became, in Abbey's words, a "death march, *marcia funebre*, the stations of the cross, *el jornado* [sic] *del muerto*."[4]

In his companion and temporary employer, Roy Scobie, Abbey provided a character utterly preoccupied with death. The seventy-year-old Scobie brooded so thoroughly about his eventual death that he was oblivious to actual hardships. Using Scobie as his foil, Abbey took for himself the role of the uncomplicated and hearty advocate of life—preoccupied with vital needs for food and water, and easily released from "the afternoon of doubt" by cooler temperatures and something to drink. Confronting Scobie's fear, Abbey claimed innocence. Sudden death in the desert seemed to him a preferable alternative to death in a hospital. "What did I know of it?" he went on. "To me death was little more than a fascinating abstraction, the conclusion to a syllogism or the denouement of a stage drama."[5]

A claim of this sort was, of course, role-playing. As a character in this particular story, Abbey had no particular interest in death, and certainly no strong feelings; but as the author, Abbey felt strongly enough about mortality to place it at the center of this and many other stories. Roy Scobie found life narrowed by an obsessive fear of death; Edward Abbey, by contrast, found life broadened and intensified by an awareness of death, to which the desert made a magnificent contribution. The experience of the Courthouse Wash cattle drive stopped considerably short of transcendence; hopelessly prosaic and grubbily commercial (each cow worth seventy dollars, as Scobie said), it left Abbey free to play temporarily with the role of a mortal unconcerned with mortality.

Abbey maintained his detachment on another outing—a search at Grandview Point for a sixty-year-old tourist who had left his car by the road and disappeared. The object of the manhunt, it turned out, had died from thirst under a juniper tree, on the edge of one of the least explored areas of the country. "Looking out on this panorama of light, space, rock and silence," Abbey said, "I am inclined to congratulate the dead man on his choice of jumping-off place." Grandview Point was virtually a shrine to the inanimate; what better site for a man's final departure? "To die in the open, under the sky, far from the insolent interference of leech and priest, before the desert vastness opening like a window onto eternity— that," Abbey said, "surely was an overwhelming stroke of rare good luck."[6]

Freedom from politeness gave Abbey's reflections a wide arc. Not only could he congratulate the dead man's taste in landscape, he could applaud his timing. "Given this man's age, the inevitability and suitability of his death, and the essential nature of life on earth," Abbey said, "there is in each of us the unspeakable conviction that we are well rid of him. His departure makes room for the living."[7] Joseph Wood Krutch could make repeated statements against crowding and congestion; Abbey, without the constraints of good taste, could extend the advocacy of room and space to a forthright celebration of death—other people's deaths. Heat and aridity at Grandview Point had made a small contribution to American population control, and Abbey would not look politely away from its significance.

Before he could be read as advocating homicide or even genocide, Abbey made clear that he had his reservations about nature's use of mortality. "Art, religion, philosophy, science and even war," he said, proclaim "that human life, in some way not easily definable, is significant and unique and supreme beyond all the limits of reason and nature." This truth, he went on, "we deny only at the cost of denying our humanity."[8]

That humane assertion, while heartening and noble, had the ring of generality and platitude. The physical and natural aspect of death, represented by the body as inanimate matter, spoke more vividly. The men in the search party suffered and joked, carrying the heavy body in its plastic bag, a bag that did not discourage the free mobility of both odors and flies. "Since he was unknown to any of us," Abbey said, "we joke about his fate, as is only natural and wholesome under the circumstances."[9] Helping to carry the body through the desert, Abbey was in another death march, *marcia funebre, jornada del muerto*. This one, like the earlier cattle drive, still left Abbey detached, considering death as a "fascinating abstraction" involving other people.

In a misadventure in Havasu Canyon, Abbey's feeling about death gained in immediacy. For a month, he lived in the ruins of an old mining camp in that branch of the Grand Canyon. "What did I do during those five weeks in Eden?" he asked. "Nothing. I did nothing." He "wandered naked as Adam," slipping by "degrees into lunacy," while "the days became wild, strange, hypnotic." As his detachment from conventional reality increased, he "worried about butterflies and who was dreaming what." In this hypnotic state, Abbey went for a hike, attempted a shortcut, and found himself trapped. He had reached the edge of an eighty-foot precipice by sliding down two rock chutes, landing in algae-covered ponds. The route, it seemed certain, could not be retraced. The future also looked certain: "death by starvation, slow and tedious."[10]

With the "blind faith of despair," he stacked rocks in the first pond, balanced his walking stick on the top of the pile, make a precarious and doubtful climb up the steep chutes, and escaped.[11] Throughout the incident, Abbey had acted on the irrational and humane proposition that his own individual human life carried significance. At Grandview Point, Abbey might admire the dead tourist's choice of death sites; he showed no particular enthusiasm for his own near luck in securing the beautiful Havasu Canyon. He chose, moreover, not to do his part for relieving the problems of overpopulation. For all of Abbey's proclamations of human insignificance, a premature eclipsing of the self was not his preferred form of closeness to nature.

Closeness, in its happiest form, came in a journey down the Colorado River through Glen Canyon. Abbey and his traveling companion could rely on the river for drinking water and for momentum; in this case, desert landscapes were available without the usual price of thirst and exertion.

This was, nonetheless, another *jornada del muerto*. Doom threatened the landscape itself. Glen Canyon was soon to be submerged, transformed by a dam into Lake Powell. In Courthouse Wash, at Grandview Point, in Havasu Canyon, the balance of power lay securely with the desert; humans narrowly defended themselves against heat, thirst, and precarious terrain. In Glen Canyon, the balance of power appeared to reverse; humans were on the offensive, while the desert canyon passively awaited drowning, and Abbey fumed over the irreversible direction of events. This was, he said, "a last voyage through a place we knew, even then, was doomed." The side canyons they left unexplored might never be seen again, "drowned beneath the dead water of the coming reservoir, buried for centuries under mud."[12]

If the submersion of Glen Canyon was a crime, who was the victim? Certainly the flooding could kill plants, and the displaced animals would have few refuges. Still, a transient claim to existence was a condition of desert life; a canyon's worth of organisms would not reverse the balance of animate and inanimate matter. And on a geological scale of the time, the building of Glen Canyon Dam hardly mattered. The river that made the canyon could take another epoch to conquer the dam or to erode another course with comparably elaborate canyons.

This was, if it was any event at all, an event in human history. The measure of the loss rested finally on a human, even an individual scale of value. Flooding Glen Canyon, the United States Bureau of Reclamation took from Edward Abbey something he valued. If the dam was a crime, he and his fellows—not nature itself—were the victims.

Defeated on a transient scale of time, Abbey found his consolation in rejecting that measure of significance. "Men come and go, cities rise and fall, whole civilizations appear and disappear—the earth remains, slightly modified," Abbey said, in clear kinship with John Van Dyke. "Turning Plato and Hegel on their heads I sometimes choose to think," he went on, "that man is a dream, thought an illusion, and only rock is real. Rock and sun."[13]

Abbey placed himself, for these reflections, on a cliff beyond the rim of Glen Canyon. On that cliff, he could hike down the way he came; a basic personal safety gave him the necessary margin for celebrating human ephemerality. On another cliff, in Havasu Canyon, with his own life at stake, Abbey would not surrender an exclusive reality to the rocks. Even a self-declared believer in the commandment "Be true to the earth" had to admit in the right circumstances that contributing his own body to the nutrient cycle was one expression of loyalty he wished to postpone.[14]

Nonetheless, it was clear that Abbey treasured the desert's associations with death—the whole package of thirst, heat, hardship, risk, and human insignificance. The risk was intrinsic to the appeal; one felt most alive when reminded of death. By the same principle, Abbey repeatedly demonstrated his preoccupation with predation—that activity in which life and death were most fully connected, with one organism's death supporting the other's life. It was precisely the starkness of this border activity, in the territory where life and death met and engaged each other, that fixed Abbey's loyalty to the desert.

III

Was Abbey a misanthrope? Did his opinions support the proposition that one loved deserts in proportion to how much one disliked humans? Like Van Dyke, Abbey comfortably condemned the collective wrongdoing of mankind. But if Van Dyke covertly retained his fondness for individuals, Abbey did not bother to make his affection covert. Companions on trails or river trips, hearty hardworking men in small towns, rural Mormon folk, and especially river guides got warm expressions of human solidarity from Abbey. In the essays published after *Desert Solitaire*, he went to some trouble to show himself domesticized, with frequent references to "my wife" and "my daughter." He evidently knew how he could be misinterpreted, and he made an earnest effort to escape the charge of misanthrope. How, "being myself a member of humanity," he asked, "could I be against humanity without being against myself . . . ?"[15]

Abbey's peace with humanity rested on an imperious division of human nature. Repressed humans were the servants and pawns of industrial society, hopelessly seeking self-realization through the manufacture and accumulation of mechanical gimmickry. Repressed humans made ideal "industrial tourists," agreeably trapping themselves in their automobiles, denying themselves authentic experience.

What, by contrast, did unrepressed humans want? They wanted very much what Edward Abbey wanted. "What most humans really desire," he said, "is really something quite different" from industrial gimmickry: "liberty, spontaneity, nakedness, mystery, wildness, and wilderness."[16] What Abbey wanted was thus in the best interests of humanity, whether or not humanity knew it. This idea carried his utter conviction; Abbey had a missionary-like certainty that, disengaged from its content, Frémont or Smythe might have envied. Purity of conviction took care of the ethical problem presented by a democratic majority that wanted the "wrong" thing. If the majority wanted a more tamed wilderness, and Abbey's minority stood in opposition, then the explanation was that the majority did not know what it really wanted or needed. Abbey did.

"The idea of wilderness needs no defense," Abbey said, drawing a cryptic distinction. "It only needs more defenders."[17] A statement guaranteed to play well at a rally of the already converted, it also dodged the need for a rationale for preservation. If pressed beyond the assertion of self-evident truth, Abbey could only offer what he felt were irresistible arguments for wilderness preservation. One approach, anthropological on the broadest scale, took on the question of human origins. Humans and nature stood in the right relation to each other when humans were honest predators. As hunters and gatherers, humans knew they were a part of and dependent on nature. In the agricultural revolution, humanity made the leap into manipulation and mastery; the industrial revolution only furthered the loss of right relations. Underneath the deformations of industrial civilization, the old hunting and gathering instincts remained strong—and in need of an outlet. Contact with untamed wilderness satisfied the primal needs left over from the earliest experience of the human race. Leaving those needs unsatisfied, humanity asked for trouble.[18]

Wilderness was thus essential to human dignity and freedom—a venerable Romantic idea pushed a step further into the twentieth century by Abbey. Totalitarian governments threatened on all fronts, Abbey argued; wilderness might prove necessary as a base for guerrilla resistance when oppression had gone too far. The core idea—that wilderness was a refuge from the burdens of civilization, a safety valve for the discontented—was conventional and familiar; the idea of the convention becoming military and political fact was a bit startling.[19]

The desert preserved was a bedrock of freedom; alone in that wilderness, individuals could recapture the origins of the human experience and recover some of the resourcefulness industrial civilization had stolen from them. As either anthropology or political science, the argument had its dubious points. But in the complicated history of humans finding meaning in nature, Abbey's philosophy had a persuasive simplicity. The desert was established in American minds as a nonconformist landscape, an environment of stubborn integrity, refusing to comply with the requirements of American materialism. If one had to pick an environment to stand for freedom from control, the desert was the leading candidate.

In their own independence, deserts had by Abbey's theory the power to revive the weak and dependent. Exposed rock, on a scale beyond human use and mastery, could shock the dulled mind back into awareness. If Delicate Arch, "a fragile ring of stone" and evidently one of the most striking features of Arches National Monument had "any significance," it lay "in the power of the odd and unexpected to startle the senses and surprise the mind out of their ruts of habit, to compel us into a reawakened awareness of the wonderful." This, of course, was precisely what George Wharton James had said: the desert was full of "surprises," with the happy effect of reviving deadened awareness. With James, the surprise had remained at the level of sensation for the sake of sensation; Abbey pushed for a wider meaning. Delicate Arch served as a reminder "that *out there* is a different world, older and greater and deeper by far than ours, a world which surrounds and sustains the little world of men as sea and sky surround and sustain a ship."[20]

Rock carried "the shock of the real." Reflecting on his spells of genuine loneliness, Abbey brought up the subject of solipsism, "the solitary confinement of the mind." Did he sometimes risk a suspicion that only the self and consciousness were real, and matter only an illusion? "To refute the solipsist or the metaphysical idealist all you have to do is take him out and throw a rock at his head; if he ducks he's a liar."[21] Rock—a thrown rock—was the vehicle of bringing philosophers back to their senses. Lost in the maze of human consciousness, they could be rescued with a forced recognition of their relationship to an inescapably genuine piece of matter.

Was this system of belief a religion? It certainly had the elements. The desert fit the category of "paradise," Abbey said, if the term were properly defined. "When I write 'paradise,' " Abbey said, "I mean not only apple trees and golden women but also scorpions and tarantulas and flies, rattlesnakes and Gila monsters, sandstone, volcanoes and earthquakes, bacteria and bear, cactus, yucca, bladderweed, ocotillo and mesquite, flash floods and quicksand, and yes—disease and death and the rotting of the flesh." Properly understood, paradise was "with us yet," in "the here and now, the actual, tangible, dogmatically real earth on which we stand."[22] Frequently the effort of Americans to appreciate the desert had meant the appreciation of light, color, and form, properties to be admired in spite of the less attractive desert life-forms and weather conditions. Abbey wanted to push past that conditional appreciation into a state of perception in which terrestrial unity came before the superficial categories of attractive and unattractive, pleasant and unpleasant. He rejected a paradise edited to suit human comfort and preference; he even wanted death, that most disturbing of physical realities, included.

Abbey's concept of paradise had its own version of virtue, sin, and restoration. "Loyalty to the earth, the earth which bore us and sustains us, the only home we shall ever know" was the touchstone of right living. Conversely, "original sin, the true original sin is the blind destruction for the sake of greed of this natural paradise which lies all around us—if only we were worthy of it."[23] By this definition, sin in late-twentieth-century America appeared as widespread as it had ever appeared to more conventional believers. Nonetheless, for Abbey as for the gloomiest Calvinist, individual moments of grace were still possible, even in the midst of universal depravity. In interludes, the true believer could at least glimpse paradise, even if humanity remained lost in self-destructive sin.

Did it add up to a religion? Abbey quoted Balzac: "In the desert, there is all and there is nothing. God is there and man is not." "God?" Abbey asked. "There is nothing here, at the moment, but me and the desert." Willing to draw a number of analogies between his beliefs and Christianity, he balked at including a Creator. "Why confuse the issue," he said, "by bringing in a superfluous entity?"[24]

Nothing in Edward Abbey's thought broke from the pattern of Romanticism described by M. H. Abrams.[25] For the Romantic, existence was a journey, leading through separation and disengagement, back to restoration to a homeland. In defining this experience, the Romantic resolutely secularized religion, keeping much of the structure of religion but stopping short of a new theology.

Writing in this tradition, Abbey carried the burden common to romantic nature-writers: how was he to make repeated declarations of wonder without sacrificing the conviction and freshness that supposedly characterized his faith? How, in fact, could he present his feelings as faith without grounding them in a bedrock of final authorship? Nature was the bedrock, and Abbey stopped there—no God, no Creation, no final causes. That conclusion may have satisfied its author, but it had the air of an inquiry cut off, a major question sidestepped.

From the idea of a lost but redeemable homeland to the secularization of religion, from the cult of the individual to the ritualized attack on materialism and industrialization, Abbey showed his kinship with the British and German Romantics of nearly two centuries before. In the Utah canyonlands, Abbey had applied an old formula to a landscape Williams Wordsworth probably never imagined.

IV

Abbey was not much concerned with charges of inconsistency. He condemned the profligate use of the automobile; he drove his own vehicles with abandon. He pled with humanity to act responsibly toward nature; he recorded his own mad trip across the Australian outback in a radically inappropriate rented Ford. He praised authenticity, finding the desert's attraction in the exposure of the essential self; he celebrated authenticity from behind the mask of a literary persona that he himself mocked.[26] His tone defied readers to be small-minded enough to find his contradictions significant.

His defense against accusations of self-contradiction lay in the idea of paradox.[27] Opposed ideas or opposed characteristics were only opposed in appearance; surface differences aside, opposites shared the same root system. Desert plants were ruggedly isolate, and they were part of a united whole; Abbey wanted solitude and he wanted kinship. These were examples of paradox, Abbey would claim, not contradiction.

Nonetheless, if readers were converted by reading Abbey's books, it would not be immediately clear what they had converted to. Abbey was fighting in defense of the arid West; somehow or other, all those words were supposed to change the direction of history and save deserts from further development. But persuasion on this matter was a precarious undertaking. If Abbey's books only convinced readers that the desert was worth seeing, he would encourage a flood of automobile tourists, compounding problems of crowding and overuse. The principal charm of the desert was the scarcity of humans; recruiting supporters to preserve that charm, Abbey had to risk destroying it with a rush of invited guests.[28]

For the full success of Abbey's mission, his readers had to agree to see the desert as an ecologically whole, life-filled world, a world with its own right to remain unimproved and unreclaimed, and also a world that they might never visit. Adopting that position required a full leap to preservationist faith, to the belief that nature had its own inherent rights, independent of use and economic value. But the preceding one hundred and fifty years had built up a powerful image of deserts as vacant, useless spaces. Pitted against that image, Abbey's voice sounded strident, unlikely to persuade anyone who was not already ripe for conversion. While he could continue to insist that humans who knew what they really wanted and needed would share his opinions, it was still obvious that he spoke for a minority whose personal needs for wilderness, he felt sure, came first.

In this apparent elitism, Abbey gave a classic demonstration of what Roderick Nash has called "full stomach environmentalism."[29] The claim that the desert had just the right amount of water could only come from someone at a safe distance from thirst or hunger. Certainly that individual could still indulge in temporary hardships, but those would be episodes of scarcity undergone by choice. Partial converts might well end up interested in deserts, but not overly interested in hardships; their version of "full stomach environmentalism" would stop short of the purity and strenuosity Abbey preferred.

One of the major sources of strain to his ideas lay, however, in the prospect of success—the danger posed by an expansion of the minority, anxious to see untouched deserts for themselves. When unmanageable numbers wanted access to wilderness, management had to step in and ration access. But a managed wilderness seemed to be a contradiction in terms, especially when Abbey had made wilderness and freedom into synonyms.[30] How would he make his peace with the prospect of wilderness licenses, waiting lists, possibly even competitive admissions exams?

When it came to the basic conceptual problems of wilderness advocacy, Abbey carried a full set. He encouraged appreciation of deserts, and yet appreciation in the late twentieth century threatened in its own way to transform wilderness. He rebelled against restraints on freedom, especially restraints imposed by a strong government, and yet preservation required forceful legislation and effective enforcement, possible only with a strong centralized authority. He wrote to encourage resistance to the commercial development of nature, and yet he gave that process of development an air of irresistible inevitability.

Abbey could on occasion match John Van Dyke in fatalism. Industrial development was "an iron glacier," bearing down on futile resistance; *Desert Solitaire*, written to defend wilderness, also recorded the fact that for its specific setting, defense came too late. Arches National Monument had over the years of Abbey's association already surrendered to development. The general picture was one of irresistible continuity: more dams, more roads, more people, with everything Abbey valued in the Southwest "going fast."[31]

And yet, Abbey would insist, "The Machine" was not beyond control; it was, after all, made up of the decisions and acts of individuals. "The world can still be rescued," Abbey argued, claiming that all his writings had exactly that goal. Once again, Abbey would use paradox as the route out of any apparent contradiction. Hope, he explained, was fatalism transmuted; "despair" could "be modulated" to "a comfortable melancholia and from there to defiance, delight, a roaring affirmation of self-existence."[32]

By that psychological alchemy, Abbey ended up with defiance in plentiful supply. The desert was his mentor; desert plants, defying the pressures of the inanimate, provided a model for his own struggle against the supposed deadness of American society—empty materialism, routinized and unresponsive government, reductive science, and ill-considered technology.

With his oppositional temperament, Abbey nonetheless held true to one long-running pattern of thought. Like Frémont and many others, he still followed the pattern of definition by opposites: deserts and society defined each other by their differences. For Frémont, the desert repelled by virtue of what it lacked; for Abbey, the desert appealed by the same qualities of absence. With human artifice removed from the picture, Abbey thought, deserts offered a restoration to authenticity. What Americans did wrong, deserts seemed to do right.

CHAPTER NINE

The Significance of Deserts in American History

When Frederick Jackson Turner searched for the meaning of the frontier, he took water for granted. At the meeting point of civilization and wilderness, Turner claimed, American pioneers developed the essential qualities of democracy and the American character. In their development, pioneers faced obstacles and hardships—Indians to remove, forests to clear, sod to break, rivers to ford. They did not face thirst or chronic drought.

In Turner's frontier, effort earned its proper rewards in opportunity and abundance. A generous, providentially arranged environment gave the United States the raw material for expansion on an extraordinary scale. The only sad news came in 1890 with the ostensible close of the frontier. Nevertheless, by that time expansion had fixed American expectations in a tone of optimism. The legacy of the frontier, on the Turner model, would be an ongoing faith in the individual's right to opportunity and the nation's right to material abundance.

Turner is known as an environmental determinist, famous for his assertion that nature changed Europeans into Americans. In fact, his presentation of nature was abstract, providing little sense of particular places with particular qualities. The wilderness may have mastered the colonist and then been mastered in turn, but this transaction took place in a realm closer to poetry than to prosaic historical reality. Mastered or mastering, Turner's wilderness took water for granted, and a large share of the continent—Nevada, Arizona, much of New Mexico, California, Utah, and eastern Oregon and Washington—vanished from frontier history.[1]

The conventions of the Turner thesis did their part to obscure the significance of deserts. Another trend in historiography had a similar effect. Exposing the exaggerated myth of the "Great American Desert," historians inadvertently drew attention away from the actual deserts.[2] Professional historians, personal experience shows, will still hear the declared intention to study the desert as an intention to explore "the Myth of the Desert." It is odd, but not altogether surprising, that environments of such powerful reality became associated in the intellectual's mind with myth and symbol.

Certainly deserts have accumulated a great deal in the way of symbolic meaning; any other conclusion would provide a very odd ending for this particular book. But that meaning rests on a very solid basis of physical actuality—aridity set against human needs for water. The history of American deserts offers a chance to revitalize questions long discredited by a simplistic environmental determinism. How do environments affect human behavior? How do people newly introduced to a particular place figure out what to make of it, both conceptually and literally? One could hardly prepare a better experiment by conscious design: Remove a crucial variable and see what changes. Reduce water, and watch how people adapt, or find an alternative to adaptation.

In 1848, when Mexico surrendered its northern territory, the United States came into possession of major tracts of desert. What made this seem a worthwhile acquisition? Why would a nation with a dominant interest in agricultural expansion want so much unwatered land?[3] California and a few river valleys in the interior were territories of recognized value. The intervening arid space had the primary function of connective tissue; something, after all, had to connect Texas to California. The deserts in the middle had value primarily as a land passage, a route for overland travel and eventually for railroads.

The American desert found its initial significance as a place to cross, to get from one livable place to another. The overland trail in general was an adventure for many participants, an experience of novelty, challenge, and opportunity. While a degree of hardship was intrinsic to the challenge, the desert went too far. In desert travel, hardship went past adventure and into ordeal. Dust and heat were burdens enough: jornadas, the utterly waterless stretches of as many as fifty miles, put the endurance of both humans and animals through a brutal test. This was, after all, a form of transportation in which the loss of the oxen, mules, or horses put the travelers in a fearful and precarious situation. The desert passage was an experience of vulnerability, discouragement, exhaustion, and, at the end, triumph and relief.

Deserts as a result put a particular strain on the optimistic expectations of pioneers. In 1849, the emigrant Peter Decker noticed this warning sign near the Humboldt Sink: "Expect to find the *worst desert* you ever saw and then find it was worse than you expected."[4] Warned or not, emigrants still found the desert a shock—the fullest proof that the overland route to profit and improvement was not an easy one. The hardships of the desert, set against expectations of a continent that made at least minimal provisions for the needs of travelers, led to the widespread perception that the desert was the most "real" of environments, the place where, as Twain put it, reality drove romance into full retreat. In the face of such intractable reality, emigrants became innocents betrayed; routes that looked clear and direct on maps turned out to be ordeals; so-called rivers were small, bitter, and given to sudden disappearances. The desert passage was an interlude of shaken confidence; the visual distortion of mirages was only one of the ways in which nature, in the desert, seemed to cheat.

For those who took time for further reflection, the significance of the desert could only become more troubling. Faced with aridity, the project of mastering the continent seemed to have reached a nonnegotiable limit. By all the conventional standards for value and habitability, the desert was an irrational environment, a betrayal of the promise of abundance fulfilled elsewhere in North America. Certainly the American agrarian ideal had never been put to a worse test.

With the discovery of minerals, beginning in the late 1850s, the significance of the desert shifted. Nature had prepared the scene for a treasure hunt, placing gold and silver in the most trying locations.

Would the Americans and their acquisitive impulses be up to the challenge, ready to follow the traces of mineral wealth despite the most discouraging travel and living conditions? The answer was a solid yes. If William Lewis Manly could be persuaded to return to Death Valley, then the prospector's urge carried as much force in deserts as in mountains. Mining gave deserts a new value, but it was the transitory value appropriate to extraction. From a place to get across, the desert had become a place to get things out of, a meaning that hardly encouraged feelings of responsibility or attachment in the new arrivals. The high hopes of prospectors also led them to see the deserts as a harsh and extreme version of reality. The man who hoped for riches and found nothing, or even the man who found minerals too difficult to extract without major investment, was a man meeting—and resenting—reality.

For both overland travelers and prospectors, deserts offered hardship and scarcity without much compensation in the form of aesthetic charm. Beauty in the desert could only be discovered with a margin of safety. As Mark Twain noted, "nothing helps scenery like ham and eggs," and nothing improved desert scenery like a reliable water supply, a refuge from heat and direct sunlight, a safe form of transportation requiring little individual exertion, and an element of choice—to visit the desert voluntarily, and to leave at will.

One further prerequisite to desert appreciation deserves mention. Most nineteenth-century Americans, those in a position to have an opinion at all, had felt that progress lay in the advance of civilization and the retreat of the desert. Along with leisure, choice, and safety, desert appreciators, from the turn of the century on, frequently had one other qualification: discontent with American society. To the degree that one found civilization unattractive, one could admire the most intractable of environments for its purity. The convention of the desert as "the most real" of landscapes carried through, although with a reversed and now positive meaning. Deserts that had not submitted to development were, to the appreciators, the most authentic of places, where existence was stripped to its essentials, without pretense and without artifice.

As turn-of-the-century appreciators began to find a new value in the unmastered desert, irrigationists began to celebrate new opportunities for mastery. Large-scale manipulation of water, with federal backing, would at last make the desert suitable for the agrarian life. Unlike emigrants, miners, and appreciators, irrigationists denied the final reality of deserts. They saw them instead as ultimately transformable; they could be remade into farms through the alchemy of irrigation.

Irrigation, it is something of a surprise to remember, fell under the category of conservation.[5] In 1900, constructing reservoirs to hold and redistribute water meant conserving resources for more efficient use. The implications here were striking: a forest, managed by conservationist, sustained-yield principles, was still a forest; a desert, managed by conservationist principles, became something else entirely—a farm, a garden, even the site of a town or city. The basic fact of low rainfall remained the same; the air might remain dry and clear, but the landscape changed character altogether.

The conditions of deserts thus made the difference between conservation and preservation noticeable from the beginning. On matters involving mountains and forests, preservationist John Muir and conservationist Gifford Pinchot could for a time imagine themselves as allies, until the Hetch Hetchy controversy divided them. In the desert, there were few possibilities for such mistaken alliances. John Van Dyke may have been the best contemporary candidate for the role of "the John Muir of desert"; he knew from the beginning that conservation, in the form of irrigation, only meant destruction of the purity he wished to preserve.

To say that the distinction was noticeable in hindsight and in the eyes of some contemporaries is not to say that everyone perceived it. A publicist like George Wharton James, alternating between praise of irrigation and praise of the untouched desert, evidently felt no sense of contradiction. The explanation lay in the apparent scale of the deserts: in 1906, with such vast spaces of arid land and such a light population, it hardly looked as if one had to make difficult choices of priority. Americans could build towns and create farms, and there would still, it seemed, be plenty of unchanged land suitable for contemplation.

For all their differences, both manipulators of water and preservationists held one hero in common. In the twentieth century, in-

dividuals of either persuasion could use the name of John Wesley
Powell with reverence. This is not to say they agreed on the proper
spirit in which Powell's name should be invoked. Federal officials
chose the name of Lake Powell for the reservoir behind the Glen
Canyon Dam; Abbey found such a use of that honored name mor-
tifying.

Who was Powell, and how did he come to be the target of such
opposed loyalties?[6] Born in New York, he grew up in Ohio and
developed a lifelong interest in nature and a loyalty to the family
farm. Civil War service in the Union Army cost him an arm, but
nothing in the way of determination. After the war, he organized
his own expeditions to little-explored areas in the West, becoming
an expert in arid lands. He eventually obtained government spon-
sorship and led one of the three main civilian surveys. In 1881, he
succeeded Clarence King as director of the United States Geological
Survey. His 1869 descent of the Colorado River was the first recorded
exploration of that river and its canyons. His 1878 Report on the Arid
Lands was also unprecedented as a sober assessment of the region's
resources and the most sensible approach to using them.

It was no mystery that Powell could appeal to such different groups.
Preservationists could admire Powell the adventurer—the sensitive,
eloquent, and courageous explorer of the river. Reclamationists could
admire Powell the planner—the practical forecaster of future uses
and value. The wise man of the arid lands worked as a patron for
both causes.

For neither group was Powell a smooth fit as elder statesman.
Preservationists had to look away from his use of phrases like "the
redemption of the Arid Region." The deserts had been lost and were
now to be saved, and this was not altogether what the preservationists
wanted to hear from Powell. While his Colorado River narrative
revealed an individual fascinated by the forms of arid terrain, his
stance in The Report was hardly that of an appreciator of deserts in
their unimproved state. Powell wanted "the legislative action necessary to inaugurate the enterprises by which these lands may be
rescued from their present worthless state." Certain areas were beyond
redemption, even for grazing. "In very low altitudes and latitudes,
the grasses are so scant as to be of no value," Powell said; "here the

true deserts are found. The conditions obtain in southern California, southern Nevada, southern Arizona and southern New Mexico, where broad reaches of land are naked of vegetation."[7] As an explorer, Powell found all terrains of value; as a policy-maker, he was willing to draw a distinction between the valuable and the valueless.

The reclamationists, on the other hand, had their reasons to quote Powell selectively. In a way that would distinguish him from many people who claimed to be his successors, Powell always admitted that water and usable lands were in limited supply. "Within the Arid Region," he said, "only a small portion of the country is irrigable." Throughout his career, according to his biographer Wallace Stegner, Powell insisted "that no more than 20% of the West could ever be reclaimed even with the most economical use of water." Powell also wanted a prolonged and careful survey of reservoir sites to precede any major developments. Congress authorized a major irrigation survey in 1888, and Powell, as the second director of the United States Geological Survey, was authorized to withhold lands in the public domain from settlement until they could be surveyed and classified. Frustrated western congressmen used budget cuts to reduce the effectiveness of the geological survey and recover access to public land.[8]

Powell earned his enemies in several ways, but certainly his prime offense was to insist on the arid character of much of the West, and on the limits aridity would place on traditional western freedom and impulsiveness. He was, on that count, something of an embarrassment to his attempted admirers. At an 1893 National Irrigation Congress meeting in Los Angeles, Powell as the featured speaker disagreed forcefully with his hosts; their visions of utterly unlimited irrigation struck him as folly. William Ellsworth Smythe, placing Powell as "first on the roll of irrigation champions," still showed scars from these battles. Powell "was a soldier, a poet, a scientist, a lover of his kind," Smythe said, "but in no sense a man of practical commercial instincts."[9]

In the twentieth century, for both reclamationists and preservationists, Powell made a less-than-manageable founding father. He wrote his major books at a time when a clash between use and appreciation did not seem inevitable. In Powell's own time, the Colorado canyonlands, the region of his adventuring, were so difficult and remote that their use was not at issue. His landscape of appreciation and his landscape of use were simply different places. When the clash came, appeals to Powell's authority predictably produced inconsistency.

There are, after all, two basic ways of looking at an isolated river canyon—two points of view comparable to the usual responses to a figure-ground drawing. With the drawing, one can see a vase in the center, or one can see the silhouettes of two faces; with a river canyon, one can see the sculptured space in the middle, an ideal place for physical and visual adventuring, or one can see the two walls of a reservoir, a construction site where nature has done the bulk of the work and humans only have to supply the plug. When flood control, storage of water for municipal use, and, most significantly, the generation of electricity provided the rationale for Colorado River dams, the point of view based on utility became for a time the politically dominant one.

By the mid-twentieth century, no standard of utility offered a clear guide to desert policy. The deserts could not sustain unlimited multipurpose use. Eventually, the purposes clashed with each other. It was only in part a matter of utility versus contemplation, hydroelectric dams and mining versus recreation. Recreation, by the 1960s had no simple meaning; between the so-called industrial tourists, dependent on access by automobile, and advocates of self-reliance and minimal intervention, there was at most a narrow strip of common ground.

A simple model of sequential phases in American attitudes toward nature had limited relevance for deserts. By this model, pioneers initially feared and hated nature in the form of wilderness; nature had them overpowered and they, sensibly, resented it. Then, in a transitional phase, pioneers fought to conquer nature, and the balance of power slowly shifted. In a final phase, pioneers had mastered nature; they were, by that very act, no longer pioneers. The completion of the conquest then made it possible to appreciate nature; and in an apparent happy ending, Americans could create national parks, museums for the last stand of a safely defeated enemy.[10]

The first two phases—fear and powerlessness, followed by a struggle for mastery—do in fact correspond to the early phases of desert history. But the existence of a final, resolved state of mastery and appreciation is simply illusory. Mastery remains partial; reckonings with the desert's basic scarcity of water have only been postponed by the mining of ground water and the usual overallocation of the Colorado Basin water.[11] Appreciation also remains partial and conditional. Like George Wharton James, the same individuals might be perfectly willing to find beauty in the exposed landscapes that alarmed people one hundred years before, and also perfectly willing to see those landscapes transformed in the higher interests of agriculture, real estate development, or recreation.

Choosing among conflicting uses of scarce resources is a difficult matter for any government, perhaps especially so for a democracy. Many square miles of the American deserts are still in public ownership; the question of their use is still a subject for public policy and for public opinion. What do the American people want to do with their desert? If few of them are going to use it, or visit it, directly, how do they want it used, and by whom? Is it in the public interest for the followers of William Ellsworth Smythe to continue the program of mastery, or is it in the public interest for the followers of Van Dyke, Krutch, and Abbey to hold the line on the side of preservation? Will the initiative instead stay in the hands of the heirs of George Wharton James, ritualizing a windy form of appreciation that permits, even facilitates, the commercial transformation of the deserts? Eventually, the depletion of ground water and excessive demands on rivers will provide a clearer conclusion to questions about the desert's future. In the meantime, the significance of the desert now centers on one question. By what principle of legitimacy are Americans to claim and allocate the desert's scarce resources?

Turner claimed that 1890 marked the close of the frontier, and yet frontier-like enterprises failed to observe that deadline. To the same degree, the prophets who defined limits on the basis of aridity spoke prematurely. Speculation, boom towns, extractive industries, major population shifts, development of vacant land—many of the central phenomena of the frontier—ran continuously past 1890 and past the borders of aridity. Nineteenth-century territorial expansion blended into twentieth-century economic expansion in a way that left few boundaries in time or space. The deserts seemed to draw a line, and Americans pushed past it. Can Americans now choose for themselves an appropriate line—and hold to it?

What, after all, are the deserts worth? The legacy of the overland trail was a judgment of arid vacancy. That legacy lasted into the twentieth century and up to the present. Describing the distinctive landscape of the Far West, the historian of the twentieth-century West Gerald Nash demonstrated the power of the overland legacy: "The only vestiges of life," he said, "could be found in towns and cities that served as oases—centers of human activity in the midst of the seemingly endless sea of nothingness."[12] From that perspective, Krutch's and Abbey's energetic attempts to popularize desert appreciation—to replace an image of vacancy with life and activity—were writings in the sand.

To add to the irony, technology and war had found new uses for vacant space. World War II redirected much of the western economy toward defense industries and military development.[13] The large-scale testing of planes, tanks, guns, and bombs required wide open spaces—unoccupied land that would be easy to acquire and suitable for simulated attack. The deserts provided ideal locations: undeveloped enough so that little in the way of improvements would be lost, isolated so that secrecy could be maintained. Since undeveloped deserts were already by popular consensus vacant and useless, bombing could hardly hurt them. In Arizona's Yuma Proving Ground and Luke Air Force Base, in California's China Lake Naval Weapons Center, Randsburgh Wash Test Range, Camp Irwin, Edwards Air Force Base, Twenty-nine Palms Marine Corps Base, and Chocolate Mountains Aerial Gunnery Range, in Nevada's Tonopah Test Range, Nellis Air Force Range, and Atomic Energy Commission Nuclear Testing Site, in New Mexico's White Sands Missile Range and Fort Bliss Military Reservation, and in Utah's Dugway Proving Grounds and Wendover Bombing and Gunnery Range, defense projects made it clear that an "endless sea of nothingness" had its uses.

When the scientists at Los Alamos needed a place to test the first atomic bomb, the New Mexico desert met the job requirements. The place called Trinity on the old *Jornada del Muerto* connecting El Paso to Santa Fe was, as Lansing Lamont wrote, "the perfect place to test the bomb." It was "isolated," "flat," "so uninhabitable that the nearest signs of civilization were a pair of abandoned coal mining towns, Troy and Carthage. . . . If disaster occurred, few besides the scientists at Trinity would be victims."[14] Even Joseph Wood Krutch commented on the fit between place and purpose: "There must be very few places in the United States so suitable for such an experiment; few, that is to say, either so remote or so devoid of anything to be destroyed."[15] It was almost providential—the way in which aridity had reserved certain regions from settlement, and therefore left them suitable for bombing.

To the north and west of Trinity, twentieth-century enterprise revealed other ways of making use of deserts. When mining proved a changeable and unreliable base for prosperity, the state legislature of Nevada entertained other routes to revenue. In 1931, the legislators added wonderfully to the resources of Nevada by legalizing gambling.[16] Here was a sensible and practical way of capitalizing on uncertainty; gambling followed symmetrically in the traditions of Americans in deserts. Overland emigrants had been gamblers, staking their lives on the uncertainties and risks of desert traveling. Prospectors had been gamblers, staking their resources and sometimes their lives on the chances and hazards of desert treasure-hunting. Irrigationists were gamblers, staking their enterprise on the unlimited extendability of desert water sources and on the changing currents of national politics. Tourist and town promoters were and are gamblers, staking their businesses on the uncertain capacity of the deserts to sustain heavy settlement and use. The eager crowds who flocked to the tables and slot machines of Las Vegas were well within the tradition of travelers in, as John W. Audubon described it in 1849, "a doubtful country."[17]

When gamblers fail to get what they want, it is second nature for them to claim betrayal. Describing contemporary Americans, Richard Barnet has analyzed the response to resource scarcity: "The new mood," he said, "is no conventional pessimism, but rather a loss of faith rooted in a sense of betrayal."[18] For four centuries nature in the New World offered Euro-Americans promises of abundance. One region reneged on that promise from the beginning. Facing the uncooperative behavior of nature in the desert, nineteenth-century Anglo-Americans experienced at least briefly a version of that "loss of faith rooted in a sense of betrayal." William Ellsworth Smythe and his heirs have done their best to shore up the faith, but the doubts aroused by aridity do not go away. This is the stage in the game in which the gamblers could profitably refrain from further bets, and reconsider their strategy.

Notes

Preface

1. Alexis de Tocqueville, *Democracy in America*, p. 25.
2. On the Great American Desert, see William H. Goetzmann, *Exploration and Empire*, pp. 49–53 and 58–64; Henry Nash Smith, *Virgin Land*, pp. 174–83; Walter Prescott Webb, *The Great Plains*, pp. 152–60; and Martyn J. Bowden, "The Great American Desert and the American Frontier."
3. On desert physiography, see Nevin H. Fenneman, *Physiography of the Western United States*, pp. 247–395; and Charles B. Hunt, *Physiography of the United States*, pp. 277–347. For exhaustive detail on the physical and biological conditions of deserts, see Gordon L. Bender, *Reference Handbook on the Deserts of North America*. For scientifically oriented descriptions, see David F. Costello, *The Desert World*; Ruth Kirk, *Desert: The American Southwest*; and John McPhee, *Basin and Range*.
4. Quoted in George H. Williams, *Wilderness and Paradise in Christian Thought*, p. 108.
5. On Indians, prehistoric and historic, living in desert areas, see C. Melvin Aikens, "The Far West," pp. 131–82, especially "The Great Basin," pp. 146–64; and William D. Lipe, "The Southwest," pp. 327–402, in Jesse Jennings, *Ancient Native Americans*; Jesse Jennings, "The Desert West," pp. 149–74, and Erik H. Red, "The Greater Southwest," pp. 175–92, in Jesse Jennings and Edward Norbeck, *Prehistoric Man in the New World*;

Robert Spencer, et al., *The Native Americans: Ethnology and Backgrounds of the North American Indians,* Chaps. 5 and 6, "Western North America–Plateau, Basin, California," and "The Southwest," pp. 164–311; Harold Driver, *Indians of North America,* pp. 17–18, 29–32, 63–66, 118–21, 142–44, 328–29, 337–39, 358–59, 366–70, 386, 397–98, 406–7, 413–17.

6. In choosing a definition and an analytic method, I have profited particularly from John Passmore, *Man's Responsibility for Nature: Ecological Problems and Western Traditions;* and Keith Thomas, *Man and the Natural World: A History of the Modern Sensibility.*

7. William James, "On a Certain Blindness in Human Beings," in *Pragmatism and Other Essays,* ed. Joseph L. Blau, pp. 252–53.

8. See Marjorie Hope Nicolson, *Mountain Gloom and Mountain Glory: The Development of the Aesthetics of the Infinite;* and Roderick Nash, *Wilderness and the American Mind,* 3rd ed., especially pp. 96–140.

9. Nash, *Wilderness,* pp. xv and xvi.

10. Ibid., p. xvi.

11. See Arthur A. Ekirch, *Man and Nature in America;* Hans Huth, *Nature and the American: Three Centuries of Changing Attitudes;* and Leo Marx, *The Machine in the Garden: Technology and the Pastoral Ideal in America* for books on attitudes toward nature that do not pay much attention to deserts.

12. See especially Eudora Welty, "Place in Fiction," in *The Eye of the Story: Selected Essays and Reviews,* pp. 116–33.

13. Tocqueville, *Democracy,* p. 435.

14. Jules Remy, *A Journey to Great-Salt-Lake City,* p. 40.

15. Ibid., pp. 95 and 79.

16. Ibid., pp. 104 and 100.

17. Ibid., pp. 53, 175, and 187.

18. Ibid., p. 95.

Introduction to Part I

1. Alfonso Ortiz, ed., Vol. IX, "Southwest," *Handbook of the American Indian,* especially p. 48; and Emil W. Haury, *The Hohokam: Desert Farmers and Craftsmen,* especially pp. 149–50. For particularly instructive portraits of specific tribal adaptations to

the desert, see Lowell John Bean, *Mukat's People: The Cahuilla Indians of Southern California;* Charles Bowden, *Killing the Hidden Waters* on the Papagos; and Jack D. Forbes, *Warriors of the Colorado: The Yumas of the Quechan Nation and Their Neighbors.* For more on Indian prehistory, see *Preface,* Note 5.

2. On Spanish exploration in deserts, see Herbert Eugene Bolton, *Kino's Historical Memoir of Pimeria Alta;* Herbert S. Auerbach, *Father Escalante's Journal,* by Silvestre Velez de Escalante; Elliott Coues, *On the Trail of a Spanish Pioneer: The Diary and Itinerary of Francisco Garces,* 2 vols.; Herbert Eugene Bolton, *Anza's California Expeditions,* 5 vols.; William Goetzmann, *Exploration and Empire,* pp. 3–78; and John Francis Bannon, *The Spanish Borderlands Frontier,* pp. 8–71, 143–66.

3. Max L. Moorhead, *New Mexico's Royal Road;* R. J. Duffus, *The Santa Fe Trail;* and the most detailed primary source, Josiah Gregg, *The Commerce of the Prairies.*

4. Goetzmann, *Exploration and Empire,* pp. 79–180; Gloria Griffen Cline, *Exploring the Great Basin,* pp. 132–80; Dale L. Morgan, *Jedidiah Smith and the Opening of the Great West.* For a particularly valuable primary source, see Zenas Leonard, *Narrative of the Adventures of Zenas Leonard.*

5. See *Preface,* Note 2.

6. Zebulon Pike, *The Expeditions of Zebulon Pike,* Vol. II, p. 525.

7. Edwin James, *Account of an Expedition from Pittsburgh to the Rocky Mountains,* Vol. II, p. 311. See also Vol. II, pp. 386–87.

8. John D. Unruh, *The Plains Across: The Overland Emigrants and the Trans-Mississippi West, 1840–1860,* pp. 119–20; and Odie B. Faulk, *Arizona,* p. 76.

9. For full information on the central trail, see David M. Potter, Introduction to *Trail to California: The Overland Journal of Vincent Geiger and Wakeman Bryarly;* George Stewart, *The California Trail;* and Unruh, *The Plains Across.*

10. For a thorough introduction to the southern trails, plus several diaries and journals, see Ralph P. Bieber, *Southern Trails to California in 1849.*

11. William Swain, quoted in J. S. Holliday, *The World Rushed In: The California Gold Rush Experience,* p. 242; Wakeman Bryarly, in David M. Potter, *Trail to California,* p. 160; Helen Carpenter in Sandra L. Myres, *Ho for California!: Women's Overland Diaries,* p.

175; Swain, in Holliday, *The World Rushed In*, p. 239. Emigrants frequently renamed the Humboldt River the "Humbug."

12. Mary Bailey, in Myres, *Ho for California!*, p. 84; Bryarly, in Potter, *Trail to California*, p. 189; Catherine Haun, in Lillian Schlissel, *Women's Diaries of the Westward Journey*, p. 182; and Bryarly, in Potter, *Trail to California*, pp. 168 and 176.

13. Bryarly, in Potter, *Trail to California*, p. 186. For information on cutoffs and their consequences, see Stewart, *California Trail*, pp. 268–85 on the Lassen Cutoff, and George R. Stewart, *Ordeal by Hunger* on the Hastings Cutoff.

14. Stewart, *The California Trail*, pp. 274–75.

15. Potter, Introduction, *Trail to California*, p. 25: "Had the Humboldt Desert been ten miles broader, only a small fraction of the emigrants would have lived to reach its Western side." Bryarly, in Potter, *Trail to California*, p. 187; Charles Tinker, quoted in Stewart, *The California Trail*, p. 268; Bryarly, in Potter, *Trail to California*, p. 195.

16. Sarah Royce, *A Frontier Lady*, pp. 34, 33–57.

17. Ibid., p. 57.

18. Rodman Wilson Paul, *Mining Frontiers of the Far West, 1848–1880*, p. 44.

19. Ibid., p. 98. For an excellent study of particular mining camp's rise and fall, see W. Turrentine Jackson, *Treasure Hill*. In a similar vein, see Russell R. Elliott, *Nevada's Twentieth Century Mining Boom: Tonopah, Goldfield, Ely*; and Elliott's *History of Nevada*. For a full survey of desert development, see W. Eugene Hollon, *The Great American Desert*.

20. Paul, *Mining Frontiers*, p. 96.

21. Ray A. Billington, Foreword to Paul, *Mining Frontiers*, p. viii.

22. Hollon, *The Great American Desert*, p. 87.

23. Paul, *Mining Frontiers*, p. 8.

24. See Note 1, above.

25. For general histories of Mormonism and the development of Utah, see Leonard J. Arrington, *Great Basin Kingdom*; Leonard J. Arrington and Davis Bitton, *The Mormon Experience*; and Thomas F. O'Dea, *The Mormons*. For a thorough discussion of Mormon irrigation, see George Lofstrom Straebel, "Irrigation as a Factor in Western History, 1847–1890."

26. On the origins of Anglo-American irrigation in the arid

West, see Alfred R. Golze, *Reclamation in the United States*, pp. 9–15; Hollon, *The Great American Desert*, p. 163; David Lavender, *The Southwest*, pp. 276–81; and William Warne, *The Bureau of Reclamation*, pp. 5–7.

27. Hollon, *Great American Desert*, pp. 141–51; Frederick Merk, *History of the Westward Movement*, pp. 467–76.

28. For a concise and thorough history of the reclamation movement, see Lawrence B. Lee, *Reclaiming the American West*, pp. 6–15.

29. On federal reclamation legislation, see Lee, *Reclaiming the American West*, pp. 12–18; Hollon, *The Great American Desert*, pp. 163–65; Warne, *Bureau of Reclamation*, pp. 6–14; Golze, *Reclamation in the United States*, pp. 16–26, 102–4; and Samuel Hays, *Conservation and the Gospel of Efficiency*, pp. 9–15.

30. Hollon, *The Great American Desert*, p. 165.

31. Donald Swain, *Federal Conservation Policy 1921–1933*, p. 78.

32. Ibid., pp. 80–85; Hollon, *The Great American Desert*, p. 167; Golze, *Reclamation in the United States*, pp. 28–30, 32–34, 69–76; Warne, *The Bureau of Reclamation*, pp. 86–103; and Paul L. Kleinsorge, *The Boulder Canyon Project: Historical and Economic Aspects*.

33. For studies in the complexities and controversies of far western water development, see Remi Nadeau, *The Water Seekers*; Norris Hundley, *Dividing the Waters: A Century of Controversy Between the United States and Mexico*; Norris Hundley, *Water and the West: The Colorado River Compact and the Politics of Water in the American West*; Elmo Richardson, *Dams, Parks and Politics: Resource Development and Preservation in the Truman-Eisenhower Era*. For contemporary controversies, see Philip L. Fradkin, *A River No More: The Colorado River and the West*; and Richard L. Berkman and W. Kip Viscusi, *Damming the West*.

Chapter One

1. John C. Frémont, *A Report of an Exploration to Oregon and North California in the Years 1843–1844*, in Donald Jackson and Mary Lee Spence, *The Expeditions of John C. Frémont*, Vol. I, p. 702.

2. Information on Frémont's life and explorations is drawn from Jackson and Spence's introduction to the edition cited above; Gloria Griffen Cline, *Exploring the Great Basin*, pp. 208–16; William H. Goetzmann, *Army Exploration in the American West 1803–1863*, pp. 65–108; William H. Goetzmann, *Exploration and Empire*, pp. 240–52; and, principally, Allan Nevins, *Frémont: Pathmarker of the West*.

3. Jackson and Spence, Introduction to *The Expeditions*, pp. xxiii–xxiv, xxv.

4. Ibid., p. xix.

5. Bernard DeVoto, *The Year of Decision: 1846*, p. 39.

6. These words are omnipresent in the sections of the *1843–1844 Report* dealing primarily with deserts, pp. 592–611 and 665–94.

7. For a full narrative of the pursuit of the Buenaventura River, see Gloria Griffen Cline, *Exploring the Great Basin*.

8. Frémont, *1843–1844 Report*, in Jackson and Spence, *Expeditions*, p. 592.

9. Ibid., pp. 575 and 658.

10. Ibid., pp. 594 and 600.

11. Ibid., p. 599.

12. Ibid., p. 600.

13. Ibid., p. 610.

14. Ibid., p. 604.

15. Ibid., p. 670.

16. Frémont, *A Report of an Exploration of the Country Lying Between the Missouri River and the Rocky Mountains on the Line of the Kansas and Great Platte Rivers*, 1842 journey, in Jackson and Spence, *Expeditions*, p. 226.

17. Ibid., p. 226.

18. Frémont, *1843–1844 Report*, in Jackson and Spence, *Expeditions*, p. 667.

19. Ibid., p. 667.

20. Ibid., pp. 674 and 686.

21. Ibid., p. 685.

22. Ibid., p. 671.

23. Ibid., pp. 677–78.

24. Ibid., pp. 680–81.

25. Ibid., p. 681.

26. Ibid., p. 684.
27. Ibid., p. 687.
28. Ibid., pp. 690–91.
29. Ibid., pp. 687, 538–39, 688, and 599.
30. Frémont, *1842 Report*, pp. 175, and 190–91.
31. Ibid., p. 187.
32. Frémont, *1843–1844 Report*, pp. 698 and 699; and
Goetzmann, *Exploration and Empire*, p. 247.
33. Ibid., pp. 699 and 700.
34. Ibid., pp. 702–3.
35. Ibid., p. 702.
36. Ibid., pp. 703 and 676.
37. Ibid., p. 679.
38. Ibid., pp. 685 and 679.
39. Ibid., pp. 702 and 674.
40. Frémont was not altogether mistaken in this assumption. In his 1842 expedition, he recorded the fact that he had carved a cross on Independence Rock; this admission was later used in the political arena to discredit him as a possible Catholic. See Jackson and Spence, *Expeditions*, p. 274, n. 75.
41. Frémont, *1843–1844 Report*, p. 702.
42. Ibid., p. 685.
43. John C. Frémont, *Memoirs of My Life*, Vol. I., p. 602.
44. Ibid.

Chapter Two

1. Most of the information on Manly's life is drawn from his book, *Death Valley in '49*. Secondary sources generally confirm his honesty and reliability of memory. See Kenneth Alexander, *Death Valley USA*, pp. 20–25; Margaret Long, *The Shadow of the Arrow: Death Valley 1849–1949*, pp. 145–66 and 216–48; and Lawrence Clark Powell, *California Classics*, pp. 31–43. For a full history, including documents, of the 1849 Old Spanish Trail emigration of which Manly was initially a part, see LeRoy and Ann Hafen, *Journals of Forty-Niners: Salt Lake to Los Angeles*.
2. Manly, *Death Valley*, pp. 11 and 12.
3. Ibid., p. 14.

4. Ibid., p. 16.

5. Ibid., p. 25.

6. Ibid., p. 30.

7. Ibid., pp. 30–32.

8. David Riesman, *The Lonely Crowd,* pp. 14–17.

9. Manly, *Death Valley,* p. 32.

10. Ibid., pp. 57, 58, and 59.

11. Ibid., p. 62.

12. Ibid., p. 73.

13. Ibid., p. 76.

14. Ibid., pp. 93–94.

15. See John Faragher, *Women and Men on the Overland Trail,* pp. 36–39.

16. Manly, *Death Valley,* pp. 107 and 108.

17. Ibid., p. 111.

18. Ibid., pp. 113 and 114.

19. Ibid., pp. 106 and 121.

20. Ibid., p. 123.

21. Ibid., pp. 131–32.

22. Ibid., p. 132.

23. Ibid., p. 142.

24. Ibid., pp. 147–48.

25. Ibid., pp. 197 and 193.

26. Ibid., pp. 214 and 234.

27. Ibid., p. 173.

28. Ibid., p. 259.

29. Ibid., p. 267.

30. Ibid., p. 254.

31. Ibid., p. 43.

32. Ibid., p. 254.

33. Ibid., pp. 146, 349, and 136.

34. Ibid., p. 126.

35. Ibid., p. 439.

36. Ibid., p. 265.

37. Ibid., p. 254.

38. William Lewis Manly, *The Jayhawkers' Oath and Other Sketches,* pp. 65 and 66.

39. Ibid., p. 70.

40. Ibid., pp. 72 and 74.

41. Alonzo Delano, *Life on the Plains,* p. 184.

Chapter Three

1. Mark Twain (Samuel L. Clemens), *Roughing It*, p. 271.
2. For biographical material on Clemens, I am much indebted to Justin Kaplan, *Mr. Clemens and Mark Twain*.
3. Quoted in Kaplan, p. 135.
4. Ibid.
5. Twain, *Roughing It*, pp. 112–13.
6. For background on transcontinental stagecoaching, see Waterman L. Ormsby, *The Butterfield Overland Mail*; Roscoe P. Conkling and Margaret R. Conkling, *The Butterfield Overland Mail*, Vols. I–III; Oscar Osburn Winther, *The Transportation Frontier: Trans-Mississippi West, 1865–1890*, pp. 44–73.
7. Twain, *Roughing It*, p. 142.
8. Ibid., p. 143.
9. Ibid.
10. Ibid., pp. 143–44.
11. Ibid., p. 144.
12. Ibid.
13. Ibid.
14. Ibid., p. 145.
15. Ibid., p. 146.
16. Ibid., p. 147.
17. Ibid.
18. Ibid., p. 149.
19. Ibid.
20. Ibid., pp. 157 and 160.
21. Ibid., p. 170.
22. Ibid., p. 173.
23. Ibid., p. 176.
24. Ibid., p. 194.
25. Ibid., p. 220.
26. Ibid., pp. 230 and 232.
27. Ibid., pp. 235, 236, and 237.
28. Ibid., p. 238.
29. Ibid., pp. 229–30 and 240.
30. Ibid., p. 265.
31. Ibid., pp. 267–68.
32. Ibid., p. 270.

33. Ibid., pp. 272 and 274.
34. Ibid., p. 203.
35. Ibid., pp. 140–41.
36. Ibid., p. 388.

Chapter Four

1. William Lewis Manly, *Death Valley in '49*, p. 14.
2. Information on Smythe's life and career is drawn from Lawrence B. Lee's excellent introduction to William E. Smythe, *The Conquest of Arid America*, 2nd ed.; and from Martin E. Carlson, "William E. Smythe: Irrigation Crusader," *Journal of the West* 7 (January 1968).
3. Smythe, *Conquest*, p. 266.
4. Ibid.
5. Ibid., p. 267.
6. On typical Progressive ways of thinking, see Richard Hofstader, *The Age of Reform*, pp. 131–271; Robert H. Wiebe, *The Search for Order 1877–1920*, pp. 111–223; and Samuel P. Hays, *Conservation and the Gospel of Efficiency: The Progressive Conservation Movement 1890–1920*, especially pp. 122–46.
7. William E. Smythe, *Constructive Democracy: The Economics of a Square Deal*, p. 78.
8. Ibid., p. 307.
9. Ibid., p. 268.
10. Ibid., Pt. 3, Chap. 4, "Plenty of Room at the Bottom," pp. 289–307.
11. Ibid., pp. 302–3.
12. Ibid., p. 306.
13. Ibid., pp. 306–7.
14. Ibid., p. 308.
15. Smythe, *Conquest*, p. 9.
16. Ibid., pp. 21–22.
17. Ibid., p. 45.
18. Ibid., p. 46.
19. Ibid., p. 328.
20. Ibid., pp. 327–31.
21. Ibid., p. xxvii.
22. Ibid., p. 43.

23. Ibid., p. xx.
24. Ibid., p. 267.
25. Smythe, *Democracy*, p. 309.
26. Smythe, *Conquest*, p. 4.
27. Ibid., pp. 17–18.
28. Ibid., p. 31.
29. Ibid., p. 272.
30. Ibid., p. 11.
31. Ibid., p. 132.
32. Ibid., p. xxv.
33. Ibid., p. xx.
34. Ibid.
35. Smythe, *Democracy*, p. 260.
36. Ibid., pp. 150–51.
37. Smythe, *Conquest*, p. xvii.
38. Ibid., p. xi.
39. Ibid.
40. Smythe, *Democracy*, p. 309, emphasis on the original.
41. Smythe, *Conquest*, p. xi.
42. Information on these colonies is drawn from Henry S. Anderson, "The Little Landers' Colonies: A Unique Agricultural Experiment in California," *Agricultural History* 5 (October 1931).
43. William E. Smythe, *City Homes on Country Lanes*, p. vii.
44. Smythe, *Conquest*, p. ix.

Introduction to Part II

1. For the best summary of twentieth-century western population growth and settlement patterns, see Gerald Nash, *The American West in the Twentieth Century: A Short History of an Urban Oasis*, pp. 77–90, 148–59, 196–201, and 218–33.

2. On the proliferation of railroads, see Robert Edgar Riegel, *The Story of the Western Railroads: From 1852 Through the Reign of the Giants*, especially pp. 179–94; Oscar Osburn Winther, *The Transportation Frontier: Trans-Mississippi West, 1865–1890*, pp. 92–133; and Keith L. Bryant, *History of the Atchison, Topeka and Santa Fe Railway*.

3. Earl Pomeroy's summary of this changing appraisal of the desert, in *In Search of the Golden West: The Tourist in Western*

America, pp. 63–67, 158–63, and 195–96, is superb. On the role of scientists and naturalists, see William G. McGinnies, *Discovering the Desert: Legacy of the Carnegie Desert Botanical Laboratory.* For primary material on the naturalists' approach, see William Hornaday, *Camp-Fires on Desert and Lava;* Godfrey Sykes, *A Westerly Trend;* Edmund Jaeger, *The California Deserts;* and Raymond Cowles, *Desert Journal.*

Chapter Five

1. John C. Van Dyke, *The Desert: Further Studies in Natural Appearances,* pp. 59 and 62.

2. Ibid., p. 62.

3. Information on Van Dyke's life is drawn from Frank Jewett Mather, Jr., "John C. Van Dyke," in the *Dictonary of American Biography* (1931); Lawrence Clark Powell, *Southwest Classics,* pp. 315–28; and a similar essay by Powell introducing the 1976 reprint of *The Desert.*

4. John C. Van Dyke, *The Open Spaces,* p. 91.

5. Quoted in Powell, *Southwest Classics,* p. 325.

6. John C. Van Dyke, *Art for Art's Sake,* pp. 5–38.

7. Van Dyke, *The Desert,* p. vii.

8. Ibid., pp. vii–viii.

9. Ibid., p. 1.

10. Ibid., p. 2.

11. Ibid., p. 7.

12. Ibid., pp. 8–9.

13. Ibid., p. 13.

14. Ibid., p. 19.

15. Ibid.

16. Ibid., pp. 24–25.

17. Ibid., p. 26.

18. Ibid., p. 27.

19. Ibid., p. 28.

20. Ibid., pp. 41–42.

21. Ibid., p. 51.

22. Ibid., pp. 52, 56, and 57.

23. Ibid., p. 57.

24. Ibid.

25. Ibid., pp. 57–58.
26. Ibid., p. 60.
27. Ibid., pp. 60–61.
28. Ibid., p. 59.
29. Ibid., pp. 61–62.
30. Ibid., pp. 87–88.
31. Ibid., p. 114.
32. Ibid., pp. 109 and 110.
33. Ibid., p. 127.
34. Ibid., p. 62.
35. Ibid., pp. 131 and 132.
36. Ibid., pp. 128 and 129.
37. Ibid., pp. 132, 133, and 141.
38. Ibid., p. 144.
39. Ibid., pp. 150 and 155.
40. Ibid., pp. 171 and 173.
41. Ibid., p. 192.
42. Ibid., p. 200.
43. Ibid., pp. 211–12.
44. Ibid., pp. 227–28.
45. Ibid., p. 228.
46. Ibid., pp. 228 and 229.
47. Ibid., pp. 230 and 231.
48. Ibid., p. 107.
49. Ibid., p. 129.
50. Van Dyke, *Open Spaces*, p. 90.

Chapter Six

1. Information on James's life is taken from Roger Joseph Bourdon, "George Wharton James, Interpreter of the Southwest." Several other sources are also helpful: Harrison G. Dwight, "George Wharton James," *Dictionary of American Biography* (1931); Lawrence Clark Powell, *California Classics*, pp. 53–65; Kevin Starr, *Americans and the California Dream*, pp. 204–7; Franklin Walker, *A Literary History of Southern California*, pp. 144–50 and 200–201.

2. George Wharton James, *The Wonders of the Colorado Desert*, Vol. I, pp. xxxi–xxxii.

3. He did in fact publish one book directly celebrating irrigation: *Reclaiming the Arid West.*

4. On the Southwest, see George Wharton James, *Arizona the Wonderland; California Romantic and Beautiful; In and Around the Grand Canyon; New Mexico: The Land of the Delight-Makers; Our American Wonderlands;* and *Utah: The Land of Blossoming Valleys.*

5. James did, in fact, dedicate *The Wonders of the Colorado Desert* to God, and similar genuflections occur throughout the book: "To the *Source,* Maker of Deserts, I dedicate this book." James, *Wonders,* Vol. I., p. vi.

6. Ibid., Vol. I, pp. 33–48.

7. Ibid., Vol. I, pp. 47 and 48.

8. Ibid., Vol. I, p. 48.

9. Ibid., Vol. I, p. 24.

10. Ibid., Vol. I, pp. 49, 270, and 24.

11. For the Salton Sea story, see Remi Nadeau, *The Water Seekers,* pp. 137–67. For a fuller sense of the way in which the Imperial Valley provided the precedent and impetus for major Colorado River projects, see also Norris Hundley, *Water and the West,* pp. 17–52.

12. James, *Wonders,* Vol. I, p. 5 and Vol. II, p. 514.

13. Ibid., Vol. I, pp. xxxii and 32.

14. Ibid., Vol. II, pp. 452 and 490.

15. Ibid., Vol. II, pp. 276, 363, and 418.

16. Ibid., Vol. II, p. 433. For background on the attribution of health of the desert, see Billy M. Jones, *Health-Seekers in the Southwest, 1817–1900.*

17. James, *Wonders,* Vol. I, p. 47.

18. Ibid., Vol. II, p. 519.

19. Ibid., Vol. I, pp. xxxiii and 15.

20. Ibid., Vol. I, p. 21.

21. Ibid., Vol. II, p. 314.

22. Ibid., Vol. II, pp. 299, 300, and 313–14.

23. Ibid., Vol. II, p. 309.

24. Ibid., Vol. II, p. 144.

25. Ibid., Vol. I, p. xxii.

26. Ibid., Vol. II, p. 532 and Vol. I, p. xxxii.

27. Ibid., Chap. 11, "Some Wild Animals of the Desert," pp. 145–56; Chap. 12, "Some Desert Birds," pp. 157–68; Chap. 13,

"Reptiles and Insects of the Desert," pp. 169–206; Chap. 14, "Plant Life of the Desert," pp. 207–32, all in Vol. I.

28. Ibid., Vol. II, p. 403.

29. Ibid., Vol. I, pp. xxii, 7, and 17.

30. Powell, *California Classics*, p. 54; and Starr, *Americans and the California Dream*, p. 206.

31. James, quoted in Walker, *Literary History*, p. 148.

Chapter Seven

1. Joseph Wood Krutch, *The Modern Temper: A Study and a Confession*, p. 142.

2. Joseph Wood Krutch, *More Lives than One*, pp. 210–11.

3. Ibid., p. 211.

4. Ibid., p. 205.

5. Ibid., pp. 294–95.

6. Krutch, *Modern Temper*, p. 249.

7. Ibid., p. 8.

8. Ibid., p. 9.

9. Ibid., pp. 84–114, especially 113.

10. Ibid., pp. 243 and 248.

11. Ibid., p. 249.

12. Ibid.

13. Ibid., p. 185.

14. Ibid., p. 8.

15. Ibid., pp. 98–125.

16. Ibid., p. 70.

17. Joseph Wood Krutch, *The Desert Year*, p. 4.

18. Ibid., p. 5.

19. Ibid., p. 11.

20. Ibid., pp. 8–9.

21. Ibid., pp. 26–27.

22. Ibid., p. 27.

23. Ibid., p. 28.

24. Ibid.

25. Ibid.

26. Ibid., p. 55.

27. Ibid., pp. 123 and 124.

28. Ibid., pp. 124 and 127.
29. Ibid., pp. 129–30.
30. Ibid., pp. 130 and 135.
31. Ibid., p. 136.
32. Ibid., pp. 147 and 150.
33. Ibid., pp. 141 and 152.
34. Ibid., p. 23.
35. Ibid., p. 95.
36. Ibid., pp. 95 and 88.
37. Ibid., p. 88.
38. Ibid., p. 183.
39. Ibid., pp. 180–82.
40. Ibid., p. 182.
41. Ibid., pp. 187–88 and 189.
42. Ibid., pp. 189 and 193–94.
43. Ibid., p. 240.
44. Ibid., p. 250.
45. Ibid., pp. 252 and 251.
46. Ibid., p. 252.
47. Ibid., p. 269.
48. Krutch, *More Lives than One*, pp. 10 and 17.
49. Ibid., pp. 57–58 and 205.
50. Ibid., pp. 177–79.
51. Ibid., pp. 179 and 250.
52. Ibid., pp. 20 and 35.
53. Ibid., pp. 4 and 5.
54. Ibid., p. 23.
55. Ibid., p. 24.
56. Ibid., p. 26.
57. Joseph Wood Krutch, *The Voice of the Desert: A Naturalist's Interpretation*, Chap. 12, "Conservation Is Not Enough," pp. 186–207.
58. Krutch, *More Lives than One*" p. 308; Krutch, *Voice of the Desert*, pp. 215 and 216.

Chapter Eight

1. Edward Abbey, *The Journey Home: Some Words in Defense of the American West*, p. 226.

2. Edward Abbey, *Desert Solitaire: A Season in the Wilderness*, pp. 29, 187, 270, and 41–42.

3. Ibid., pp. 273, 300–301, and 270.

4. Ibid., p. 102.

5. Ibid., pp. 105 and 94.

6. Ibid., p. 240.

7. Ibid., p. 242.

8. Ibid.

9. Ibid., pp. 241–42.

10. Ibid., pp. 224, 225, and 227.

11. Ibid., p. 229.

12. Ibid., pp. 174 and 187. For background on the Glen Canyon Dam, see Elmo Richardson, *Dams, Parks and Politics: Resource Development and Preservation in the Truman-Eisenhower Era*, pp. 59–70, 129–153, and 194–200; and Roderick Nash, *Wilderness and The American Mind*, 3rd ed., pp. 228–37 and 332–33.

13. Abbey, *Desert Solitaire*, p. 219.

14. Ibid., p. 208.

15. Ibid., p. 274.

16. Edward Abbey, *Abbey's Road*, p. 127.

17. Abbey, *Journey Home*, 223; and Abbey, *Down the River*, pp. 119–20.

18. Abbey, *Down the River*, pp. 114–16 and 120; Abbey, *Abbey's Road*, p. 40.

19. Abbey, *Desert Solitaire*, pp. 149–51; and Abbey, *Journey Home*, p. 231.

20. Abbey, *Desert Solitaire*, pp. 40–42.

21. Ibid., pp. 42 and 111–12.

22. Ibid., p. 190.

23. Ibid.

24. Ibid., p. 208.

25. M. H. Abrams, *Natural Supernaturalism: Tradition and Revolution in Romantic Literature*, pp. 12–13, 91, 145, 182, 187–91, 201, 207, 217, 225, 255, 375, 385, and 411.

26. Abbey, *Desert Solitaire*, pp. 246–48; Abbey, *Abbey's Road*, pp. 46–68 and xv.

27. Abbey, *Desert Solitaire*, pp. 6, 297, and 114.

28. Nash, *Wilderness and the American Mind*, pp. 316–41 and 384.

29. Ibid., p. 343.

30. Ibid., pp. 339–41. As Nash puts it, "The paradox of wilderness management is that the necessary means defeat the desired ends."

31. Abbey, *Desert Solitaire,* pp. 145, ix, 51, and xii.

32. Abbey, *The Journey Home,* p. 226; Abbey, *Abbey's Road,* pp. xxi and 195.

Chapter Nine

1. Frederick Jackson Turner, "The Significance of the Frontier in American History," in *The Early Writings of Frederick Jackson Turner,* pp. 183–229. In Ray Allen Billington, *Frederick Jackson Turner: Historian, Scholar, Teacher,* Billington notes that Turner set out to write an essay called "The Significance of the Great Plains, The Rocky Mountains and the Deserts in American History" but evidently never completed it to his satisfaction. The essay would, Billington remarked, have added "a new dimension to [Turner's] scholarship (p. 329)." For a tradition in western history that fully recognized aridity, although focused on the region of the Great Plains, see Walter Prescott Webb, *The Great Plains;* and especially Webb's essay, "The American West: Perpetual Mirage," *Harper's* 214 (May 1957): 25–31.See also W. Eugene Hollon, *The Great American Desert.*

2. Henry Nash Smith, *Virgin Land: The American West as Myth and Symbol* is a superb study, unjustly held responsible for giving the symbolic West greater significance than the actual West. In fact, Smith pointed out the power and influence of images and did not discount actuality.

3. On the acquisition of Mexican territory and American responses to the acquisition, see Odie B. Faulk, *Too Far North . . . Too Far South;* Paul Neff Garber, *The Gadsden Treaty;* Frederick Merk, *Manifest Destiny and Mission in American History: A Reinterpretation;* and Howard R. Lamar, *The Far Southwest,* pp. 56–82 and 415–18.

4. Peter Decker, *The Diaries of Peter Decker: Overland to California in 1849 and Life in the Mines, 1850–1851,* p.125.

5. Samuel P. Hays, *Conservation and the Gospel of Efficiency: The Progressive Conservation Movement, 1890–1920,* pp. 5–26.

6. For information on Powell, see Wallace Stegner, *Beyond the Hundredth Meridian: John Wesley Powell and the Second Opening of the West;* and William Goetzmann, *Exploration and Empire,* pp. 530–76.

7. John Wesley Powell, *Report on the Lands of the Arid Region of the United States,* pp. 7, 8, and 30.

8. Ibid., p. 16; and Stegner, Introduction to Powell, *Report,* p. xxiii.

9. Stegner, *Beyond the Hundredth Meridian,* pp. 342–43; and Williams Ellsworth Smythe, *The Conquest of Arid America,* p. 261.

10. For an example of this model, see Hans Huth, *Nature and the American: Three Centuries of Changing Attitudes;* or Arthur A. Ekirch, *Man and Nature in America.*

11. For a contemporary survey of this situation, see Philip L. Fradkin, *A River No More: The Colorado River and the West;* and for a vivid case study, see Charles Bowden, *Killing the Hidden Waters.*

12. Gerald Nash, *The American West in the Twentieth Century: A Short History of an Urban Oasis,* p. 5.

13. Ibid., pp. 201–14 and 233–38; James L. Clayton, "Defense Spending: Key to California's Growth," *Western Political Quarterly* 15 (June 1962); and James L. Clayton, "An Unhallowed Gathering: The Impact of Defense Spending on Utah's Population Growth," *Utah Historical Quarterly* 34 (Summer 1966).

14. Lansing Lamont, *Day of Trinity,* p. 75.

15. Joseph Wood Krutch, *The Desert Year,* p. 85.

16. Russell R. Elliott, *History of Nevada,* pp. 278–79.

17. John W. Audubon, *Audubon's Western Journal, 1849–1850,* p. 160.

18. Richard J. Barnet, *The Lean Years: Politics in the Age of Scarcity,* p. 15.

Bibliography

Primary Sources

Abbey, Edward. *Abbey's Road*. New York: E. P. Dutton, 1977.

————. *Desert Solitaire: A Season in the Wilderness*. New York: Ballantine Books, 1975.

————. *Down the River*. New York: E. P. Dutton, 1982.

————. *The Journey Home*. New York: E. P. Dutton, 1977.

Albert, Herman W. *The Odyssey of a Desert Prospector*. Norman: University of Oklahoma Press, 1967.

Audubon, John W. *Audubon's Western Journal*. Edited by Frank Heywood Hodder. Cleveland: Arthur H. Clark Co., 1906.

Austin, Mary. *Earth Horizon*. New York: Literary Guild, 1932.

————. *The Land of Journey's Ending*. New York: Century Co., 1924.

————. *The Land of Little Rain*. 1903. Reprint. Albuquerque: University of New Mexico Press, 1974.

————. *Lost Borders*. New York: Harper and Brothers, 1909.

Banham, Reyner. *Scenes in America Deserta*. Salt Lake City: Peregrine-Smith, 1982.

Bartlett, John Russell. *Personal Narrative of Explorations and Incidents in Texas, New Mexico, California, Sonora and Chihuahua*. New York: D. Appleton and Co., 1854.

Beale, Edward F. *Wagon Road from Fort Defiance to the Colorado River*. 35th Cong., 1st sess. House Ex. Doc. 124, pp. 1–87.

Bidwell, John. *Echoes of the Past*. Edited by Milo Milton Quaife. Chicago: Lakeside Press, 1928.

Bieber, Ralph, ed. *Exploring Southwestern Trails: 1846–1854.* Glendale, Calif.: Arthur H. Clark Co., 1938.

————, ed. *Southern Trails to California in 1849.* Glendale, Calif.: Arthur H. Clark Co., 1937.

Bishop, W. H. *Mexico, California and Arizona.* New York: Harper and Brothers, 1900.

Bolton, Herbert Eugene, ed. and trans. *Anza's California Expeditions.* 5 vols. Berkeley: University of California Press, 1930.

Bowles, Samuel. *Across the Continent: A Summer's Journey to the Rocky Mountains, the Mormons and the Pacific States, with Speaker Colfax.* Springfield, Mass.: Samuel Bowles and Co., 1865.

Brewer, William. *Up and Down California in 1860–1864.* Edited by Francis P. Farquhar. Berkeley: University of California Press, 1949.

Brewerton, George Douglas. *Overland with Kit Carson.* Edited by Stallo Vinton. New York: A. L. Burt Co., 1930.

Browne, J. Ross. *Adventures in the Apache Country.* 1871. Reprint. New York: Promontory Press, 1974.

Bruff, J. Goldsborough. *Gold Rush.* Edited by Georgia Willis Read and Ruth Gaines. New York: Columbia University Press, 1949.

Bryant, Edwin. *What I Saw in California.* New York: D. Appleton and Co., 1848.

Burdick, Arthur James. *The Mystic Mid-Region: The Deserts of the Southwest.* New York: G. P. Putnam's Sons, 1904.

Burton, Richard F. *The City of the Saints and Across the Rocky Mountains to California.* New York: Alfred A. Knopf, 1963.

Calvin, Ross. *Sky Determines: An Interpretation of the Southwest.* Albuquerque: University of New Mexico Press, 1965.

Camp, Charles, ed. *James Clyman Frontiersman: The Adventures of a Trapper and Covered-Wagon Emigrant As Told in His Own Reminiscences and Diaries.* Portland, Ore.: Champoeg Press, 1960.

Carvalho, Solomon Nunes. *Incidents of Travel and Adventure in the Far West.* Edited by Bertram W. Korn. Philadelphia: Jewish Publication Society of America, 1954.

Chandless, William. *A Visit to Salt Lake.* London: Smith, Elder and Co., 1857.

Chase, J. Smeaton. *California Coast Trails.* Boston: Houghton Mifflin Co., 1913.

————. *California Desert Trails*. Boston: Houghton Mifflin Co., 1919.

————. *Yosemite Trails*. Boston: Houghton Mifflin Co., 1911.

Clemens, Samuel. *The Innocents Abroad: Or the New Pilgrim's Progress*. Hartford: American Publishing Co., 1869.

————. *Life on the Mississippi*. New York: Harper and Brothers, 1899.

————. *Roughing It*. Hartford: American Publishing Co., 1872.

————. *A Tramp Abroad*. Hartford: American Publishing Co., 1880.

Couts, Cave Johnson. *Hepah, California! The Journal of Cave Johnson Couts from Monterrey to Los Angeles*. Edited by Henry F. Dobyns. Tucson: Arizona Pioneers' Historical Society, 1961.

Cowles, Raymond. *Desert Journal*. Edited by Elna S. Bakker. Berkeley: University of California Press, 1977.

Cremony, John C. *Life Among the Apaches*. San Francisco: A. Roman and Co., 1868.

Cronkhite, Daniel. *Recollections of a Young Desert Rat: Impressions of Nevada and Death Valley*. Verdi, Nev.: Sagebrush Press, 1972.

Decker, Peter. *The Diaries of Peter Decker: Overland to California in 1849 and Life in the Mines, 1850–1851*. Georgetown, Calif.: Talisman Press, 1966.

Delano, Alonzo. *Life on the Plains*. New York: C. M. Saxton, Barker and Co., 1861.

Dellenbaugh, Frederick S. *A Canon Voyage*. 1906. Reprint. New Haven: Yale University Press, 1962.

Derby, George Horatio. *Derby's Report on the Opening of the Colorado*. Albuquerque: University of New Mexico Press, 1969.

Didion, Joan. *Slouching Toward Bethlehem*. New York: Farrar, Straus, Giroux, 1968.

Dunne, John Gregory. *Vegas: A Memoir of a Dark Season*. New York: Warner Books, 1974.

Emory, W. H. *Notes of a Military Reconnaissance*. 30th Cong. 1st sess. House Ex. Doc. No. 41, pp. 1–126.

————. *Report on the United States and Mexican Boundary Survey*. 34th Cong., 1st sess. Sen. Ex. Doc. 108, Vol. 1.

Escalante, Fray Francisco Silvestre Velez de. *Father Escalante's Journal*. Edited and translated by Herbert S. Auerbach. N.p.: Utah Historical Quarterly, 1943.

Faunce, Hilda. *Desert Wife*. Boston: Little, Brown and Co., 1934.

Fletcher, Colin. *The Man Who Walked Through Time*. New York: Random House, 1972.

————. *The Thousand-Mile Summer: In Desert and High Sierra.* Berkeley: Howell-North Books, 1964.

Font, Pedro. *Font's Complete Diary.* Edited and translated by Herbert Eugene Bolton. Berkeley: University of California Press, 1933.

Frémont, John Charles. *Memoirs of My Life,* Vol. 1. Chicago: Belford, Clarke and Co., 1887.

————. *The Expeditions of John C. Frémont,* Vol. 1. Edited by Donald Jackson and Mary Lee Spence. Urbana: University of Illinois Press, 1970.

Garces, Francisco. *On the Trail of a Spanish Pioneer: The Diary and Itinerary of Francisco Garces.* Edited by Elliott Coues. New York: Francis P. Harper, 1900.

Geiger, Vincent, and Wakeman Bryarly. *Trail to California.* Edited by David Potter. New Haven: Yale University Press, 1967.

Greeley, Horace. *An Overland Journey.* Edited by Charles T. Duncan. New York: Alfred A. Knopf, 1969.

Gregg, Josiah. *The Commerce of the Prairies.* Edited by Max L. Moorhead. Norman: University of Oklahoma Press, 1954.

Hafen, LeRoy and Ann, eds. *Journals of Forty-Niners, Salt Lake to Los Angeles.* Glendale, Calif.: Arthur H. Clark Co., 1954.

————. eds. *The Old Spanish Trail.* Glendale, Calif.: Arthur H. Clark Co., 1954.

Hardy, R. W. H. *Travels in the Interior of Mexico.* London: Henry Colburn and Richard Bentley, 1829.

Henderson, Randall. *On Desert Trails: Today and Yesterday.* Los Angeles: Westernlore Press, 1961.

————. *Sun, Sand and Solitude: Vignettes from the Notebook of a Veteran Desert Reporter.* Los Angeles: Westernlore Press, 1968.

Hogner, Dorothy Childs. *Westward, High, Low and Dry.* New York: E. P. Dutton, 1938.

Hornaday, William T. *Camp-Fires on Desert and Lava.* New York: Charles Scribner's Sons, 1908.

Humphrey Zephine. *Cactus Forest.* New York: E. P. Dutton, 1938.

Jaeger, Edmund. *The California Deserts.* Stanford: Stanford University Press, 1938.

James, Edwin. *Account of an Exploring Expedition from Pittsburgh to the Rocky Mountains.* 1832. Reprint. N. p.: Readex Microprint, 1966.

James, George Wharton. *Arizona the Wonderland.* Boston: Page Co., 1917.

———. *California Romantic and Beautiful.* Boston: Page Co., 1914.

———. *In and Around the Grand Canyon.* Boston: Little, Brown and Co., 1900.

———. *New Mexico: Land of the Delight-Makers.* Boston: Page Co., 1920.

———. *Our American Wonderlands.* Chicago: A. C. McClurg and Co., 1915.

———. *Reclaiming the Arid West.* New York: Dodd, Mead and Co., 1917.

———. *Utah: The Land of Blossoming Valleys.* Boston: Page Co., 1922.

———. *What the White Race May Learn from the Indian.* Chicago. Forbes and Co., 1908.

———. *The Wonders of the Colorado Deserts.* 2 vols. Boston: Little, Brown and Co., 1906.

James, William. *Pragmatism and Other Essays.* Edited by Joseph L. Blau. New York: Washington Square Press, 1963.

Johnston, A. R. *Journal of Captain A. R. Johnston.* 30th Cong., 1st sess. House Ex. Doc. 41, pp. 567–614.

Jungk, Robert. *Tomorrow Is Already Here.* New York: Simon and Schuster, 1954.

King, Clarence. *Mountaineering in the Sierra Nevada.* 1872. Reprint. Lincoln: University of Nebraska Press, 1971.

Kino, Eusebio. *Kino's Historical Memoir of Pimeria Alta.* Edited and translated by Herbert Eugene Bolton. Cleveland: Arthur H. Clark Co., 1919.

Krutch, Joseph Wood. *The Desert Year.* New York: William Sloane Associates, 1951.

———. *The Forgotten Peninsula.* New York: William Sloan Associates, 1961.

———. *Grand Canyon: Today and All Its Yesterdays.* New York: William Sloane Associates, 1958.

———. *The Modern Temper: A Study and a Confession.* New York: Harcourt, Brace and Co., 1929.

———. *More Lives than One.* New York: William Sloane Associates, 1962.

———. *The Twelve Seasons*. New York: William Sloane Associates, 1949.

———. *The Voice of the Desert: A Naturalist's Interpretation*. New York: William Morrow, 1955.

Leonard, Zenas. *Narrative of the Adventures of Zenas Leonard*. Edited by Milo Milton Quaife. Chicago: Lakeside Press, 1934.

Luhan, Mabel Dodge. *Edge of Taos Desert, An Escape to Reality*. New York: Harcourt, Brace and Co., 1937.

Lumholtz, Carl. *New Trails in Mexico*. New York: Charles Scribner's Sons, 1912.

Lummis, Charles Fletcher. *The Land of Poco Tiempo*. New York: Charles Scribner's Sons, 1902.

———. *Mesa, Canon and Pueblo: Our Wonderland of the Southwest*. New York: Century Co., 1925.

———. *A Tramp Across the Continent*. New York: Charles Scribner's Sons, 1892.

Manly, William Lewis. *Death Valley in '49*. San Jose: Pacific Tree and Vine Co., 1894.

———. *The Jayhawkers' Oath and Other Sketches*. Edited by Arthur Woodward. Los Angeles: Warren F. Lewis, 1949.

Metcalfe-Shaw, Gertrude. *English Caravanners in the Wild West: The Old Pioneers' Trail*. London: William Blackwood and Sons, 1926.

Miller, Henry. *The Air-Conditioned Nightmare*. New York: New Directions, 1945.

Myres, Sandra, ed. *Ho for California! Women's Overland Diaries*. San Marino, Calif.: Huntington Library, 1980.

Ormsby, Waterman L. *The Butterfield Overland Mail*. Edited by Lyle H. Wright and Josephine M. Bynum. San Marino, Calif.: Huntington Library, 1942.

Pattie, James Ohio. *Personal Narrative*. 1833. Reprint. N. p.: Readex Microprint, 1966.

Paxton, June. *My Life on the Mojave*. New York: Vantage Press, 1957.

Perkins, Edna Brush. *The White Heart of Mojave: An Adventure with the Out-of-Doors of the Desert*. New York: Boni and Liveright, 1922.

Pike, Zebulon. *The Expeditions of Zebulon Montgomery Pike to the Headwaters of the Mississippi River, Through Louisiana Territory, and in New Spain During the Years 1805–06–07.* 3 vols. Edited by Elliott Coues. New York: F. P. Harper, 1895.

Powell, John Wesley. *Canyons of the Colorado.* Meadville, Pa: Flood and Vincent, 1895.

———. *Report on the Arid Region of the United States.* Edited by Wallace Stegner. Cambridge, Mass.: Harvard University Press, 1962.

Powers, Stephen. *Afoot and Alone: A Walk from Sea to Sea.* Hartford: Columbian Book Co., 1872.

Preuss, Charles. *Exploring with Frémont.* Norman: University of Oklahoma Press, 1958.

Price, Edna Calkins. *Burro Bill and Me.* Idyllwild, Calif.: Strawberry Valley Press, 1973.

Priestley, J. B. *Midnight on the Desert.* New York: Harper and Brothers, 1937.

Reid, John C. *Reid's Tramp, or a Journal of the Incidents of Ten Months' Travel Through Texas, New Mexico, Arizona, Sonora and California.* Austin: Steck Co., 1935.

Remy, Jules. *A Journey to Great Salt Lake.* 2 vols. London: W. Jeffs, 1861.

Royce, Sarah. *A Frontier Lady.* Edited by Ralph Henry Gabriel. New Haven: Yale University Press, 1932.

Schlissel, Lillian, ed. *Women's Diaries of the Westward Journey.* New York: Schocken Books, 1982.

Simpson, James Hervey. *Report of Lt. J. H. Simpson of an Expedition into the Navajo Country in 1849.* 31st Cong., 1st sess. Sen. Ex. Doc 64, pp. 55–139.

Sitgreaves, Lorenzo. *Report of an Expedition Down the Zuni and Colorado River.* 32nd Cong., 2nd sess. Sen. Ex. Doc. 59, pp. 1–21.

Smythe, William Ellsworth. *City Homes on Country Lanes: Philsophy and Practice of the Home-in-a-Garden.* New York: MacMillan Co., 1921.

———. *The Conquest of Arid America.* 1st ed. New York: Harper and Brothers, 1900.

———. *The Conquest of Arid America.* 2d ed. 1905. Reprint. Seattle: University of Washington Press, 1970.

———. *Constructive Democracy: The Economics of a Square Deal.* New York: MacMillan Co., 1905.

————. *History of San Diego.* San Diego: History Company, 1907.

Strobridge, Idah Meacham. *In Miners' Mirage Land.* Los Angeles: Baumgardt Publishing Co., 1904.

Summerhayes, Martha. *Vanished Arizona: Recollections of My Army Life.* Philadelphia: J. B. Lippincott Co., 1908.

Sykes, Godfrey. *A Westerly Trend.* Tucson: Arizona Pioneers' Historical Society, 1944.

Thompson, Hunter. *Fear and Loathing in Las Vegas: A Savage Journey to the Heart of the American Dream.* New York: Popular Library, 1971.

Tocqueville, Alexis de. *Democracy in America.* Edited by J. P. Mayer. Garden City, N.Y.: Doubleday and Co., 1969.

Van Dyke, John Charles. *Art for Art's Sake: Seven University Lectures on the Technical Beauties of Paintings.* New York: Charles Scribner's Sons, 1893.

————. *The Desert: Further Studies in Natural Appearances.* 1903. Reprint. Tucson: Arizona Historical Society, 1976.

————. *The Grand Canyon of the Colorado: Recurrent Studies in Impressions and Appearances.* New York: Charles Scribner's Sons, 1920.

————. *In Egypt: Studies and Sketches Along the Nile.* New York: Charles Scribner's Sons, 1931.

————. *The Mountain: Renewed Studies in Impressions and Appearances.* New York: Charles Scribner's Sons, 1916.

————. *Nature for Its Own Sake: First Studies in Natural Appearances.* New York: Charles Scribner's Sons, 1898.

————. *The Opal Sea: Continued Studies in Impressions and Appearances.* New York: Charles Scribner's Sons, 1906.

————. *The Open Spaces: Incidents of Nights and Days Under the Blue Sky.* New York: Charles Scribner's Sons, 1922.

Whipple, A. W. *A Pathfinder in the Southwest: The Itinerary of Lt. A. W. Whipple During his Explorations for a Railway Route from Ft. Smith to Los Angeles in the Years 1853 and 1854.* Edited by Grant Foreman. Norman: University of Oklahoma Press, 1941.

Wright, William (Dan DeQuille). *The Big Bonanza.* Reprint. New York: Thomas Y. Crowell Co., 1947.

————. *Washoe Ramblings.* 1861. Reprint. Los Angeles: Westernlore Press, 1963.

Secondary Sources

Abrams, M. H. *Natural Supernaturalism: Tradition and Revolution in Romantic Literature.* New York: W. W. Norton and Co., 1971.

Alexander, Kenneth. *Death Valley USA.* South Brunswick, N.J.: A. S. Barnes and Co., 1969.

Anderson, Henry S. "The Little Landers' Colonies: A Unique Agricultural Experiment in California." *Agricultural History* 5 (October 1931).

Arrington, Leonard J. *Great Basin Kingdom.* 1958. Reprint. Lincoln: University of Nebraska Press, 1966.

Arrington, Leonard J., and Davis Bitton. *The Mormon Experience:* New York: Alfred A. Knopf, 1979.

Bannon, John Francis. *The Spanish Borderlands Frontier, 1513–1821.* New York: Holt, Rinehart and Winston, 1970.

Barnet, Richard J. *The Lean Years: Politics in the Age of Scarcity.* New York: Simon and Schuster, 1980.

Baur, John E. *The Health Seekers of Southern California, 1870–1900.* San Marino, Calif.: Huntington Library, 1959.

Berger, Peter, and Thomas Luckman. *The Social Construction of Reality: A Treatise in the Sociology of Knowledge.* Garden City, N.Y.: Doubleday and Co., 1966.

Bean, Lowell John. *Mukat's People: The Cahuilla Indians of Southern California.* Berkeley: University of California Press, 1972.

Bender, Gordon L., ed. *Reference Handbook on the Deserts of North America.* Westport, Conn.: Greenwood Press, 1982.

Berkman, Richard L., and W. Kip Viscusi. *Damming the West.* New York: Grossman Publishers, 1973.

Billington, Ray Allen. *The Far Western Frontier, 1830–1860.* New York: Harper and Row, 1956.

———. *Frederick Jackson Turner: Historian, Scholar, Teacher.* New York: Oxford University Press, 1973.

Bourdon, Roger Joseph. "George Wharton James: Interpreter of the Southwest." Ph.D. diss. University of California, Los Angeles, 1965.

Bowden, Charles. *Killing the Hidden Waters.* Austin: University of Texas Press, 1977.

Bowden, Martyn J. "The Great American Desert and the American Frontier," in *Anonymous Americans*, edited by Tamara Harevan. Englewood Cliffs, N.J.: Prentice-Hall, 1971.

Bryant, Keith L. *History of the Atchison, Topeka and Santa Fe Railway*. Lincoln: University of Nebraska Press, 1974.

Buber, Martin. *I and Thou*. Translated by Walter Kaufmann. New York: Charles Scribner's Sons, 1970.

Burch, William R. *Daydreams and Nightmares: A Sociological Essay on the American Environment*. New York: Harper and Row, 1971.

Burke, Kenneth. *A Grammar of Motives*. Berkeley: University of California Press, 1969.

———. *Permanence and Change: An Anatomy of Purpose*. 1954. Reprint. Indianapolis: Bobbs-Merrill Co., 1965.

———. *A Rhetoric of Motives*. Berkeley: University of California Press, 1969.

Butcher, Devereux. *Exploring Our National Parks and Monuments*. Boston: Houghton-Mifflin Co., 1951.

Carlson, Martin E. "William Ellsworth Smythe: Irrigation Crusader." *Journal of the West* (January 1968).

Clayton, James L. "Defense Spending: Key to California's Growth." *Western Political Quarterly* 15 (June 1962).

———. "An Unhallowed Gathering: The Impact of Defense Spending on Utah's Population Growth." *Utah Historical Quarterly* 34 (Summer 1966).

Cline, Gloria Griffen. *Exploring the Great Basin*. Norman: University of Oklahoma Press, 1963.

Collingwood, R. G. *The Idea of Nature*. New York: Oxford University Press, 1976.

Conkling, Roscoe P., and Margaret B. Conkling. *The Butterfield Overland Mail*. 3 vols. Glendale, Calif.: Arthur H. Clark Co., 1947.

Corle, Edwin. *Desert Country*. New York: Duell, Sloan and Pierce, 1941.

———. *The Gila: River of the Southwest*. Lincoln: University of Nebraska Press, 1964.

Costello, David F. *The Desert World*. New York: Thomas Y. Crowell Co., 1972.

DeVoto, Bernard. *The Year of Decision: 1846*. 1942. Reprint. Boston: Houghton Mifflin Co., n.d.

Driver, Harold. *Indians of North America*. Chicago: University of Chicago Press, 1961.

Duffus, R. J. *The Santa Fe Trail.* London: Longmans, Green and Co., 1930.

Ekirch, Arthur A. *Man and Nature in America.* Lincoln: University of Nebraska Press, 1973.

Eliade, Mircea. *The Sacred and the Profane: The Nature of Religion.* New York: Harcourt, Brace and World, 1959.

Elliott, Russell R. *History of Nevada.* Lincoln: University of Nebraska Press, 1973.

————. *Nevada's Twentieth Century Mining Boom: Tonopah, Goldfield, Ely.* Reno: University of Nevada Press, 1966.

Faragher, John Mack. *Women and Men on the Overland Trail.* New Haven: Yale University Press, 1979.

Faulk, Odie B. *Arizona: A Short History.* Norman: University of Oklahoma Press, 1970.

————. *Tombstone: Myth and Reality.* New York: Oxford University Press, 1972.

————. *Land of Many Frontiers: A History of the American Southwest.* New York: Oxford University Press, 1972.

————. *Too Far North . . . Too Far South.* Los Angeles: Westernlore Press, 1967.

Fenneman, Nevin H. *Physiography of the Western United States.* New York: McGraw-Hill, 1931.

Fleming, Donald. "Roots of the New Conservation Movement," *Perspectives in American History* 6 (1972):5–91.

Forbes, Jack D. *Apache, Navajo, Spaniard.* Norman: University of Oklahoma Press, 1971.

————. *Warriors of the Colorado: The Yumas of the Quechuan Nation and Their Neighbors.* Norman: University of Oklahoma Press, 1965.

Fradkin, Philip L. *A River No More: The Colorado River and the West.* New York: Alfred A. Knopf, 1981.

Freud, Sigmund. *Civilization and Its Discontents.* Translated by James Strachey. 1930. Reprint. New York: W. W. Norton and Co., 1961.

————. *The Future of an Illusion.* Translated by James Strachey. 1927. Reprint. New York: W. W. Norton and Co., 1961.

Garber, Paul Neff. *The Gadsden Treaty.* Philadelphia: University of Pennsylvania Press, 1923.

Gates, Paul Wallace. *History of Public Land Law Development.* Washington, D.C.: U.S. Government Printing Office, 1968.

George, Uwe. *In the Deserts of This Earth.* New York: Harcourt, Brace, Jovanovich, 1977.

Ghent, W. J. *The Road to Oregon: A Chronicle of the Great Oregon Trail.* New York: Longmans, Green and Co., 1929.

Glass, Mary Ellen. *Water for Nevada: The Reclamation Controversy, 1885–1902.* Carson City: University of Nevada Press, 1964.

Goetzmann, William. *Army Exploration in the American West: 1803–1863.* New Haven: Yale University Press, 1959.

————. *Exploration and Empire: The Explorer and the Scientist in the Winning of the American West.* 1966. Reprint. New York: Random House, 1972.

Golze, Alfred. *Reclamation in the United States.* Caldwell, Idaho: Caxton Printers, 1961.

Haury, Emil W. *The Hohokam: Desert Farmers and Craftsmen.* Tucson: University of Arizona Press, 1978.

Hays, Samuel P. *Conservation and the Gospel of Efficiency: The Progressive Conservation Movement, 1890–1920.* 1959. Reprint. New York: Atheneum, 1974.

————. "From Conservation to Environment: Environmental Politics in the United States Since World War II." *Environmental Review* 6, no. 2 (Fall 1982):14–41.

Heilbroner, Robert. *An Inquiry into the Human Prospect.* New York: W. W. Norton and Co., 1975.

Heimlert, Alan. "Puritanism, the Wilderness and the Frontier." *New England Quarterly* 26 (September 1953).

Hoffman, Abraham. *Vision or Villainy: Origins of the Owens Valley–Los Angeles Water Controversy.* College Station: Texas A and M University Press, 1981.

Hofstader, Richard. *The Age of Reform: From Bryan to FDR.* New York: Random House, 1955.

Holliday, J. S. *The World Rushed In: The California Gold Rush Experience.* New York: Simon and Schuster, 1981.

Hollon, W. Eugene. *The Great American Desert: Then and Now.* Lincoln: University of Nebraska Press, 1975.

Hundley, Norris. *Dividing the Waters: A Century of Controversy Between the United States and Mexico.* Berkeley: University of California Press, 1966.

————. *Water and the West: The Colorado River Compact and the Politics of Water in the American West.* Berkeley: University of California Press, 1975.

————. "The Dark and Bloody Ground of Indian Water Rights: Confusion Elevated to Principle." *Western Historical Quarterly* 9 (October 1978):454–82.

————. "The Politics of Reclamation: California, the Federal Government, and the Origins of the Boulder Canyon Act—A Second Look." *California Historical Quarterly* 52 (1973):292–325.

Hunt, Charles B. *Physiography of the United States*. San Francisco: W. H. Freeman and Co., 1967.

Huth, Hans. *Nature and the American: Three Centuries of Changing Attitudes*. Lincoln: University of Nebraska Press, 1972.

Jackson, John Brinckerhoff. *American Space: The Centennial Years: 1865–1876*. New York: W. W. Norton and Co., 1972.

Jackson, William Turrentine. *Treasure Hill: Portrait of a Silver Mining Camp*. Tucson: University of Arizona Press, 1963.

Jennings, Jesse, ed. *Ancient Native Americans*. San Francisco: W. H. Freeman and Co., 1978.

Jennings, Jesse, and Edward Norbeck, eds. *Prehistoric Man in the New World*. Chicago: University of Chicago Press, 1964.

Johnson, Allen, and Dumas Malone, eds. *Dictionary of American Biography*. New York: Charles Scribner's Sons, 1931.

Jones, Billy M. *Health-Seekers in the Southwest, 1817–1900*. Norman: University of Oklahoma Press, 1967.

Jungk, Robert. *Brighter than a Thousand Suns*. New York: Harcourt Brace, 1958.

Kaplan, Justin. *Mr. Clemens and Mark Twain: A Biography*. New York: Simon and Schuster, 1966.

Kirk, Ruth. *Desert: The American Southwest*. Boston: Houghton Mifflin Co., 1973.

Kleinsorge, Paul L. *The Boulder Canyon Project: Historical and Economic Aspects*. Stanford: Stanford University Press, 1941.

Laird, Carobeth. *The Chemehuevis*. Banning, Calif.: Malki Museum Press, 1976.

Lamar, Howard Roberts. *The Far Southwest, 1846–1912: A Territorial History*. New York: W. W. Norton and Co., 1970.

————, ed. *The Reader's Encyclopedia of the American West*. New York: Thomas Y. Crowell Co., 1977.

Lamont, Lansing. *Day of Trinity*. New York: Atheneum, 1965.

Langer, Suzanne. *Philosophy in a New Key: A Study in the Symbolism of Reason, Rite and Art*. 1942. Cambridge, Mass.: Harvard University Press, 1976.

Lavender, David. *The Southwest.* New York: Harper and Row, 1980.

Laxalt, Robert. *Nevada.* New York: W. W. Norton and Co., 1977.

Lee, Lawrence B. *Reclaiming the American West: An Historiography and a Guide.* Santa Barbara: ABC-Clio, 1980.

Leopold, Aldo. *Sand Country Almanac.* New York: Ballantine Books, 1966.

Long, Margaret. *The Shadow of the Arrow: Death Valley, 1849–1949.* Caldwell, Idaho: Caxton Printers, 1950.

Lovejoy, Arthur O. *The Great Chain of Being.* 1936. Cambridge, Mass. Harvard University Press, 1974.

McGinnies, William G. *Discovering the Desert: Legacy of the Carnegie Desert Botanical Laboratory.* Tucson: University of Arizona Press, 1981.

McIntosh, James. *Thoreau as Romantic Naturalist: His Shifting Stance Toward Nature.* Ithaca, N.Y.: Cornell University Press, 1974.

McPhee, John. *Basin and Range.* New York: Farrar, Straus, Giroux, 1982.

Marx, Leo. *The Machine in the Garden: Technology and the Pastoral Ideal in America.* New York: Oxford University Press, 1972.

Meinig, D. W. *Southwest: Three Peoples in Geographical Change, 1600–1970.* New York: Oxford University Press, 1971.

Merk, Frederick. *History of the Westward Movement.* New York: Alfred A. Knopf, 1978.

———. *Manifest Destiny and Mission in American History.* New York: Random House, 1966.

Miller, Perry, *Errand into the Wilderness.* Cambridge, Mass. Harvard University Press, 1976.

Monagham, James. *The Overland Trail.* Indianapolis: Bobbs-Merrill Co., 1947.

Moorhead, Max. *New Mexico's Royal Road.* Norman: University of Oklahoma Press, 1958.

Morgan, Dale L. *The Humboldt: Highroad of the West.* New York: Farrar and Rinehart, 1943.

———. *Jedediah Smith and the Opening of the West.* Lincoln: University of Nebraska Press, 1971.

———. *Overland in 1846: Diaries and Letters of the California-Oregon Trail.* 2 vols. Georgetown, Calif.: Talisman Press, 1963.

Nadeau, Remi. *The Water Seekers.* Garden City, N.Y.: Doubleday and Co., 1950.

Nash, Gerald. *The American West in the Twentieth Century: A Short History of an Urban Oasis.* Englewood Cliffs, N.J.: Prentice-Hall, 1973.

Nash, Roderick. *Wilderness and the American Mind.* 3d ed. New Haven: Yale University Press, 1982.

Nevins, Allan. *Frémont: Pathfinder of the West.* New York: Longmans, Green and Co., 1955.

Nicolson, Marjorie Hope. *Mountain Gloom and Mountain Glory: The Development of the Aesthetics of the Infinite.* New York: W. W. Norton and Co., 1963.

O'Dea, Thomas F. *The Mormons.* Chicago: University of Chicago Press, 1957.

Ortiz, Alfonso, ed. *Southwest: Handbook of the American Indian,* Vol. 9. Washington, D.C.: Smithsonian Institution, 1979.

Ostrander, Gilman, *Nevada: The Great Rotten Borough.* New York: Alfred A. Knopf, 1966.

Palmer, Tim. *Stanislaus: The Struggle for a River.* Berkeley: University of California Press, 1982.

Passmore, John. *Man's Responsibility for Nature: Ecological Problems and Western Traditions.* London: Duckworth, 1974.

Paul, Rodman Wilson. *Mining Frontiers of the Far West 1848–1880.* 1963. Reprint. Albuquerque: University of New Mexico Press, 1974.

Polanyi, Michael. *Personal Knowledge: Towards a Post-Critical Philosophy.* Chicago: University of Chicago Press, 1962.

———. *The Tacit Dimension.* Garden City, N.Y.: Doubleday and Co., 1967.

Pomeroy, Earl. *In Search of the Golden West: The Tourist in Western America.* New York: Alfred A. Knopf, 1957.

Potter, David. *People of Plenty: Economic Abundance and the American Character.* Chicago: University of Chicago Press, 1969.

Powell, Lawrence Clark. *Arizona.* New York: W. W. Norton and Co., 1976.

———. *California Classics: The Creative Literature of the Golden State.* Los Angeles: Ward Ritchie Press, 1971.

————. *Southwest Classics: The Creative Literature of the Arid Lands.* Los Angeles: Ward Ritchie Press, 1974.

Powledge, Fred, *Water: The Nature, Uses and Future of Our Most Precious and Abused Resource.* New York: Farrar, Straus, Giroux, 1982.

Pringle, Laurence, *Water: The Next Great Resource Battle.* New York: Macmillan, 1982.

Richardson, Elmo. *Dams, Parks and Politics: Resource Development and Preservation in the Truman-Eisenhower Era.* Lexington: University Press of Kentucky, 1973.

————. *The Politics of Conservation: Crusades and Controversies, 1897–1913.* Berkeley: University of California Press, 1962.

Riegel, Robert Edgar. *The Story of the Western Railroads: From 1852 Through the Reign of the Giants.* 1926. Reprint. Lincoln: University of Nebraska Press, 1967.

Riesman, David, with Nathan Glazer and Reuel Denney. *The Lonely Crowd: A Study of the Changing American Character.* 1950. Reprint. New Haven: Yale University Press, 1977.

Rogers, Peter. "The Future of Water," *Atlantic Monthly* (July 1983):80–92.

Ronald, Ann. *The New West of Edward Abbey.* Albuquerque: University of New Mexico Press, 1982.

Safer, Thomas H., and Orville E. Kelly. *Countdown Zero: GI Victims of U.S. Atomic Testing.* New York: G. P. Putnam's Sons, 1982.

Schmitt, Peter J. *Back to Nature: The Arcadian Myth in Urban America.* New York: Oxford University Press, 1969.

Sears, Paul. *Deserts on the March.* Norman: University of Oklahoma Press, 1935.

Sheridan, David. *Desertification of the United States.* Washington, D.C.: Council on Environmental Quality, 1981.

Sibley, George. "The Desert Empire." *Harper's* (October 1977).

Smith, Henry Nash. *Virgin Land: The American West as Symbol and Myth.* 1950. Reprint. Cambridge, Mass. Harvard University Press, 1976.

Spencer, Robert, with Charles E. Dibble, Jesse D. Jennings, Elden Johnson, Arden R. King, Theodore C. Stern, Kenneth M. Stewart, Omar C. Stewart, and William Wallace. *The Native Americans: Ethnology and Backgrounds of the North American Indians.* New York: Harper and Row, 1977.

Starr, Kevin. *Americans and the California Dream, 1850–1915.* New York: Oxford University Press, 1973.

Stegner, Wallace. *Beyond the Hundredth Meridian: John Wesley Powell and the Second Opening of the West.* Boston: Houghton Mifflin Co., 1954.

Stewart, George R. *The California Trail: An Epic with Many Heroes.* New York: McGraw-Hill, 1962.

———. *Ordeal by Hunger.* 1936. Reprint. New York: Simon and Schuster, 1971.

Straebel, George Lofstrom. "Irrigation as a Factor in Western History, 1847–1890." Ph.D. diss. University of California, Berkeley, 1965.

Swain, Donald C. *Federal Conservation Policy, 1921–1933.* Berkeley: University of California Press, 1963.

Thomas, Keith. *Man and the Natural World: A History of the Modern Sensibility.* New York: Pantheon, 1983

Turner, Frederick Jackson. *The Early Writings of Frederick Jackson Turner.* Compiled by Everett E. Edwards. Madison: University of Wisconsin Press, 1938.

———. *The Significance of Sections in American History.* Edited by Max Farrand. New York: Peter Smith, 1950.

Unruh, John D. *The Plains Across: The Overland Emigrants and the Trans-Mississippi West, 1840–1860.* Urbana: University of Illinois Press, 1979.

Walker, Franklin. *A Literary History of California.* Berkeley: University of California Press, 1950.

Warne, William. *The Bureau of Reclamation.* New York: Praeger Publishers, 1973.

Waters, Frank. *The Colorado.* 1946. Reprint. New York: Holt, Rinehart and Winston, 1974.

Webb, Walter Prescott. *The Great Frontier.* 1951. Reprint. Austin: University of Texas Press, 1964.

———. *The Great Plains.* 1931. Reprint. New York: Grosset and Dunlap, 1971.

———. "The American West: Perpetual Mirage," *Harper's* 214 (May 1957).

Welty, Eudora. *The Eye of the Story: Selected Essays and Reviews.* New York: Random House, 1979.

White, Gilbert F. *Strategies of American Water Management.* Ann Arbor: University of Michigan Press, 1969.

Whitehead, Alfred North. *Science and the Modern World.* 1925. Reprint. New York: Macmillan, 1967.

Wiebe, Robert H. *The Search for Order: 1877–1920.* New York: Hill and Wang, 1967.

Williams, George H. *Wilderness and Paradise in Christian Thought: The Biblical Experience of the Desert in the History of Christianity and the Paradise Theme in the Theological Ideal of the University.* New York: Harper and Brothers, 1962.

Williams, Raymond. *The Country and the City.* New York: Oxford University Press, 1973.

Winther, Oscar Osburn. *The Transportation Frontier: Trans-Mississippi West 1865–1890.* 1964. Reprint. Albuquerque: University of New Mexico Press, 1974.

Worster, Donald. *Dust Bowl: The Southern Plains in the 1930's.* New York: Oxford University Press, 1979.

———. *Nature's Economy: The Roots of Ecology.* Garden City, N.Y.: Anchor Books, 1979.

———. "Hydraulic Society in California: An Ecological Interpretation," *Agricultural History* 56 (July 1982):503–15.

Index

Abbey, Edward, 10, 92, 94, 149–
63, 170, 173, 174; *Abbey's
Road*, 150, 157, 158, 161, 163,
193–94; *Desert Solitaire*, 150–
63, 193–94; *Down the River*,
150, 158, 193; *The Journey
Home*, 149, 150, 158, 163,
192–94
American society, 10–11, 43–44,
79–81, 93–94, 102–3, 123–
24, 126, 129–30, 147, 150–
51, 157–58, 161–63, 168
animality, 37–39, 43, 56, 66,
108, 129–30, 133–35
appreciation (of desert), 6–8, 10–
11, 18, 41, 75, 91–163; 168–
73
Arizona, 4, 18, 27, 91, 113, 128,
139, 147, 165–66, 171
atomic bomb, 174–75
Audubon, John W., 175

Barnet, Richard, 175
Billington, Ray Allen, 21–22
Buenaventura River, 29–30, 49

California, 4, 15, 16, 17, 18, 20,
21, 26, 27, 29, 31, 48, 51,
52, 54, 55, 57–58, 91, 96,
108–9, 112, 166, 171
Carnegie, Andrew, 110
Carson, Kit, 32, 35
Clemens, Samuel (Mark Twain),
10, 61–75, 88, 98, 103, 118,
119, 132, 134, 167, 168;
Roughing It, 61–75, 185–86
Colorado River, 12, 24, 49, 102,
119–20, 124, 155–56, 170,
172
complacency (toward desert), 13,
91, 124–26
conquest (of desert), 20, 28, 77,
81, 84–85, 88, 89, 101, 104,
124, 173

dams, 22–24, 89, 94, 141–50,
155–56, 163, 172
death (and desert), 5, 6, 18, 19,
22, 30, 35–37, 43, 51–52, 54,
58, 59, 61–62, 63, 64, 70–
74, 99–101, 104, 105–6, 110–
11, 117, 121–22, 129, 131,
152–56, 159–60

Death Valley, 46, 54, 55, 58–59, 168

Delano, Alonzo, 59

environmental determinism (in desert), 4–5, 16–17, 23, 30, 39, 43, 106–7, 165, 166

food, 6, 19, 22, 37–39, 44, 51–52, 56, 58–59, 66, 68, 69, 71–72, 75, 82, 99, 103, 107, 129–30, 132, 134, 140, 142, 144, 153, 156, 158, 162, 168

Frémont, Jessie Benton, 26, 28

Frémont, John C., 10, 17, 25–44, 45, 46, 55, 56, 57, 59, 62, 63, 64, 66, 67, 75, 86, 98, 105, 111, 118, 134, 157, 163; *Report of an Exploration to Oregon and North California in the Years 1843–44*, 26–43, 181–83; *Report on an Exploration of the Country Lying Between the Missouri and the Rocky Mountains*, 26–28, 32, 38, 182–83; *Memoirs, Vol. I*, 27, 43–44, 183

Glen Canyon, 155–56, 170

Goetzmann, William, 39

Grand Canyon, 49, 149

Great American Desert, 3, 16, 166

Great Basin, 4, 15, 16, 21, 23, 26, 29, 39–41, 43

Great Plains, 3–4, 8, 16–17, 23

Hollon, Eugene, 22, 23

Humboldt Desert, River and Sink, 4, 11, 17–18, 19–20, 73–74, 167

Indians, 5, 11–12, 15, 16, 19, 22, 28, 31–33, 34–39, 42–43, 46, 49, 56, 66–67, 68, 69, 71, 99, 103, 135, 142

individual (the), 9, 10–11, 84–85, 92, 93, 105, 107, 109–10, 129, 133, 135, 136, 137–39, 148, 151

irrigation (reclamation), 7, 9–10, 15, 20–21, 22–24, 40, 77–90, 91, 94, 102–4, 108, 114, 115, 116, 117, 119–20, 125, 150, 168–72, 175

Jackson, Donald, 26

James, George Wharton, 10, 92, 113–26, 159, 169, 173; *The Wonders of the Colorado Desert*, 113–26

James, William, 7

Kaplan, Justin, 62

Krutch, Joseph Wood, 10, 92, 94, 127–48, 149, 151, 154, 173, 174, 175; *The Desert Year*, 128, 147, 132–42, 191–92; *Forgotten Peninsula*, 128; *Grand Canyon*, 128; *The Modern Temper*, 127–28, 132–33, 137, 142, 143–44, 145, 191; *More Lives than One*, 127–28, 143–48, 191–92; *The Twelve Seasons*, 128; *The Voice of the Desert*, 128, 147–48, 192

Long, Stephen, 16–17, 139

Manly, William Lewis, 10, 45–59, 62, 71, 75, 77, 90, 98, 105, 118, 121, 134, 151, 152, 168; *Death Valley in '49*, 46–58, 183–84; *The Jayhawkers' Oath and Other Sketches*, 58–59, 184

Mexico, 4, 15, 31, 33, 34–36, 166

mining, 7, 10, 20–22, 48–49, 53, 57–58, 68–69, 74–75, 91, 122–23, 141, 167–68, 175

misanthropy (and desert-loving), 93, 95, 97–98, 103–4, 110, 112, 157

Mono Lake, 61, 71–72

Mormons, 22, 40, 46, 50, 62, 67

Muir, John, 92, 169

Nash, Roderick, 8, 162

nature (attitudes toward), 6, 9, 18, 28, 39, 43–44, 55, 59, 68, 75, 84, 95–97, 103–4, 105–9, 110–11, 120, 127, 129, 130, 132–33, 137–39, 147, 151, 160, 162, 172–73

Nevada, 4, 17, 21, 26, 29, 31, 33, 45, 59, 61, 67, 68, 91, 165, 171, 175

New Mexico, 4, 15, 113, 166, 171

Newlands, Francis, 23

obstacle (desert as), 6, 16–17, 27, 30, 139, 151, 167, 171, 173–74

Old Spanish Trail, 31–37, 45, 50–51

Overland trail, 6, 10, 17–20, 21, 45–59, 63, 73, 75, 77, 91, 112, 124, 125, 166–67, 174, 175

Paul, Rodman, 21–22

Pike, Zebulon, 16, 139

Pinchot, Gifford, 169

Powell, John Wesley, 170–72

railroads, 91, 117, 152, 166

reality (desert as), 64–67, 72–73, 92, 123, 131–32, 136–37, 148, 151, 166, 167, 168

Remy, Jules, 11–12

Riesman, David, 47–48

rivers (and desert), 4, 17–18, 22, 24, 29, 40, 49, 69, 78, 94, 102, 118–20, 124, 155–56, 167, 170–72

Royce, Sarah, 19–20

Salton Basin and Sea, 12, 101–2, 105, 119–20, 124

science, 40–42, 82, 84–85, 92, 128, 129, 131, 134, 136–37, 142, 144–45

shortcuts (through desert), 18–19, 46, 49–55

Smythe, William Ellsworth, 9–10, 23, 77–90, 95, 97, 101, 103, 104, 111, 115, 118, 119, 139, 150, 151, 157, 171, 173, 176; *City Homes on Country Lanes*, 89–90, 187; *The Conquest of Arid America*, 78, 81–90, 186–87; *Constructive Democracy*, 78–80, 84, 87, 88, 186–87

Spanish (and desert), 15, 22, 29

Spence, Mary Lee, 26

stagecoach, 63–66, 73, 117

Swain, Donald, 24

Tahoe, 68
Tocqueville, Alexis de, 3, 11
Turner, Frederick Jackson, 27,
    165–66, 173

Utah, 4, 22, 26, 49–50, 141–
    42, 149, 161, 166

vacancy (of desert), 4, 5, 8, 18,
    34, 41, 55–56, 64, 66, 88, 92,
    102, 114–15, 142, 162, 174
Van Dyke, John, 10, 92, 94, 95–
    112, 115, 118, 120, 151, 157,
    163, 169, 173; *Art for Art's
    Sake*, 96, 188; *The Desert*, 95–
    112, 188–89; *Nature for Its
    Own Sake*, 96–97; *The Open
    Spaces*, 96, 111–12, 188–89

Williams, George, 5